Inside Canada's Nursing Homes

END OF THE LINE

Maria Bohuslawsky

James Lorimer & Company, Publishers
Toronto, 1989

Front cover photo: Pauline Comeau

Canadian Cataloguing in Publication Data

Bohuslawsky, Maria.
  End of the line: Inside Canada's nursing homes

ISBN 1-55028-292-1 (bound). - ISBN 1-55028-290-5 (pbk.)

1. Nursing homes - Canada. 2. Nursing home patients - Canada.
I. Title.

RA998.C3B63 1989   362.1'6'0971   C89-094959-X

James Lorimer & Company Limited
Egerton Ryerson Memorial Building
35 Britain Street
Toronto, Ontario
M5A 1R7

Printed and bound in Canada
6 5 4 3 2 1 89 90 91 92 93 94

*For my parents, Andrey and Sarafima
Bohuslawsky, who taught me that
there's no place like home*

Contents

Acknowledgements

I am indebted to the people who are profiled in this book. I thank them for their patience, cooperation, courage and friendship.

I also thank all other nursing-home residents, their families and staff who were kind enough to allow me to interview them. Although there was not enough room in the book to profile all of them, they provided invaluable information on the workings of the nursing-home system.

Many experts on long-term care generously sent information on the strength of a phone call or letter and were available for interviews. I am grateful for all their help.

A special thanks is extended to the *Winnipeg Free Press* for assigning me to nursing-home stories and for granting me a leave of absence in order to write this book.

I would also like to thank Curtis Fahey, Pauline Comeau and especially Geoffrey York.

Preface

This is the inside story of life in nursing homes, told by people who live and work in these institutions or visit them regularly. Each chapter looks at nursing homes through a different set of eyes — from the elderly resident who keeps hoping that "things will get better," to the families who visit daily, to the nurse who is too busy to stop when a resident is calling her.

The issues examined in the book are timely, because Canada's population is aging. In 1986, about one in ten Canadians — about 2.7 million — were over the age of sixty-five, compared to 1.5 million in 1966. The numbers will continue to grow. It is estimated that by 2001 every fifth Canadian will be over sixty-five. That is nearly six million people.

But these demographic trends are not a reason to build more nursing homes. For one thing, the trends are not necessarily permanent. The aging of Canadian society is a result of the post-war baby boom between 1946 and 1960. When the baby boomers reach the end of their life span by 2030, the age distribution will probably become more evenly distributed.

Furthermore, even if the demographic trends were permanent, investing more public money in nursing homes would be a mistake. By their very nature, as this book attempts to show, nursing homes are ill-equipped to deal with elderly people who are physically and mentally disabled. To make matters worse, nursing-home residents are often the victims of understaffing, overuse of drugs and restraints, boredom and a regimented, institutional atmosphere.

Not all homes, admittedly, are nightmares. There are dedicated, caring people in the system. The heroes are the advocacy groups, staff and families who are fighting to change the homes; the health-care aides who give up their coffee breaks to read and talk to lonely people; and the residents who survive by maintaining their sense of humour and their capacity to dream. In this book, readers will meet a nursing-home administrator in Niagara Falls who has fulfilled his dream by building a high-quality nursing home, and a nurse in Winnipeg who refuses to give unnecessary drugs. The problem is the system itself. Nursing homes are no longer just retirement homes; they have become chronic-care hospitals. But staffing and funding have not kept pace with the change.

The nursing-home system is immense; indeed, Canada has one of the highest rates of institutionalization in the world. In 1987, there were 2,627 special-care facilities for the aged in Canada, containing 168,447 beds, and thousands of other elderly people were living in long-term care units of general and special hospitals. The significance of these figures becomes apparent when placed in a comparative framework. In 1981, Canada institutionalized 7.5 per cent of all its citizens over the age of sixty-five. Almost 36 per cent of Canadians over the age of eighty-five were shipped to nursing homes. By comparison, the United Kingdom institutionalized only 5 per cent of people over the age of 65 and only 21 per cent over the age of 85. Its ability to minimize the numbers of people sent to institutions was the result of a model home-care system.

The value of home-care programs, and the need to expand their scope in Canada, is one of the principal themes of this book. Increasingly, elderly people are finding that there's no place like home; they have no wish to end their lives in an institution — and most of them should not have to. It is time for us as a society to think long and hard about what the institutionalization of our elderly really means, and what the options are.

I became interested in nursing homes after writing about them for the *Winnipeg Free Press*. Long after the newspaper articles appeared, I was still receiving phone calls and letters in response, and I realized there was a longer story to be told.

To paint a fuller picture of nursing-home life, I spent about a year interviewing residents, staff, families, clergy and members of advocacy groups, mostly in Manitoba and Ontario. From the spring of 1988 to the spring of 1989, I visited nursing-home residents at regular intervals, and they told me about their experiences, thoughts and feelings. During visits to nursing homes, I was able to observe — over an extended period of time — the residents' surroundings, what they ate and how staff treated them. I spoke with other residents of the homes, and saw what happened to them as well. I have spent hundreds of hours in nursing homes — probably more than any other journalist in this country

To supplement these personal accounts, I read scholarly literature, books, newspaper and magazine articles, inquest reports, union contracts, nursing-home legislation and various studies and reports about nursing homes from across the country. I tapped a broad range of sources: federal and provincial governments, social planners, gerontologists, health-care researchers and practitioners, unions, professional associations, advocacy groups and the nursing-home industry. I also interviewed dozens of professionals in the field, including physicians, nurses, government officials, scholars, nursing-home administrators, clergy and union leaders.

To learn more about conditions in nursing homes, I obtained about seventy-five government inspection reports on twenty-one homes in Manitoba and Ontario. (In Manitoba, the inspection reports were obtained under the Freedom of Information Act.) The literature substantiated the experiences described by individuals.

The terms used for institutions for the elderly vary from province to province. The phrase "nursing home" is used in this book for the sake of uniformity.

Throughout this book, I have used pseudonyms for nursing-home residents, their families and staff. Their fear of reprisal for speaking out is unlike any I have seen in ten years of journalism.

Maria Bohuslawsky
July 1989
Winnipeg

1

Mrs. Sinclair

Who goes into nursing homes today? Many more women than men. This is not surprising, since women live longer. Almost 60 percent of Canadians aged sixty-five and over are women. If present trends continue, by 2001 two-thirds of those aged seventy-five and over will be women.

One of the thousands of Canadian women now in a nursing home is Eunice Sinclair. Her small room overlooks the neighbourhood "hooker lane." From her window, the retired schoolteacher can sometimes see male and female prostitutes plying their trade. Mrs. Sinclair, eighty-four, is one of about 300 residents of a decaying high-rise nursing home in Winnipeg's rundown inner city. "Just like anyone else who goes into a home, I thought it would never come to this," she says, looking surprised at the tears that suddenly soak her cheeks.

"I don't usually blubber," she apologizes. And it is true. Mrs. Sinclair normally faces the trials of old age, disability and institutional life with spunk and dignity.

But she gets emotional talking about the events that led up to her placement in the nursing home eleven years ago.

Her beloved husband, Andrew, a retired accountant and avid golfer, suffered a debilitating stroke and was bedridden. She was the only person looking after him. "I slept with one eye open," she recalls. The stress was too much. Just before his death, she was also felled by a massive stroke. It paralyzed her left arm. It also affected her mind. She spent a week in the psychiatric ward of a hospital. "I realize I was in poor shape," Mrs. Sinclair admits.

"I was grieving." Mrs. Sinclair's stepchildren were cool to her. She had married their father the day after the first Mrs. Sinclair died. Eunice and Andrew had been in love — "without doing anything about it" — for about thirty years. She had no children of her own.

Her elder stepson had her declared mentally incompetent and she became a ward of the public trustee. "I went to write a cheque and they'd frozen my account," she said, her eyes again filling with tears. "I thought I was in Russia. After the stroke I relied on him a lot and I guess he thought I was bothering him too much."

The staff at the hospital decided that Mrs. Sinclair should go into a nursing home. She did not argue. It seemed the only alternative, although she was financially comfortable, with her husband's assets, her own teacher's pension and government pensions. "I didn't want to be a burden on the children," she says.

After several months in the nursing home, she felt strong enough to go to the public trustee's office. An official there told her that she seemed fine. For $285, a lawyer finally got the order of supervision annulled.

But Mrs. Sinclair stayed in the nursing home. By then, she had sold or given away most of her possessions and furniture, and had given up her apartment. As a widowed, childless woman, she had few people in her life. And after suffering a stroke, she felt intimidated at the idea of looking after herself. She was unaware of any alternative to the nursing home, especially since community support services such as home care were practically unknown. Besides, she had grown fond of the nurses who had coaxed her back to health. "They say you can get in these places but you can't get out," Mrs. Sinclair muses. "The reason I stayed was because I thought it would get better. It couldn't get worse."

A Winnipeg nurse who worked in a nursing home says she saw many people recuperate and become well enough to leave. "But they never left," she says. "The longer they're there, the less relevance the community has."

Mrs. Sinclair's only disability is her paralyzed left arm, which causes her a little difficulty when she dresses. "I can't do up my bra," she explains. Nobody thinks to give her a brassiere that can be unhooked from the front with one hand.

The staff at the nursing home do little for her. They bathe her once a week. She is given an unidentified vitamin pill every day at lunch. Each night, the staff give her a sleeping pill; sleeping pills are routinely handed out to many residents of nursing homes.

In contrast to many of her co-residents, Mrs. Sinclair tidies her room and feeds herself. She goes shopping once a week, and visits the donut shop with friends. She is president of the residents' council. She has enough strength in her one good arm to push a large upholstered chair toward a visitor. She does not always swallow the sleeping pills that the nurse brings her. They lie collecting dust in various corners of her room where she has flung them.

Almost half of the people who land in a nursing home are sent there from hospital after they have suffered an injury or illness. Often, relatives or hospital staff are concerned about the elderly person's ability to cope in his or her own home. Medical experts and social workers size up the individual's abilities and physical condition; they and the family often decide if the patient will go to a nursing home.

But a hospital is the worst possible place to evaluate people's ability to manage at home, according to Dr. Neena Chappell, a University of Manitoba gerontologist.

"They've just come out of a bad health experience and are in a sterile, inhumane and unfamiliar institution. Most likely they will be assessed as requiring an environment other than home," she says.

"If you can get them back home for a few weeks — that's all — evidence suggests the difference will be absolutely amazing."

One study found that 72 per cent of nursing-home residents had been in a hospital shortly before entering the nursing home. "Frail, elderly persons experience rapid loss of functional skills when left in acute-care hospitals for even a few weeks," another study says.

The fact that Mrs. Sinclair is still almost completely independent after more than a decade in a nursing home is proof that she did not belong there in the first place.

She is not alone. Manitoba statistics for 1987-1988 show that more than 40 per cent of residents in nursing homes require only minimal or partial assistance in activities such as bathing, dressing and feeding. Some need as little as twenty minutes of attention a day.

Manitoba statistics for 1987-1988 show that more than 40 per cent of residents in nursing homes require only minimal or partial assistance in activities such as bathing, dressing and feeding. Some need as little as twenty minutes of attention a day.

Similarly, a 1988 Ontario study concluded that 55 per cent of nursing-home residents do not need the level of care provided in those institutions, and shouldn't be there. All of these residents need less than ninety minutes of care a day. Elderly people in Ontario are not supposed to ender a nursing home unless they require at least ninety minutees of care each day — the minimum standard for nursing-home admission in that province. While most nursing-home residents in Canada have one or more chronic illnesses or disabilities, "many are relatively independent," notes a recent book on institutionalization of the elderly in Canada.

People like Mrs. Sinclair would be far better off at home, with support services such as Meals on Wheels, housekeeping and home visits by a nurse. Not only is home care more economical for the taxpayer, it is also more humane. The dilemma is that there is a shortage of community services, and of group homes or seniors' apartments that provide helpful services. As a result, Mrs. Sinclair and others like her are forced into institutions.

Chappell says that elderly patients like Mrs. Sinclair should be using a nursing home on a temporary basis, as a convalescent home. "A lot of us argue that our institutions would better serve the elderly if there was a good rehabilitation program, so they can return to the community," she says.

The Registered Psychiatric Nurses Association of Manitoba also likes this approach. "The goals of personal-care homes should be reviewed," says Annette Osted, executive director of the organization. "Their goals should be to stop deterioration. We should use them as a general hospital and return people to the community."

For years, Mrs. Sinclair was not permitted to have a key to her room in the nursing home. It was officially described as a "private" room, but she could not even lock the door. She was finally given a key to her room — a few months before her tenth anniversary in the building.

When she first moved in, she was promised new furniture to replace the shabby relics she inherited from the previous tenant — a single bed with wooden headboard, a twenty-four-year-old mattress covered in tattered sheets, a desk-and-dresser set, a chest of drawers and a kitchen chair. All the wooden surfaces were scratched and stained, and the drawers were stubborn — impossible to handle for someone with only one good arm. Throughout the years, the administrator of the home renewed his promises, but no new furniture arrived.

"I've been living on promises for ten years," Mrs. Sinclair says. "I'm sick and tired of looking at that stuff."

Eventually, she sent a letter to Toronto, to the head office of the wealthy, multinational corporation that owns the nursing home. "My furniture looks like Queen Victoria's trousseau," she wrote in a neat hand. (The staff in the business office of the nursing home had refused to let her use their typewriter.)

She never received a reply. But the administrator found out about her correspondence and made a point of telling Mrs. Sinclair he knew about it. "There are no secrets here," she says.

Finally, Mrs. Sinclair called a consumer columnist at the local newspaper and complained about her furniture. The next day, a brand-new chest of drawers and night table appeared. "I guess they were afraid of getting into the *Free Press*," she says. But the replacement for the desk-and-dresser set was second-hand, and just as dilapidated as the first. Unwilling to complain further, Mrs. Sinclair plans to buy some paint stripper and refinish the piece herself.

Ironically, the same nursing-home administration refused to let her bring in her own furniture. All she was allowed was an easy chair from home. A treasured oriental rug was forbidden. The home also objected to a large TV that Mrs. Sinclair had received as a wedding gift. "If the TV doesn't come in, neither do I," she told them. "It's the only pleasure I have left." After much haggling it was permitted.

When the administrator found out she had been storing five suitcases of clothes in her room, he asked her to get rid of most of them. She did. Her few remaining dresses bulge out of a closet only two feet wide.

Later, the administrator thanked her for her co-operation.

People entering a nursing home have usually experienced profound loss. They've lost their health, a spouse, a community, a home, friends, a driver's licence — control over their lives. Their world is ever-shrinking; they move from a house or apartment into one room, leaving behind many prized belongings.

Giving up personal possessions is an added hardship, on top of the loss of independence and the sorrow of leaving a lifelong home, says Milada Disman, an assistant professor in the behavioural sciences department at the University of Toronto. Disman says an elderly person's possessions have sentimental value: they provide memories of happier times. However, for "hygienic" reasons, many nursing homes do not allow residents to "clutter" a small space with their belongings. The institution may not see the value of those possessions to the resident, Disman says.

Other experts on nursing-home environments have stressed the importance of personal possessions. "Allowing residents to personalize their space gives them a sense of control over their environment in a setting where opportunities for this are not extensive," says Toronto psychologist Myra Schiff, a consultant to designers of facilities for the elderly. "It gives them a vehicle for expressing their personality and individuality."

"I'm paying $10,000 a year to live in a dump," Mrs. Sinclair declares. "It's a heck of a lot for what I get."

Each resident pays a daily residential charge of $20.50. This amount is set by the provincial government and increases by twenty cents four times a year to coincide with increases in pensions. Mrs. Sinclair also pays an extra seven dollars a day for a "private" room which includes sink and toilet. In addition, to Mrs. Sinclair's payment, the nursing home receives about sixty-two dollars a day for each resident from the provincial government.

In other words, the nursing home received about $33,000 in 1989 for giving Mrs. Sinclair food, shelter and supervision.

But when she dared ask the nursing home staff for a hot-water bottle and a basin to soak her aching feet, she was told to go out and buy them herself. She also had to pay five dollars for an I.D. bracelet and fifteen dollars to get her name marked in her clothing with black ink.

The daughter of another resident at the same home was astonished when her mother's telephone was disconnected. It turned out that the nursing home had disconnected the phone because of a fifteen-dollar debit in her account. The daughter investigated the incident and learned that the nursing-home office — which handles her mother's money — was putting fifteen dollars a month aside for a funeral and another sum for a wheelchair. Her mother was fifty years old and mobile. "I thought, 'My God, the woman is still alive.'" Another twenty dollars was removed from her mother's account in December to buy her a Christmas gift.

When the daughter wanted to discuss these deductions, the nursing home's social worker scoffed at her concerns. "This is too piddly," he said. "Other people in the nursing home have millions of dollars." Her mother's pension income was about $750 a month and she was paying $620 to live in the home.

Mrs. Sinclair has tried to give her room a homey feel. She installed a couple of African violets that refuse to bloom, pictures on the wall and framed photos. A portrait of herself taken on D-Day stands on the dresser. In it, she is gazing off into the distance looking happy and hopeful — a glamorous blonde with soft curly hair, big blue eyes and perfect teeth.

But there are constant reminders that she is in an institution. While cleaning, a clumsy staff member accidentally cracked the glass over a handsome portrait of her husband. Mrs. Sinclair's clothing is put away in drawers marked "night" and "day" to make it easier for rushed staff to pull out the appropriate items. Staff are constantly barging in — sometimes without knocking — bringing juice or laundry. The intercom in the hallway is blaring twenty-four hours a day. The noise from the intercom is clearly audible in her room. Members of the staff walk off with her newspapers, or coupons that she has clipped for free samples or savings in stores. "The nurses seem to think that because I get the paper they can grab it."

Mrs. Sinclair likes a few cigarettes a day. Not only is smoking prohibited in her room, but for years she was not allowed to have a lighter or a book of matches. "I've never set fire to anything," she says in disbelief. Every time she wanted a smoke, she had to ask a nurse for a light. Finally, on the basis of seniority in the home, she finagled her own lighter — albeit one with the nursing-home corporation logo imprinted on it. But another resident, who had also received permission to carry a lighter, was later denied that privilege. "That's how it works around here," Mrs. Sinclair explains. "You get permission from one person and then someone else comes along and says, 'No, it's not the policy of the home.'"

Cigarettes are not sold in the home. During a three-week cold snap when visitors stayed away, Mrs. Sinclair had to borrow cigarettes from staff and other residents.

Mrs. Sinclair finds it humiliating that the nursing-home office knows so much about her life. A file on her, kept by the nursing home, contains the information that she was once legally considered mentally incompetent and under the supervision of the public trustee. "It's a terrible feeling," she says. And when she sold her TV to a health-care aide for fifteen dollars, the office had to be notified.

"If you sell anything here, you have to go to the office and say what you're selling, who you're selling it to and for how much. You feel like saying, 'None of your goddamn business.'"

Mrs. Sinclair broached the idea of purchasing a scatter rug to place by her bed because the grey tile floor is cold on her feet in the the morning. It was not allowed. The nursing home decided that the rug might become smelly because of the incontinence of other elderly residents who might wander into her room.

Mentally impaired residents, often suffering from Alzheimer's Disease, are integrated with the residents who are mentally alert. As a result, clear-headed residents are frequently victimized by their confused neighbours. An elderly lady came to Mrs. Sinclair's room one night and urinated in the doorway. "They run you ragged," she says.

A 1988 survey of nursing home physicians in Ontario found that 83 per cent of the doctors suspected their patients had been abused by other residents — another good argument for keeping nearly independent people out of nursing homes.

One room on Mrs. Sinclair's floor has four elderly residents who suffer from Alzheimer's Disease. One of the residents wanders up and down the hall shouting, "Crazy people! Crazy people!"

"If you get too close she'll hit you," Mrs. Sinclair warns. "And she's got a hand like a board."

Before Mrs. Sinclair was allowed to lock her room, it was routinely ransacked by demented people. One woman would enter the room as soon as Mrs. Sinclair left for a meal. "I caught her in my lingerie drawer. I said, 'There's nothing in there that belongs to you.'"

"Oh yes," the woman replied. "This, this and this."

"I never saw you before," Mrs. Sinclair retorted, before taking the woman by the arm and giving her a little shove towards the door. "I was upset," she said.

One night, she forgot to lock her door. "I was standing without a stitch on. Before I could put my nightgown on, I looked up, and she's standing at the door watching me. After all, some things should be private and sacred." Sometimes, she would return to her room to find that someone had used her toilet and not flushed it.

Mrs. Sinclair has a few buddies in the home, but finds it hard to find compatible people. "You're happy if you get one who can talk to you." She knows of about ten other schoolteachers in the home, but none of them can communicate with her, because they have some form of dementia or paralysis.

Mrs. Sinclair's doorknob rattles at least several times an hour. "It's the wanderers," she explains. "If it's open they come in. And things go missing." That is how she lost a sterling-silver comb, brush and mirror set.

She also lost a set of luggage. It disappeared from the storage room in the basement. But it was not the wanderers who took the luggage. It was the staff, Mrs. Sinclair believes.

Permanent disappearance of residents' clothes and personal possessions is one of the most common complaints in nursing homes. Not only is it traumatic for the resident who has so little to begin with, but it is a serious issue because stealing is a criminal offence. Families and residents say they are going broke trying to replace lost items.

"I haven't found anyplace where I can hide something and be sure it'll be there when I go for it," Mrs. Sinclair says. "At Christmas-time I got numerous chocolates. They were never there when I went to get them. It's just a den of thieves, really. I'd notice a few out of a box and then I'd come back and the whole box would be gone from a drawer." She adds: "It's a common disease to these places. My sister knows the president of the residents' council at another home, and she says she can put something down, turn around and it's gone."

Items of clothing get "lost" in the laundry to such an extent that some residents are afraid to hand over cherished articles. They end up washing the clothing themselves in their small sinks. "The laundry likes to lose your stuff," Mrs. Sinclair observes wryly. "I have two pairs of slacks down there and I don't ever expect to see them again."

These losses disturb Mrs. Sinclair. She takes pride in her appearance. She wears rouge, red lipstick and matching nail polish, and attractive wash-and-wear dresses. It embarrasses her that, because of a hammertoe, she cannot find a comfortable pair of dress shoes, and instead must wear slippers around the nursing home.

In one bizarre incident, the strap on Mrs. Sinclair's white vinyl purse broke. The maintenance man offered to mend it. "Crazy Glue will fix anything," he assured her. Four months later, she still didn't have her purse back. Again, Mrs. Sinclair telephoned the consumer columnist for the local newspaper. Within five minutes of her call, the administrator sent for Mrs. Sinclair to demand what was going on. "What other recourse did I have?" she asked the official, referring to her call to the columnist. The administrator gave fifty dollars to an activity worker to buy Mrs. Sinclair a new purse. "What I want to know is why didn't he give the money to me?" Mrs. Sinclair fumed. "That makes me mad. The activity worker is not my age. How does she know what I want?"

Concerned Friends of Ontario Citizens in Care Facilities, a consumer and advocacy group for nursing-home residents, recommends reporting thefts and other incidents to police. "If you lived in an apartment building and your superintendent offered to fix your purse and didn't bring it back, you'd call the police," says Patricia Spindel, past president of Concerned Friends. "But in nursing homes, people talk to the administrator. It just doesn't make sense."

Not only is there is no protection for Mrs. Sinclair from theft by residents and staff, but there is also virtually no security system at the home to deter criminals from outside the home. Mrs. Sinclair has been robbed twice. The first time, a young man gained entrance to her room by passing himself off as a maintenance worker. He took thirty-five dollars from her room. Forty-five minutes later, when she realized what had happened, she began to shake uncontrollably. "It was traumatic."

On the second occasion, Mrs. Sinclair was hanging up a bird cage in the lounge. When she turned around, her purse, containing thirty dollars, had disappeared from a couch. "That shows how quickly they move and how closely they watch you here," she says.

In some homes, "security" measures are little more than a pretext to keep tabs on the friends and relatives who are visiting the residents. In most homes, visitors are required to sign their name and indicate whom they are visiting; this helps the nursing homes discourage visits from journalists, advocacy groups and other potential troublemakers. In one Winnipeg home, clergy are required to indicate the reason for their visit. The nursing homes like to know as much as possible about everything that happens inside the walls of their buildings.

Mrs. Sinclair remembers sitting in the lounge with a friend one day. A member of the staff approached her. Without acknowledging her friend, the employee demanded: "Who's your visitor today?" Mrs. Sinclair made polite introductions. Later she sputtered in frustration. "She's got some nerve."

Not only do visitors sign in, but families taking residents out must sign them out. "You feel like a little kid that's being taken out of school. You feel like a prisoner," Mrs. Sinclair says.

Concerned Friends accepts the sign-in policy of most homes as a safety measure, although the group does not agree with it. "I suspect they have other motivations for doing it," Spindel says. "But we do accept it because there have been incidents in inner-city nursing homes where some pretty peculiar people have walked in."

There have been attempts by some nursing-home administrators to use the sign-in information to bar visitors such as members of Concerned Friends and the media. So far, it appears that they are able to use trespass laws to keep out whomever they wish, except a resident's legal counsel.

"Nursing homes are private institutions, and as such, the owners and agents for these owners have control over the property, and in turn control over who may come into the nursing home," says Judith Wahl, executive director of the Advocacy Centre for the Elderly in Toronto.

However, in the United States, the denial of access by visitors has been considered a breach of constitutional rights to free assembly and communication. Wahl says a similar argument could be made under Canada's Charter of Rights and Freedoms. "The residents, by virtue of the fact that they are living in the nursing home and are paying fees to receive the services of the home, may have the power to authorize the visitor to remain on the premises." Furthermore, nursing homes are nearly public institutions because they receive public funding.

But the question does not appear to have been decided, at least not in Ontario or Manitoba courts.

About seventy-five elderly men and women are wedged around a strip of carpet in the activity room of the nursing home. Every Wednesday is carpet bowling day. The residents sit in wheelchairs, or chairs in rows four deep. A few chat, others stare down at their laps. Only those in the front row can see the game. "The people in the back don't have a clue what's going on," one nursing-home employee comments to another. The activity worker wheels a man in a wheelchair to the front of the carpet runway, and hands him a ball. He flings it, and it bounces randomly down the carpet runway.

Large, mindless group activities such as carpet bowling do not appeal to Mrs. Sinclair. She prefers to read in her room — romance novels from the library, or the newspaper. She also enjoys visiting with her friends. However, the pressure to participate is often difficult to withstand.

"If a nurse comes up and says,'You're going to stroke club today' you're not going to say,'The hell I am,'" she explains.

The stroke club is an activity dreamed up by two activity workers who are under the age of forty. "How can they see through the eyes of someone over seventy?" Mrs. Sinclair demands. "If you have a stroke you don't want to talk about it. You don't want to be reminded. I don't see how it helps someone else to tell them I had a stroke. Several of those who attended their meetings ended up crying before it was over."

A young man from the activities department races up to Mrs. Sinclair while she is escorting a visitor to the door. "Going to the birthday party, Mrs. Sinclair?" he asks in a babyish sing-song voice. She glares at him and gives him her stock answer. "I never go to those things. I don't even go to my own."

Birthday parties are a major event in most nursing homes. They are typically held once a month, and everyone who has a birthday that month is honoured. A band is brought in, and a few residents get up and dance. Cake and ice cream are served. There are no presents or liquor. "They're like kids' parties," Mrs. Sinclair says. "I expect them to start singing, 'Gathering Nuts in May.'"

In another Winnipeg nursing home, residents who do not attend birthday parties are punished. "The administrator makes them eat in their room," a former staff member at the home said. "She says, 'You're here and you're supposed to participate.'"

The only activity Mrs. Sinclair attends is the glee club, once a week. But even there, the confused residents ruin it for the rest. "It sort of disgusts me because they all sing a different tune. The old ladies get all mixed up."

Win Lindsay is a former life-enrichment consultant to the Manitoba Health Services Commission, which funds and monitors nursing homes. She does not approve of mixing confused and lucid residents. "If you do that, you cannot give the specific kind of care and stimulation and environment that's best for certain types of people."

Although nursing homes are required to provide an activity program, they tend to spend as little as they can. The Manitoba Health Services Commission requires that homes of more than forty beds spend ten cents a day per resident for activity programs. At Mrs. Sinclair's home, supplies for the activities department come from the sale of residents' handiwork at the home's annual spring tea. On one occasion, $2,000 from the tea went to fix the piano in the lounge. Recently the home received a federal government grant to get a complete kitchen set for the activity room. In the meantime, the company that owns the home shows a healthy profit margin on its annual reports.

Lindsay says some Winnipeg nursing homes have imaginative activity programs, but most stick to the basics: crafts, church, bingo, exercise and entertainment. Most homes have slim libraries with old books. "There should be a lot more in any home," she says. "By putting a person in a personal care home, you have intervened. It's a duty to give them quality of life." She says some people commit slow suicide without meaningful activity. "They just will themselves to die and they do it over a period of months if they have decided there is no point in living any more." Lindsay argues that activity workers should have more training and higher pay. Currently, they are paid about $18,000 a year.

One Winnipeg woman, whose mother is in a Winnipeg nursing home, observes that the activities seem to be geared to accommodate the lower-functioning residents. "They are pretty childlike," she says. "There are crafts and a lot of entertainment, as opposed to discussion groups. In the main lounge, there's the TV. Period. It distresses me to see people just sitting around doing nothing."

In another home, a resident who enjoyed painting was forced to stop because his hobby was taking up too much room. "They were short of space so they stopped the painting," he said. "So I haven't done any more since."

There is an exercise program several times a week at Mrs. Sinclair's home. She does not find it challenging enough. "They throw a beach ball from three feet away. You can't miss it." Her friend Miss Bell, eighty-six, complains that the exercise class, a low priority for the staff, is postponed or cancelled at the slightest pretext. Most recently, it was cancelled to prepare the activity room for a bazaar.

Many people in nursing homes could benefit from physiotherapy and occupational therapy. Instead, they get no more than an exercise class — sometimes. Mrs. Sinclair's damaged arm was not given any rehabilitation in the nursing home, and the muscles have contracted to such an extent that the arm is now curled up on her breast.

And Mrs. Sinclair's home is not unique. Most homes in Ontario do not offer rehabilitative care. In Manitoba, the government pays a private, non-profit agency for therapy services in nursing homes. But there is a shortage of therapists. Moreover, the nursing homes seem to be a low priority for the therapists, who focus their efforts on people who are living independently. The average nursing home sees a therapist approximately once every two weeks. In theory, the therapist trains the nursing home staff to give residents therapy, but the staff are often too busy to do this.

A 1986 federal government study recommended an expansion of rehabilitation services for the elderly in institutions. "It is now recognized that rehabilitation therapy of many chronic conditions associated with older adults can delay institutionalization, reduce the burden of family caregivers and improve the quality of life of older adults," the study said. "However, in Canada there is a shortage of therapists such as physiotherapists, occupational, speech and recreation therapists. In the training of such professionals, little emphasis is placed on the benefits of rehabilitation with older adults."

Because of the absence of recreational activities in the nursing home, Mrs. Sinclair kills time by smoking in the lounge with a couple of men. Together they make up "the old fogey group," she says. "We just yack." The ashtray provided to them by the nursing home is a plastic fruit-juice jug with a hole ripped into it. It is rarely emptied and usually contains about six pungent inches of ashes.

Life in a nursing home is a thousand small indignities. Tea and coffee are available in the lounge for twenty-five cents a cup, but both are served in glass coffee pots, making it impossible to tell which is the tea and which is the coffee. You have to sniff the pots to tell the difference. A little basket of synthetic creamers is provided. The beverages are so weak and tasteless that Mrs. Sinclair is unsure which drink she has poured into her beige plastic mug — even after she has taken a sip.

If Mrs. Sinclair wants a soft drink during the day, she must purchase it from a vending machine in the lounge for eighty cents. She and one of her smoking pals — Mr. Miller — occasionally split a pop for the sake of thrift.

There is a colour TV in the lounge but no books or magazines, as the provincial government considers books and magazines a fire hazard. A government memo to nursing-home administrators says: "In the interests of safety, it is requested that lounges be kept clear of excessive amounts of flammable material, such as bookcases, magazine racks, etc."

And so the residents sit and smoke. Mr. Miller complains that staff have forbidden him to roll his own cigarettes, although they are half the price of packaged ones and he is on a fixed income. "A nurse came in and said,'You can't do that anymore. It makes too much of a mess.'"

Their conversation is interrupted every few minutes by the public-address system. "Would Mrs. So-and-So go to such-and-such a department."Or: "A message to all staff. Dr. Leach is in the building and will be doing rounds in a few minutes."

Mr. Miller scowls. "Dr. Leach. Big bloody deal." He says he doesn't like being examined by a stranger. He would prefer to see his long-time family doctor, but that is discouraged. Dr. Leach is one of several house doctors in the nursing home. Although residents have the right to see their own physicians, the nursing-home administration encourages residents to use Dr. Leach or one of the other house doctors. It is more convenient for the administrators.

Just before supper, the nursing home opens its bar for an hour. Mr. Miller goes in for his daily whisky. Mrs. Sinclair never goes, because the liquor is too expensive. "A dollar twenty-five for a whisky, and you only get a jiggerful."

When her male friend leaves, Mrs. Sinclair is joined by Brenda, a nursing-home resident who is a former stripper. She parades through the home singing all her former show songs. Brenda is a large, busty woman bursting out of worn red polyster slacks and a red blouse. She has a ring on every finger and dyed blonde hair up in a ponytail. She walks with a cane. "Sometimes I just don't feel like living," she says, her face crumpling. But at the Christmas party, she got up to sing a carol.

One reason Mrs. Sinclair spends so much time in the downstairs lounge is because it is the only attractive place in the nursing home. It is spacious and abundantly decorated with silk plants. The carpet and numerous couches harmonize in tones of brown and beige. Many homes spend considerable effort to beautify the lobby area. It's a showcase meant to impress visitors — too often at the expense of other areas of the home.

The rest of the old downtown building has a tired, institutional look. The corridors are long and cold, with grey tile floors and white concrete walls. The paint is chipped and the handrails worn. The elevators are tiny and choppy and more often than not, the stench of urine greets the visitor who gets off on a resident floor. Residents wander aimlessly up and down the halls or perch on a kitchen chair by the elevator in what's known as the "designated smoking area." Signs providing information about the month's activities are scrawled on a piece of construction paper. Decoration is of the kindergarten variety — for example, paper hearts taped to the corridor wall on Valentine's Day.

While the lounge is comfortably air-conditioned in summer, residents' rooms are "like an oven" during Winnipeg's scorching summers, says Mrs. Sinclair. When she purchased an air conditioner for her room, she became the only resident to have one, prompting a steady stream of company. "Boy, was I popular," she recalls.

The record-breaking heat wave in the summer of 1988 probably contributed to the deaths of thirteen residents of nursing homes and homes for the aged in Ontario. In buildings without air conditioning, many residents suffered from heat and dehydration. The Ontario Ministry of Health was forced to issue guidelines for keeping residents cool, and for identifying and relieving symptoms of heat stroke and heat exhaustion.

About a dozen elderly residents — some sitting in wheelchairs, others leaning on walkers or canes — are waiting outside the dining room. The doors are shut and will not open for another half an hour, and lunch will not be served for another hour. Lining up in advance is a common sight in many nursing homes. Meals are the highlight of the day: since there are few other activities, meals break the monotony.

The food is rarely worth the wait. Liver and onions are a frequent offering. "The liver is tough. They don't take the membrane off when they cook it," Mrs. Sinclair says. "The other night I had liver and onions, and my liver was burned black. I was indignant that they would serve it to me like that. But it didn't get me anywhere."

Fresh salad or fruit is rare. If a bit of lettuce appears on Mrs. Sinclair's plate, she feeds it to the budgie in the lounge. "Some days they'll bring a bowl full of macaroni. Awful stuff. Not cooked. Looks horrible. I enjoy my breakfast here and that's about all. I have oatmeal porridge or a hardboiled egg, toast, jam, coffee."

In many homes, the milk is powdered. "Sometimes it looks like milk, sometimes it doesn't," one kitchen worker comments. "It depends on how much water they put in." Drink crystals are often used instead of real juice. Eggs are often served twice a day because they are a cheap source of protein.

Nursing homes in Manitoba spend about ninety-three cents on each meal for a resident. Daily food costs are about $2.80 a day per resident.

Jerry Fontaine, administrator of a nursing home at the Fort Alexander Indian Reserve in Manitoba, complained angrily to the federal Indian Affairs Department when the department asked him to limit his food costs to the same level as the provincial nursing homes, eighty-eight cents a meal. The Fort Alexander home spends about $2.20 meal. "It's ludicrous to think that any human being can be provided with a well-balanced and nutritious meal at ninety-three cents per meal," says Fontaine.

Anne Hrenchuk, a dietetic consultant to the Manitoba Health Services Commission, inspects up to fifty nursing homes a year. She says she receives complaints about instant potatoes, or beef being too tough or too greasy. "Some people say the food is rotten," she says.

Lindsay, the life-enrichment consultant, notes that nursing-home food is often not as spicy as many older people would like. "Somehow there's a feeling that older people can't have spicy food," she says. But in reality, the residents often prefer spicy food. Age and constant medication have dulled their taste buds, so they cannot taste their food unless it is well seasoned.

Nursing-home residents tend to be lumped together, especially at mealtime. They are not treated as individuals. Miss Bell, for instance, says there is always too much food on her plate. She asks for less, but she is ignored. "I suppose they're sort of dishing them out one after another," she sighs. "But a big piled plate turns off my appetite."

Mrs. Sinclair eats with the confused residents — upstairs in the lounge on her floor — because she doesn't like eating in the main dining room, with over 100 people. "They're just herded in like sheep," she says. "They fit in wherever." The food also takes too long to arrive, and residents are left to gape at each other.

The 1985 Manitoba Conference on Aging condemned "herding," which is the term used by gerontologists to describe the common practice of gathering large groups of elderly residents together for meals and recreation activities. Conference participants called it depersonalizing.

In one rural Manitoba nursing home, the dining room is in the basement of an eighty-three-year-old building. The elderly and infirm residents line up and wait at the elevator. Employees lead them inside and they descend to the basement to eat amid fluorescent lights, pipes and cement.

About ten people eat in the small lounge on Mrs. Sinclair's floor. They are lined up around the walls, each with a small table in front of them. The elderly men and women stare straight ahead or down at their tables without uttering a word. About half are in wheelchairs with a tray across their chair handles. Most of the men are wearing jogging pants. One worried-looking woman is dressed in a red jogging suit with hot pink pantyhose peeking out at the ankles. A set of large faux pearls completes the ensemble.

A young woman with long swinging hair brings brown plastic trays holding thick, institutional crockery and brown plastic mugs of coffee. Lunch is a western omelette with toast. Because Mrs. Sinclair had eggs for breakfast, she requests a substitute, and is given chicken salad spread thinly on white sandwich bread without lettuce. Her tray also contains a four-ounce plastic cup of apple juice and a small glass of milk. Meanwhile, the confused residents are fed scrambled eggs and mashed potatoes.

The staff members are picking up the tiny bowls of dessert and trying to guess what they contain. They giggle, give up, and slap down the mystery substance — apparently a blob of oatmeal smeared with pink jelly.

Those who can feed themselves eat quickly and wordlessly, their eyes glued to their plates. The young woman feeds several residents while standing over them, hair dangling into their trays. "C'mon, you gotta eat something," she tells an old man, sounding irritated. Her eyes wander to a stormy love affair unfolding on the television in the lounge. After a few mouthfuls, a confused woman pushes her table away with a loud scrape and bolts from the lounge. A minute later there's a commotion in the hall. "Don't you dare!" a member of the staff can be heard shouting. "I know what you were going to do. You were set to hit her. Now, get back to your room!" Nobody in the lounge so much as looks up. After about twenty minutes, Mrs. Sinclair pushes her table away and leaves in silence.

Food is the number-one complaint of residents. Their grievances include cold food, poor cooking and lack of variety. However, their attempts to improve the situation through their official voice — the residents' council — have met with little success. "We talked to the dietary fellow but things go on just the same," Mrs. Sinclair says. "He agrees with everything and goes on doing the same thing."

Other complaints do not even get that far. Mrs. Sinclair says many residents are afraid to speak their minds. Their perception is that if they complain too loudly, they will suffer retaliation. Most prefer to be quiet about most issues because they don't want to deal with reprisals.

"They're all hidden away in their own little worlds, too scared to say anything," she says. "They talk about their beefs outside the meeting of the residents' council. If I went to court and needed a witness, not one person in here would say I'm right."

According to Patricia Spindel of Concerned Friends, the fears of retaliation are well founded. Concerned Friends has had reports of the following reprisals: mail held up; food not arriving; residents scolded, threatened, left on the toilet for extended periods of time, ignored when they ring the call bell. "There are a million different ways that people can get even with people in nursing homes," she says. "And it's impossible to prove. I've had a number of residents say to me, 'It's easy for you. You can leave at night.'"

Residents' councils, which represent the people in each nursing home, are legislated in Ontario and encouraged in Manitoba through government guidelines.Theoretically, incidents of abuse or neglect can be reported to these bodies. But the residents who are most likely to be abused — those who are physically and mentally frail — are usually unable to participate in the councils.

Mrs. Sinclair says the residents' council in her nursing home has been a disappointment. "It has no teeth," she says. "It's the deadest thing you ever saw." According to a report by a union in Alberta, the residents' councils in many nursing homes are run by the activity director or the administrator of the home. This arrangement, given the residents' fear of reprisals for speaking out, casts serious doubt on their ability to express their opinions at council meetings.

In Mrs. Sinclair's home a resident was elected secretary of the council, but he suffered a stroke and is unable to speak or hear. "Communication is sort of restricted," Mrs. Sinclair says. "But we can't really kick him out. It would hurt his feelings." His duties are currently performed by a nursing-home employee.

Improvements in the nursing homes are often temporary. The administrators are given advance warning of the scheduled visits by teams of inspectors from the Canadian Council on Health Facilities Accreditation, an independent standards agency which assesses nursing homes for accreditation.

Mrs Sinclair always knows when the inspectors are scheduled to arrive, because her nursing home is spotless. "You don't know the place," Mrs. Sinclair says. "You don't recognize the meals you get that day. You're looking around to see if you're in the right place."

A 1986 report on crimes against the elderly in institutions in Ontario — by Toronto criminologist Dr. Birthe Jorgensen — found sufficient grounds for criminal charges in almost half of the fifty-six detailed complaints which were studied. Theft was one of the charges that could have been laid. Among the other potential charges were assault or breach of legal duty to provide the essentials of life or proper medical care.

One of the most dramatic examples was a case where residents of a home were so hungry that they were begging for food from visitors and eating paper from wastepaper baskets. In another case, a ninety-nine year-old woman with a broken leg was denied X-rays and medical attention by nursing-home staff — including the doctor — for more than eleven days. And a ninety-one-year-old blind woman suffered a large bruise and cut on her forehead after being assaulted by staff.

Of the fifty-six complaints, only one was made by a resident. The rest came from families and staff members of nursing homes. Jorgensen says that the victims' fear of retaliation makes them too scared to come forward with complaints. Furthermore, they have no other place to go, as there are waiting lists for nursing homes, and few community alternatives.

None of the complaints were made to the police. Instead, Jorgensen found that complaints were made to the staff and administration of the nursing home or the Ministry of Health (which licenses and regulates nursing homes) or the Ministry of Community and Social Services (which oversees publicly owned Homes for the Aged).

Jorgensen says criminal prosecutions can and should be initiated for offences perpetrated in nursing homes. "Criminal prosecutions probably will be more likely to effect positive changes in conditions in nursing homes at present than the current enforcement mechanisms of the Ministry of Health," she concluded in her report.

The release of this report sparked a furor. It led to an investigation by the Ontario Provincial Police and the Metropolitan Toronto Policeinto some of the more notorious nursing homes.

Amazingly, the investigation concluded that there was no evidence that poor medical treatment had resulted in actual endangerment of the lives or health of the residents. However, these cases were reported to the College of Physicians and Surgeons for investigation.

Police were not able to lay criminal charges in homes with unsanitary conditions because "the failure to provide a clean and pleasant environment for those residents by owners of care facilities does not necessarily amount to a failure to provide the 'necessaries of life', nor does such a failure show a 'wanton or reckless disregard to the lives or safety' of the residents," Attorney-General Ian Scott wrote in a February 1989 letter to Patricia Spindel of Concerned Friends. Furthermore, criminal negligence in cases of poor conditions and inadequate housing care cannot be proven if the accused has an honest belief that the life or safety of the victim was not at risk. "It should be noted that in criminal law an 'honest belief' does not have to be a reasonable belief," Scott wrote.

Although police found "questionable nursing care," they concluded that staff were not recklessly or intentionally negligent in a criminal sense. "In many cases the evidence was equally consistent with staff being overworked or not properly trained for the duties which they were required to perform."

As a result of the investigation, a memorandum was issued to all chiefs of police advising them of the importance of thorough investigations of alleged criminal offences in nursing homes.

In his letter to Spindel, Attorney-General Scott explained how difficult it is to collect evidence and lay charges in nursing-home incidents. Many of the police officers assigned to this case visited nursing homes for the first time as a result of the investigation. In many cases, police found, conditions at the homes had improved greatly since the complaints arose. In some cases, the homes were under new management or had closed down. In other cases, residents or relatives were unwilling to co-operate with police in providing a statement. The greatest difficulty was the passage of time since the alleged offences had occurred.

Usually, Mrs. Sinclair gets out of bed at around 7:30 a.m.. But sometimes she's awake at 5:30 a.m., when the staff start jabbering in the corridor. "It gets pretty darn noisy when one of the women starts," she says. The resident whose room is above Mrs. Sinclair's is constantly re-arranging her furniture. Sometimes the scraping of chairs and dressers can be heard at 6:30 a.m. When Mrs. Sinclair complained to a staffer, she was asked: "What do you want me to do about it?"

Although Mrs. Sinclair is supposed to have help getting undressed, staff only came to her room twice during a recent week. "I had to get undressed myself. And it's a burden, believe me. When I get to my bra I can't undo it, because I need two hands."

While some members of the staff are wonderful, others are rude and indifferent, she says. They make her life at the home uncomfortable. "They're officious and self-opinionated, always diagnosing someone else's case and forgetting their own," Mrs. Sinclair says bitterly.

Before Christmas she had ordered several boxes of chocolates from a drugstore to give to friends and favourite members of the staff as Christmas gifts. When they were delivered, she went to the front desk and asked for them. "What's the magic word?" demanded the receptionist. "Buzz off," Mrs. Sinclair spat.

Despite her bravado, Mrs. Sinclair is all too aware that she is in the hands of the nursing-home administration. She frets about what they will or will not let her do. When a nearby shopping centre opened, Mrs. Sinclair went to see it but fell down several stairs in the mall. As other shoppers hovered over her and discussed calling an ambulance, she leapt up and fled. She was shaken, scraped and embarrassed. "I said I wasn't hurt. Oh, but I was. But if I came back here and told them I fell, they'd never let me out again."

She had an invitation to go to Ontario for Christmas. "I don't think they'll let me go," she said gloomily. She went to Vancouver a few years ago, but the administrators are stricter now, she says. She ended up spending Christmas at the nursing home, commiserating with another resident, whose elderly sister had been murdered a year earlier. "We wept together."

One Christmas, a health-care aide promised to take her home to visit the aide's family. Mrs. Sinclair bought some books for the woman's children and sat in the lounge, waiting to be picked up. The aide never came. When she finally called in mid-March to apologize, Mrs. Sinclair was curt with her. "There's only so much a person can take," she explained.

Forming attachments in the home too often leads to heartbreak. Mrs. Sinclair befriended a thirty-seven-year-old female epileptic "because she had so little." But the woman died a short time ago. Another good friend of hers was recently diagnosed with throat cancer.

Deaths are a common occurrence in nursing homes, but the residents are the last to find out. They eventually learn the news from the rumour mill. "There's very little mentioned in the building about death, even on your floor." Miss Bell says. "A lady across the hall died, and I didn't know all morning. I guess they figure you'll get depressed."

Mrs. Sinclair's visitors have grown few and far between. "When I first came in here, I had so many visitors I didn't know what to do with them. But they've dwindled over the years. I guess I'm losing my charm."

She has a ninety-year-old sister who still lives in her own home. And she has a fun-loving sixty-year-old divorced niece who visits her and takes her shopping.

Mrs. Sinclair is dressed in a green and gold sparkly two-piece outfit. She expertly opens her bag with one hand, removes a cigarette, lights it and smokes elegantly. "Never take up smoking unless you enter a nursing home," she advises. "Then you'll want something to pass the time. Better yet, when you get old, don't let them put you in a place like this."

2

MRS. LEARY

There are two dining rooms in Mary Leary's nursing home. One is for residents who can feed themselves; Mrs. Leary calls it the "Royal Highness Room." She eats in the other dining room — the one for mentally and physically handicapped residents, who need help eating or who must be fed by the staff.

Mrs. Leary knows she is in the wrong place when she is sent to have meals with the elderly, demented residents. However, she is confined to a wheelchair, paralyzed on her left side by a stroke, weakened by a heart condition and further disabled by an amputated right leg. She needs help eating. So she is assigned to the room for the confused and crippled.

"There's nothing wrong with my mind," she says. "But I have to sit in this room with all these people screaming. By the time you look at that noise and all that around you, you're not hungry."

The "Royal Highness Room" has tablecloths on the tables. In Mrs. Leary's dining room, by contrast, the tables are covered with plastic sheeting to guard against spills and drooling. Even the food served in the two rooms sometimes differs. One evening, when the residents of the "Royal Highness Room" were served pork chops for supper, Mrs. Leary and her fellow-diners were given small shreds of pork roast — a cheaper cut of meat. The roast was accompanied by half a potato. "Would you mind bringing me a magnifying glass so I can see how many pieces of meat are here?" Mrs. Leary sarcastically asked the food server.

The comment is typical of the dark humour and bitterness Mrs. Leary feels about her life in an institution. At age sixty, she is one of the younger residents of what is sometimes called "the old folks' home."

"It's depressing," she says. "I was fifty-two when I came in. Right now I feel like I'm ninety. You feel old before your time. I've lost interest in everything."

Nursing homes in Canada house not only the elderly, but also thousands of younger people with psychiatric problems, physical handicaps, mental retardation or cerebral palsy. Across the country, thousands of people under the age of sixty-five live in nursing homes. In Manitoba alone, a total of 398 people under the age of sixty-five were living in nursing homes in 1988. They represented almost 5 per cent of all nursing-home residents in the province. And these younger residents included seventy-two people under the age of forty-five.

The Fourth Manitoba Conference on Aging in 1985 recommended that the provincial government develop special facilities for young disabled people. But so far, little has been done. There is one special apartment complex in Winnipeg: Ten Ten Sinclair, a transitional residence where people with disabilities can gain practical skills in daily living, so that they can function independently. Other young disabled people live in their own homes with personal-care services provided by the provincial home-care program. For others, there is no alternative to a nursing home.

A nursing home cannot offer a satisfying life to a young person. "A nursing home is supposed to be for older people for care until they die," says Lise, a thirty-five-year-old former schoolteacher from rural Manitoba. She has multiple sclerosis. "I find myself growing old before my time." Her room in a large Winnipeg nursing home overlooks a cemetery.

"The needs of the younger residents are different from those of the elderly," says Renald Massicotte, executive director of Tache Nursing Centre in Winnipeg. "They have a greater desire for autonomy, socialization." Tache is one of two Winnipeg homes with a concentration of younger people. In 1988 more than one-fifth of the 316 residents were under the age of sixty-five.

"This is not the right setting for young people," agrees Mollie Willard, director of nursing at Bethania Mennonite Personal Care Home in Winnipeg. "They need someone to go out and have a beer with. Their sexual needs are different. It's difficult to bring in girlfriends and boyfriends. It's like a small town. It wouldn't take long for word to get around."

Concerned Friends is strongly opposed to mixing people of vastly different ages and health problems in the same nursing home. Anne-Marie Johnston, past president of the organization, calls this practice warehousing. "Whether it's multiple sclerosis, muscular dystrophy, Alzheimer's, Parkinson's, mental retardation; it doesn't matter," she says. "We grab these people and stick them in a warehouse. We close the door, and forget about them, and make sure they never come out."

"It's disastrous to put all these people together," says Patricia Spindel of Concerned Friends. "When you start mixing people with different needs nobody gets their needs met."

To avoid the elderly residents of the nursing home, Mrs. Leary has become a recluse. She only ventures out of her tiny bedroom for meals. "I got my own problems," she growls. "You ask some of those old people how they are and some of them won't bother talking to you. Others tell you their problems, and by the time they're finished, you're sick."

Mrs. Leary has no friends her own age in the nursing home. The only other younger resident is a fifty-two-year-old woman who is mentally impaired. Mrs. Leary used to chum around with a woman in her thirties who had multiple sclerosis, but that woman moved to Tache: she, too wanted to be with people her own age.

Mrs. Leary always sits in the same corner of her room in front of her 14-inch television. Her bedroom is about twelve feet by fourteen feet — considerably less than the size recommended by provincial guidelines. It is much too small for her. She wheels back to her room from supper and tries to manoeuvre the wheelchair into her favourite corner. As the mechanical chair swings around, Mrs. Leary's foot gets caught under her hospital bed. "Ouch!" Her face is twisted with pain. A visitor helps dislodge her foot, and she tries again. This time, the wheelchair rams into the narrow closet containing Mrs. Leary's few dresses. No members of the nursing-home staff come to help. "There's nobody ever around," she mutters angrily. After five minutes, she is finally in position.

Mrs. Leary's room contains a bedside table, a little sink, a small desk and a chair. A collection of stuffed animals is displayed on the desk. A small print of The Last Supper hangs over her bed. Colour photographs of a grinning little girl with jaunty blonde pigtails and a swaddled baby boy hang in a prominent position on the wall. "I haven't given up hope of seeing my grandchildren," Mrs. Leary says. Because of a quarrel with her son, she hasn't seen the two youngsters for six years. "I think my son has told them I've passed away," she says.

Mrs. Leary is divorced. She once lived by herself in an inner-city rooming house. When she lost her leg due to poor circulation, she moved to a wheelchair suite in a special apartment for disabled people. She did her own shopping, attended wrestling matches and went for drives in the country with a friend. It was a pleasant life. But a crippling stroke eight years ago ended all that. Like many poor, single women, she found herself in a nursing home.

Mrs. Leary is worried she's becoming like her elderly neighbours. "My mind is starting to go," she says. "Someone tells me something and I'll forget five minutes later. In a nursing home, you take on an older person's life. You just don't want to do anything or you figure you can't do it."

Twice a year, Mrs. Leary goes to the activity room, where travelling salesmen from a clothing manufacturer for the handicapped ply their wares, spring and fall. She is wearing one of the company's flowered polyester dresses, which cost thirty dollars of her income-tax refund. It was money well spent: the dress is practical — it fastens with velcro — and complements her short red hair and smooth white skin. Her outfit is set off by a knitted legwarmer.

Mrs. Leary's favourite entertainment is watching films on video. She rents them from a nearby video store, which provides free delivery to her on Saturday afternoons. She doesn't get to pick which video she wants to watch. But a sympathetic saleswoman has learned her taste over time and can make an educated guess.

Another pastime is reviewing the films for the nursing-home newsletter. If visitors express a suitable degree of interest, Mrs. Leary can be persuaded to roll down the hall past the constant sing-songs, which she loathes ("We're so happy," the residents sing) to the bulletin board, where her cryptic reviews of films are tacked. The film "Three Men and a Baby" gets five stars and the comment: "It goes to show that men can't do without us women."

This is the only way she can read the film reviews in the newsletter. Her hands are too disabled to turn pages or hold a book. Years ago, she asked the physiotherapist, who sometimes comes to the nursing home, for a mechanical page-turner. But she never got it. "I used to love to read," she mourns. Romance and animal stories were her favourites.

But now her life's passion unfolds on her TV screen. She loves the antics of the professional wrestlers. And she uses wrestling videos as a form of therapy. "When I get mad, I put on my tapes of Wrestlemania, and fantasize I've got one of the aides or the doctor and I'm beating them up," Mrs. Leary confesses. "That makes me feel better."

Mrs. Leary became a wrestling fan at the age of thirteen when her mother took her to a match. For the next thirty years, mother and daughter attended wrestling matches, often obtaining front-row seats. "Yukon Eric, Hardboiled Haggerty, Whipper Billy Watson, Pretty Boy," she recites. "I could name them all."

The Wrestlemania tapes were Christmas gifts from her sister and brother-in-law who visit every Wednesday afternoon and all day Christmas. Although she is not close to her sister, Mrs. Leary appreciates the contact with people close to her age. "If you've got family to back you up, you're doing pretty good," she says. "If you haven't got family you might as well give up and die."

When she wants to listen to music, Mrs. Leary flips on the TV weather channel, which plays easy listening tunes as news and weather information scroll across the screen.

Mrs. Leary's life-line is a small white control unit, about the size of a pack of cards. By pressing down on it with the slight mobility she has in her right hand she can operate her phone, TV, video-cassette recorder and call bell. A box that looks like a compact disc player contains the controls.

Any diversions are up to her because the nursing home has cut back on activities she used to enjoy. The home used to provide occasional entertainment, such as a children's choir or live dance band. "Now there's nothing," Mrs. Leary says. "It's gone to the dogs."

Mrs. Leary believes the home cancelled the social programs as a cost-cutting measure. The nursing home once had pub nights for the residents, but those were also terminated. There was once a shop that sold cigarettes and candy, but it was replaced with vending machines, which Mrs. Leary is too disabled to operate.

Mrs. Leary does not take pleasure in the few activities that are available, because they are not intended for adults who have their full mental faculties. These childish programs include sing-songs and such crafts as making Easter bonnets out of tissue paper.

Other activities are not appropriate for Mrs. Leary because they are toned down to accommodate the elderly. For example, the church service is only fifteen minutes long, because the nursing-home administrators feel a longer service would tire the elderly residents. Mrs. Leary, a Roman Catholic, does not attend Mass because it takes her more time to get to and from the room where the service is held than she actually spends at the service. So she stays in her room.

A group of nursing-home residents, including Mrs. Leary, once went to an outdoor theatre to see a play. But the staff returned them to the nursing home at intermission, because it was time for the older people to go to bed. Mrs. Leary was extremely disappointed.

The primary entertainment fixture of every nursing home is the TV. Television is the constant background noise of almost every nursing home — canned laughter, children's shows, game shows and soap operas.

One evening, the local cable company was experiencing technical difficulties. In the lounge of a Winnipeg nursing home, the television screen was blank except for a series of wavy lines. The staff of the home made an announcement over the public-address system to inform the residents that the TV programs were being interrupted. But the elderly residents still sat in front of the TV, watching the test pattern.

Not only is Mrs. Leary mentally stagnating in the nursing home, but she has also physically deteriorated. When she first went into the home, she was still able to slide herself out of her wheelchair and onto her bed. But now she cannot. At one time, she was able to feed herself. Now she cannot lift her arm. Mrs. Leary believes this is the result of a shortage of physiotherapy in the nursing home.

When Mrs. Leary applied for admission to the home, she asked if physiotherapy was available. It was important to her. The administration of the nursing home assured her that a therapist would visit. Mrs. Leary soon learned that a therapist arrives only once every two weeks — mainly to help the elderly residents get fitted for devices such as walkers. Although she is supposed to receive assistance with arm-movement exercises twice a day, she is lucky if she gets the required exercise once a week. Worried about her deteriorating abilities, she requested more therapy. "I'll see about it," the administrator of the nursing home promised. But that was as far as it went. "I just gave up," Mrs. Leary admits.

A member of the staff in another Winnipeg nursing home observes that most of the residents end up in wheelchairs. "They come in walking or with a cane or a walker, and in a few months, they're all in wheelchairs," she says.

Mrs. Leary feels her health needs are being neglected because she is considered one of the elderly people. She does not get an annual physical examination, breast examinations or Pap tests. However, she does receive a veritable cornucopia of medication — about ten different kinds, including an anti-flatulent, valium and assorted heart medications. The list of pills keeps growing longer. "If one disagrees with you, they give you another, but they don't take away the first," she says.

A Winnipeg study of residents of a nursing home found that all the residents interviewed took medication ranging from two to twelve pills a day. One woman described what was a common scenario for many residents: "I take half a green pill for my stomach. I had an operation years ago and the veins don't open very good. I take calcium pills, a stool softener and pain pills...I take Gravol for my upset stomach and a nerve pill — valium."

Because Mrs. Leary lives with elderly people, she tends to get the same poor medical care that they do. She has had an ongoing battle with the house doctor who visits the nursing home and is responsible for its residents. She has been having pains in her stomach for two years, and wants them diagnosed. But the doctor does not usually come to the residents' rooms. The elderly people are expected to line up at the nursing station, where he examines them. "I told him I wasn't going to kiss his backside," Mrs. Leary says. "He's getting paid for this."

Furthermore, Mrs. Leary is annoyed at the doctor's short memory. "I got so sick of telling him how I lost my leg I finally told him I was a wrestler and I lost it in the ring," she says. "I said I was in a leg lock, and it was twisted so hard it came right off." The doctor was intrigued, and wanted to know how she got out of the ring.

In Ontario, inquest juries have repeatedly recommended that physicians working in nursing homes should receive training in the special needs of the elderly. The Canadian Medical Association has called for improved training of medical students to help them learn how to care for the elderly.

"Although more than 20 per cent of physician services are directed at people over age sixty-five, only a small part of the curricula of Canadian medical schools is devoted to geriatric teaching," the CMA wrote in a 1987 report on health care for the elderly. Of the sixteen Canadian faculties of medicine, only one includes compulsory training in the care of the elderly, the CMA noted.

The biggest complaint of nursing-home residents is that doctors do not spend enough time with them. In one case in Ontario, a doctor admitted to visiting about forty nursing-home residents in a single morning.

The inadequate care provided by doctors to nursing-home residents can also be attributed to the payment system. Physicians are usually paid between ten dollars and fifteen dollars for each visit to a nursing-home resident. That does not include travelling time. "That buys about five to ten minutes of a physician's time," says Dr. James Kirkland, chief of geriatric services at the Queen Elizabeth Hospital in Toronto. "Eventually, that will create a degree of resentment or reluctance to visit a person in a nursing home."

Mrs. Leary is demoralized by her ever-increasing dependence on the members of the staff. "It hurts," she says. "Especially if you're alert and you have to rely on others to do things for you."

"We want to promote their independence," says Sandra, a Winnipeg nurse who works in a nursing home. "But certain rules are applicable in an institution because we need to maintain order."

A frail, elderly resident of a Winnipeg nursing home says she tries to do as much as possible for herself. "That's my therapy," she says. "While I can do it, I have the upper hand."

Mrs. Leary is categorized as a heavy-care resident. She must be fed, taken to the bathroom, and lifted on and off her bed. She is washed by staff, and cleaned up when she has an accident. When she is in bed or in her wheelchair, she must be repositioned periodically to prevent pressure sores. All of these tasks are performed by health-care aides.

"Some of the girls are all right," Mrs. Leary says. "Others make you feel like you gotta get on your hands and knees and beg 'em to do something for you. They don't realize how embarrassing it is if we have an accident."

Mrs. Leary is showered twice a week. To avoid thinking about the indignity of being bathed, she tries to have some fun. "If I have a nice aide who knows what she's doing, we more or less fool around in the shower," Mrs. Leary says. "She gets more wet than I do."

She is hoisted by a mechanical lift into the shower, where she sits on a chair with a hole in the seat. The aide soaps her with a washcloth, then hoses her down. The water is turned on outside the shower by the aide. "I gotta be alert," Mrs. Leary says. "They try it first on themselves. My circulation is not as good. What's warm on them is boiling hot on me."

The staff have labelled Mrs. Leary a "difficult resident" because she complains if she feels she is not getting proper care. "If they do anything I don't like I just tell them right to their face," she says. "I don't care if they like me or they don't. I always say to the girls: 'You're going to get old. How do you know you won't be like me?' They get quite annoyed."

Many nursing homes hire health-care aides with little or no training. It is cheaper than hiring aides who have a certificate from a community college. On-the-job training is usually minimal as well. At Mrs. Leary's home, the new aides are given one day of orientation, during which they stand and watch an experienced health-care aide. The following day, they are on their own.

The Christian Labour Association of Canada, in a report on conditions in Alberta nursing homes in 1988, noted that aides are trained by reading manuals for one day and working alongside an experienced aide for two days. "After this small amount of training, new employees carry a full workload and are expected to be fully knowledgeable about how to care for the residents, some of whom are fully bedridden, partially paralyzed or suffering from such crippling ailments as Alzheimer's Disease," the Alberta report said.

The new aides often learn poor work habits from already overburdened staff. There is a risk of injury to both the aide and the resident.

As the recipient of hands-on care, Mrs. Leary is worried about the inexperienced health-care aides the nursing home hires. "They're getting so many new girls off the street," she says. "They don't know what they're doing. It's scary. They open the blanket and you got one leg and you can't move and the poor kid doesn't know what to do."

Inexperienced aides cause pain to Mrs. Leary when they fail to seat her properly in the sling of the mechanical lift to hoist her in and out of bed. It also hurts when she is not properly placed in her wheelchair, and she slides out. "The other day I was crying, I was so uncomfortable," she says. "The nurse was just about to say, 'Go back to your room and wait,' but my niece showed up. The nurse came as soon as she saw her."

Mrs. Leary is acutely aware that the home does not have enough staff. She must always ask to be repositioned in her chair or bed, because the staff are too busy to notice. "I could be completely hanging over my chair in the hall and they won't bother unless I ask," she says. "Some just give my shoulder a push. Others do it the proper way. They lift under the arms."

Although the air in the home is very dry, Mrs. Leary has stopped using her humidifier because the workers are too busy to keep it filled with water. "One girl will fill it up and the next one won't."

Nor does she get enough to drink. "I keep asking and asking the girls for a drink and they say, 'Yeah, okay,' and they forget." Between meals, juice is available only in half-empty four-ounce glasses. "They get mad if I ask for more juice," she says. Yet dehydration is a serious health problem in nursing homes.

In her younger days, Mrs. Leary worked as a health-care aide in a community hospital. So when student nurses are sent to the nursing home for six weeks of training, they are told to practise on her. "I can train them," she says. "I teach them how to put a sling on, how to dress a handicapped person, how to feed a handicapped person."

Some members of the staff — experienced or not — are good. Others get jaded and callous. "A lot of them just shovel the food into your mouth, instead of putting it to your lips so you can test it with your tongue to see if it's hot," Mrs. Leary says. "There's some that are here because they care, but others are here just for the money. They don't care how you sit or how they treat you.

"The caring ones will make you comfortable, and they'll laugh with you and joke with you while they're doing their work. The other ones just slap you around, bang you here and there trying to get you where you're going fast — to the bed or to the washroom. They scratch you or hit you with their elbow. They yell at the residents."

The insensitivity of some staff is astounding. While Mrs. Leary talked to a visitor, a nurse marched into her room. Ignoring the visitor, the nurse placed a plastic cup under Mrs. Leary's chin and ordered her to remove her teeth for cleaning. Mrs. Leary meekly obeyed. The teeth fell out with a clack.

It is suppertime on Good Friday. Mrs. Leary sits at a dining table with three elderly women. She is the last at the table to get her portion of battered fish, green beans and hash browns. "Nothing tastes the same as in your own home," one nursing-home resident says. "Sometimes they mix it all up like for a dog or a cat."

Another woman at Mrs. Leary's table gets a pureed dinner. It consists of a green glob and two beige globs. The food is served on thick institutional china. Most residents are wearing white terrycloth bibs. A member of the dietary staff rushes up to Mrs. Leary's table and, without saying a word, snatches away the salt shaker and gives it to a resident at another table.

One of the women eating with Mrs. Leary gulps her food and leaves the dining room before dessert is served. "Good evening, ladies," she says, beating a hasty retreat. Another woman at the table picks at her food. When the plate is whisked away at the end of the meal, it is nearly untouched. The faces of the elderly diners in the room are sad. There is no chatter or laughter. A demented woman at another table loudly demands: "What is wrong here? Will you tell me what is wrong here?" Another woman asks for dessert and is told by a member of the staff: "You'll have to wait."

There are too few workers in the dining room to help feed the residents. Mrs. Leary sits and waits until an aide is available. "Sometimes I'm the last one out," she says.

The aide sits between Mrs. Leary and another resident and alternates feeding them: a spoonful into one mouth, and a spoonful into the other. Mrs. Leary only eats soup for supper, because her stomach is sore. She consumes half a bowl. "Too salty," she grimaces.

The Christian Labour Association report found that many nursing homes in Alberta were "shamefully understaffed," especially at mealtimes. "In several institutions it is impossible to feed a resident in a relaxed way," the report said. "There is no time to ensure that the soup or other food is not too hot or too cold, so some residents refuse to eat or cannot keep up and consequently do not get adequate nutrition."

The food has an institutional sameness to it. But Mrs. Leary is amazed at all the different appellations dreamed up in the kitchen to gussy up their offerings. "All this week, we had chicken, but they had three different names for it."

Although it is an especially chilly March, a fan overhead is blowing cold air throughout the dining room. Many of the elderly residents are wearing sweaters and have covered their legs or shoulders with afghans. A confused woman in a wheelchair sits with her dress up around her waist, exposing bare legs in knee-high stockings. As Mrs. Leary leaves the dining room she passes a disoriented man who has made several unsuccessful attempts to escape from the nursing home. "I want to get to know him," she quips. "Maybe he'll hold the door open for me."

Mrs. Leary keeps her bedroom door open because she feels claustrophic. The halls hum with activity. Staff bellow to each other. Residents and visitors parade back and forth. Two members of the staff burst in at once: "Hi, Mary!" One plops a cookie on her bedside table, while the other hangs a dress in the closet. The staff routinely barge into Mrs. Leary's room without knocking on the open door to let her know that they would like to enter.

The din in the hall is nerve-wracking. The call bells, which are rung by residents needing assistance, emit a shrill insistent burble every minute or so, with jarring consistency. "That goes on twenty-four hours a day," Mrs. Leary says wearily. The institutional atmosphere of the nursing home is emphasized by the use of call bells, which can be heard in Mrs. Leary's room as well as in the corridors. Adding to the cacophony is an intense buzz that signals the opening of the nursing home's front door.

Not only is the noise annoying, but it is disturbing for elderly people who are hard of hearing. The buzzers and the noise of the public address system often interfere with their hearing aids, and make it difficult for them to hear ordinary conversations.

Douglas Rapelje, the director of the municipally-run Senior Citizens Department in Niagara Falls, is an expert on the design of nursing homes. He believes new homes should be built with design features that reduce background noises and buzzers. "There is very little evidence that staff are particularly aware of the noise they make while they are working," Rapelje adds. Because of short-staffing, the call bells are often ignored for up to twenty minutes. "You could have a heart attack and be dead before they come," Mrs. Leary says. Sometimes when she triggers the call bell she can hear staff say: "Nothing wrong there," or, "She can wait."

Although Mrs. Leary has a private room, there is no real privacy. One of the supervising nurses once demanded to know the name and occupation of a visitor. When Mrs. Leary refused to tell her, she was punished. Her call bell went unanswered, and staff performed tasks in an unfriendly manner.

Neighbours can also be intrusive: confused residents frequently wander into Mrs. Leary's room, and she is powerless to evict them. "I get worried when they go and touch my control mechanism," she says.

The integration of mentally alert residents with confused people "leads to peer abuse, and often to the denial of many of the basic human rights," Douglas Rapelje has written.

Lise, the schoolteacher with multiple sclerosis, lives on a floor in the nursing home where there are numerous elderly residents suffering from Alzheimer's Disease. Hers is a frustrating existence. One confused woman is constantly wandering into her room and walking out with books and other things that belong to Lise. "All I can do is say, 'Get the hell out of here,'" she says.

In another Winnipeg nursing home, a lucid woman in her seventies was forced to share a semi-private bedroom with a roommate who was blind and demented, and who screamed night and day.

The lucid woman had one joy in life — reading. Because she was blind in one eye, she brought a special reading lamp with her into the nursing home. But the administrator removed the lamp, because her disoriented roommate was crashing around the room with a walker. The staff felt it was unsafe to have the lamp located where the roommate could knock it over. When an activity worker suggested to the administrator that the woman be paired with a more suitable roommate or that the lamp be nailed down, both requests were refused.

The lucid elderly woman "was getting angry, depressed and withdrawn," the activity worker said. "She wouldn't participate in any group activities any more and she wouldn't converse. Two years later, she was basically a vegetable. They stole the last few years of this woman's life from her, because it was inconvenient to make a room reassignment. She would have thrived with someone on her own level."

One frail eighty-six-year-old nursing home resident says she dislikes being with other old people. "I don't like old people unless they got a good sense of humour," she says. "I love young people. I love babies. My house used to be full of them."

Several of the residents in the nursing home are acquaintances from her old neighbourhood. But she does not go near them now. They have various forms of dementia. "If I take up with them, I'll become like them," she says. "The only thing I hope is that I keep my mind. When that goes, I hope I die."

It is not unusual for alert residents of nursing homes to become withdrawn and depressed. In one dramatic case, an elderly woman did not speak to anyone for eight years after she entered a Toronto nursing home. She was visited by Anne-Marie Johnston of Concerned Friends, who asked the nursing-home staff whether they knew anything about the woman's background. They said, vaguely, that she used to play the piano. That was all they knew.

Johnston visited regularly. She kept chatting to the woman, although the woman never responded. One day, Johnston began humming a piece of classical music. The woman finally spoke: she named the piece of music. It turned out that she had once been a world-famous concert pianist who played command performances for the royal houses of Europe. She was as alert as ever, but she had turned inward to avoid the horrible reality of life in a nursing home.

Johnston was dumbfounded at the discovery. "You're outfoxing everyone," she gasped. The woman replied: "My child, don't you see I have to?"

During their visits, the woman was careful to watch the bedroom door. Whenever a staff member appeared, she would cease speaking and slump back into her chair. It remained their secret until the elderly woman's death.

When mentally confused residents are integrated with lucid ones, the staff sometimes treat all the residents as if they are confused.

Two elderly women who have been friends for thirty years live in the same Winnipeg nursing home, but not in the same room. So the mobile one visits her disabled friend each day. In the evening, she washes her friend's false teeth for her. Sometimes, they sit and enjoy a bag of potato chips.

One winter evening, a health-care aide walked into the room with a snack of tea and cookies. "This is not your room," she said to the friend. "C'mon, dear. You're in the wrong room."

"Oh shut up," the old woman snapped. "I know where I am." The aide rolled her eyes and left. A tear trickled down the face of the elderly woman. "Too many bosses," she explained to her friend.

At Mrs. Leary's home, possessions have gone missing. During the Christmas season, she hangs a wreath on her door and decorates her room with a few baubles. "I count all my decorations," she says. "They try to blame the residents, but I think it's the staff."

Cans of diet soft drinks brought by Mrs. Leary's sister have disappeared from a fridge in the medication room. Now, her sister is forced to mark Mrs. Leary's name on the cans with a black marker.

In another Winnipeg nursing home, a resident has written her name in black ink on everything — including her walker, a bottle of cologne, and a tin of biscuits.

Mrs. Leary's young friend with multiple sclerosis lost money in the nursing home. While she was in the bathroom, someone stole it from a small bag attached to her wheelchair. "We were going to order pizza, and it was gone," Mrs. Leary recalls.

She keeps her money in the office. "Every once in a while I ask how much is there, and that's how I keep track of it."

Her total income — $7,230 in 1988 — comes from welfare. "I don't see my cheque. It goes straight to the office." By the end of 1988, she was paying a daily residential charge of $20.20 a day. She pays extra for cable TV and her telephone, and is also responsible for purchasing an over-the-counter lotion for her stump. Another expense is decaffeinated coffee: Mrs. Leary prefers it, but the nursing home does not provide it free of charge. Virtually all of her annual income goes to the nursing home for her daily residential fee. Her income-tax refund is her only source of pocket money.

Like many people, Mrs. Leary fantasizes about winning a lottery. What would she do if her fantasy came true? "I would build a place for the middle-aged and young," she says.

Mrs. Leary is angered by the plight of young and middle-aged disabled residents in nursing homes. "They have no one to talk to their own age," she says. "They get depressed, and next thing you know they're shoving nerve pills."

She dreams of a nursing home with enough room for younger handicapped people to move around comfortably. It would provide interesting and suitable activities. It would ensure transportation, so that the residents could occasionally leave the nursing home. Most important, it would allow the younger residents to mingle with their peers.

She believes a special facility for young and middle-aged disabled people would save money currently spent on psychiatry and medication.

"Maybe I'll hit the jackpot," she muses. "I always ask my sister to buy me a ticket, but she never does. I hope and pray — that's my last wish — that they stop putting middle-aged in with the elderly."

A 1984 task force on young disabled Manitobans found that young disabled adults living in nursing homes were lonely and bored. Their health was deteriorating. They felt stigmatized by being in a nursing home, they told task-force members, and they were convinced that the homes represented the end of the line.

Their attitudes ranged from resignation to total dissatisfaction. They spent little time with the elderly in the nursing homes, especially since their privacy was frequently invaded by wandering and disoriented elderly people. They ran into trouble with elderly residents and staff when they became sexually active. They hated living in a fishbowl where everybody knew their every move.

Administrators of nursing homes told the task force that their facilities weren't equipped to deal with young disabled people, especially when the young residents were venting their anger and frustration. The task force's report concluded: "The disabled adults in personal care homes are felt to require more than the elderly in terms of rehabilitation, therapy and recreational opportunities, activities, job opportunities and community contacts and involvement," the report said.

The task force recommended the establishment of a wide range of options for young disabled people, based on their varied needs. Some of the young adults told the task force that they would be content with a wing in a nursing home designated for people like themselves; others requested a smaller nursing home, designed for younger people.

The task force also recommended transitional housing to help nursing-home residents develop skills for independent living. Other recommendations included group homes and independent apartments with personal-care attendants. Some of these alternatives exist in various parts of Canada, but there are not enough facilities.

The Canadian Association for Community Living is calling for the de-institutionalization of younger people living in nursing homes. The organization estimates that in 1988 there were at least 20,000 people with mental handicaps living in Canadian institutions, including nursing homes. About 1,400 were children. "There is ample evidence that those same persons traditionally institutionalized can lead rich and full lives when accommodated in the community regardless of their physical needs," the association said in a June 1988 brief to the Canadian government. It called for the closure of institutions, and financial assistance to provinces to set up alternative housing and community programs.

The association believes that the rights of nursing-home residents are not respected in institutions. These include "the right to choose what to eat (and) wear ... the right to be free from abuse and not to be punished — rights which are not respected in any sense in an institutional setting," the report said.

Gordon Sones is a rehabilitation counsellor who works for the Society for Manitobans with Disabilities Inc. He is currently designing a proposal for a transitional living residence for people with brain injuries who make a physical recovery. At this facility, such people could re-learn how to function in the world — how to go to the bank or to cook, for example.

Sones says a nursing home is inappropriate for young disabled people because of the lack of stimulation and the loss of dignity. "Young people don't want to play bingo every night," he says. "They lose privacy and dignity even if the home is really well-run. People come in without knocking. Young people have a hard time with that."

Young disabled people tend to rebel against the regimentation of an institution, Sones says. "It's almost inherent in the system to have some depersonalization." And they don't want to be with the elderly. "They don't see themselves as different from their age peers except for special needs," Sones says.

Tim Thurston, thirty-eight, is one of the few who got away. He entered a Winnipeg nursing home at the age of twenty — a furious, devastated young man. Four years later, he left the institution to embark on an independent life.

Once an all-star football player, Thurston had had a good chance at a football scholarship at the University of North Dakota. When he wasn't playing ball, he was drinking beer with his buddies, and chasing girls. "Everything that I was, and everything that I was going to be, was tied up in my body," Thurston says. "And in a twinkling of an eye, all that was snatched away."

In October 1968, Thurston was playing junior football when he broke his neck during a game. He became a quadraplegic. After leaving hospital, Thurston lived in his parents' three-bedroom townhouse. He lay in his bed because there was nowhere to go. His father was an alcoholic and his family moved frequently. "It was just a nightmare," Thurston remembers. It seemed to him that a nursing home might be an improvement. "But I was not happy about going into a nursing home," he says. "I did not have happy prospects."

Thurston recalls entering the nursing home and seeing all the old people. "I was feeling like I had just been thrown onto the scrapheap," he says. "I was embarrassed to be there. I didn't care how nice it looked or how friendly the people were. When you look around and see only people who are eighty years old, it destroys the spirit."

Thurston met some wonderful older people at the home. "But at twenty it was not appropriate to live twenty-four hours a day with people whose life experiences are largely behind them," he says. "They're at a different stage in life."

Thurston plunged into despair and considered suicide. "The thing that's worse than physical pain is the icy grip of despair," he says. Most times, he sat in his private room in the nursing home, reading books and watching TV. "I just want to be left alone," he once told members of the staff.

He was the first young person admitted to the nursing home, and the administration made him their "project." They expressed personal interest in him, and were constantly interviewing him and bringing visitors to his room. Thurston knew their intentions were good; but he resented the invasion of privacy. "I told them to go fuck themselves, to get out of my face."

To the dismay of the nursing-home staff and management, the ex-football star continued his drinking and womanizing. "I would drink to oblivion," he says. "I wanted to escape." Girls who worked at the nursing home began to hang around him. He had sexual encounters. Staff considered him a problem because he demanded that they knock before entering his room. Once he was caught with a woman in his arms.

The loss of privacy and control enraged Thurston. "The institution makes regular incursions into your sense of self," he says. "I was forced to eat with the same people at the same time." He was not treated as an adult. Because he was sitting in a wheelchair, some members of the staff used to pat him on the head as if he was a child. "They would talk to me as if I didn't understand English."

Thurston was offended by the treatment received by some elderly residents of the nursing home. "They were treated like meat," he says. "They put people in bed at 8:00 p.m. because it was convenient for the staff. It's pretty much a factory. These people couldn't preserve their dignity like I could."

For personal care such as bathing, Thurston had to develop a psychological distance to preserve his sanity. "It takes a while to get used to it," he says. By giving directions to the staff, he was able to feel some control over what happened to his body. "You gotta protect yourself. You could die in an environment like that. It's insidious. You become part of the furniture. Your horizons shrink to the perimeter of the building."

Thurston fell in love with a young woman whose mother worked at the nursing home. Their love affair was the spark he needed to change his life. He went to university and studied psychology while still living in the home.

Fed up with the nursing home, he eventually gained enough willpower to leave. First, he moved to Ten Ten Sinclair. Now, he lives in a two-bedroom apartment in a downtown, wheelchair-accessible apartment building. "It's not an institutional setting. There is no comparison to the nursing home," he says.

He and seven other disabled people living in the apartment building share an attendant service. Attendants funded by the provincial home-care program are available on a twenty-four-hour basis on a pager system. "The attendant only shows up when I call him," Thurston says. "I control what happens to me. No one else." An attendant assists Thurston in dressing, bathing and preparing meals. "His hands become an extension of my brain."

Thurston is able to pursue more challenging activities than those offered by the nursing home. He has worked as a social worker since 1977. Currently, he is the co-ordinator of services at Ten Ten Sinclair.

Thurston's story is proof that a nursing home is not the only solution for the disabled. Instead of stagnating in an institution, he was capable of leading a satisfying life in the community. A wheelchair is not necessarily a prison. Although he was younger than most nursing-home residents, his return to the community could be duplicated by middle-aged residents of nursing homes — if only there were enough options and services.

In his leisure time, Thurston goes kayaking and fly-fishing in remote northern areas of the province. "My scope of activities is large, and I'm happy with it."

3

The Family

Arthur Wolfe, seventy-five, visits his wife, Sarah, in the nursing home twice a day. Just to keep an eye on... well, things. It was not long after he placed Sarah in a Winnipeg nursing home that Arthur realized strange things do happen.

One day, Arthur found Sarah lying on the floor unconscious, face bruised, ears thickening and crumpled like a boxer's. A demented resident had taken a flying run at her and pushed her down: she had hit her head on the concrete floor, and it also seemed she had been beaten. Sarah was taken to hospital, where tests revealed a large blood clot on her brain. Arthur insisted the doctors operate. After surgery, Sarah began to suffer seizures.

Another time, Arthur found a gash on Sarah's thigh that no one on the nursing-home staff could explain. It was an odd occurrence, because Sarah is not mobile. There were other things, too; small, but annoying. Sarah's false teeth were stolen. Her good wool sweater was thrown in the laundry where it shrunk to a child's size.

And given Arthur's personality — he admits to being hot-tempered and bitter — all this is fuel to the fire.

"It's a snake pit," he barks when asked to describe the nursing home. "Their civil rights are being violated twenty-four hours a day. The residents are all treated like hunks of meat."

The last time Arthur was able to get out of the city was in 1972, to attend his sister's funeral in Edmonton. Since then, his life has revolved around caring for Sarah. For ten years, he looked after her in their small North End house. And now — to his disbelief — he must monitor the care in the nursing home.

"I remember the shock," he says. "I put her in there and figured, gee, I was going to take a trip to Israel. I put money away. I figured once I put her in there things were going to be wonderful. Doesn't work that way."

Sarah is seventy-seven years old and has Alzheimer's Disease, a fatal illness that slowly destroys the intellectual functions of the brain. It is marked by progressive memory loss and dementia.

Because of the nature of the disease, Arthur's efforts are thankless. "She can't communicate," Arthur says. "Or else she starts talking gibberish. She must know me, but she wouldn't know the relationship. It got to the point where she couldn't remember her own kids' names or her birthday. These are questions they ask to determine the extent of the disease."

Arthur is trim and fit, but he is under tremendous stress worrying about Sarah's well-being. Their daughter Dominique says her father is nearly apoplectic most of the time. Much of his anger has to do with fighting the nursing home to get better care for Sarah. Some of the practices of the institution seem senseless, if not downright unjust or harmful. Some of the members of the staff are wonderful, but others do not seem to care much. It has been an unwelcome learning experience.

Studies show that most elderly people are not abandoned by family and friends. "Elderly parents and their children still rely on each other for companionship and assistance, especially in times of crises. In fact, the elderly are more likely to turn to their family and friends for both emotional and concrete support than to community services or professionals," one study on aging says.

Unfortunately, for some people there is no option other than a nursing home. Canada is a large country, and family members are scattered from coast to coast. Adult children of elderly people often still have jobs and their own children at home. Others, like the Wolfes, look after their relatives at home as long as possible. "These people are in a bind and nearly going bonkers — physically, emotionally and financially," says Anne-Marie Johnston of Concerned Friends.

In addition to Arthur's twice-a-day vigil, Dominique and her daughter also visit regularly. They — like many other families across the country — do the work of nursing-home staff who are too busy to provide proper care. They walk Sarah, feed her and put her to bed. They do their best to ensure she is not neglected. "Staff do as they please with those who don't have family," says a woman who worked as a paid companion to an elderly nursing-home resident. She used to see other residents lying in their beds, wet in urine, in front of open windows, their calls for help going unheeded.

It is a cool, wet March morning, and Arthur strides purposefully down the hall past the nursing station where two overweight women in uniforms call out a cheerful, insincere-sounding greeting. By now, Arthur is certain he has earned a reputation as a troublemaker. Staff do not like "difficult" and "demanding" relatives. Arthur glares at them and continues past the gaping, drooling mouths of residents; past the blaring televisions in the lounges.

Sarah is sitting in a chair outside her sparsely furnished private room. She wears beige slacks and a pink sweater. Dominique was shocked to discover that, from time to time, some of the clothes sent up to Sarah's room by laundry staff belonged to deceased residents of the home.

Arthur kneels beside Sarah and caresses her cheek with his knuckles, crooning softly: "Sarah, Sarah." There's a dreamlike quality to her response. Her head turns languidly, sloe eyes glazed.

Arthur rises, enters Sarah's room and rifles a drawer, emerging with a tube of red lipstick and a rouge compact in his hand. He deftly applies the color. "I want her to look nice. It gives me a lift," he says. "There's one hell of a girl that works here. When I come, she's got Sarah all gussied up. But the rest of them don't give a damn. Those that have been here too long get jaded.

They're very careless." Sometimes he finds Sarah with food encrusted on her mouth, or her short grey hair unkempt.

Arthur and Sarah have been married fifty-six years. He remembers falling in love. He was a friend of her elder brother, a mechanic. One night, he and the mechanic were tinkering in the garage. "When she walked in — this never happened to me before and never happened since — I couldn't catch my breath. God, she was gorgeous."

Arthur's routine rarely changes. It is a twenty-minute bus ride to the nursing home, and Arthur is normally there by nine o'clock in the morning. He takes Sarah for a walk; if the weather is good, they go outside. "The whole thing is to keep her walking. Sometimes it's easy. Sometimes she'll walk by herself, and I just gotta watch her. They could do the same with a lot of others. But they don't. The physiotherapy here is a bloody joke. They toss a ball to each other."

Three gerontologists at the University of Waterloo and Queen's University, in a recent study of institutionalization of the elderly in Canada, conclude that the elderly can gain dramatic improvements in their lives if they have access to physical and occupational therapists, speech therapists, recreationists, music therapists and activity directors. Physiotherapy has "the potential to assist many of those suffering from the residuals of stroke, fractures, or arthritis. Although restorative goals must be realistic, considerable functional improvements are possible," the gerontologists say.

Proper therapy and activities can prevent dementia brought on by over-drugging, and by lack of activity and stimulation. Even incontinence is not an inevitable consequence of old age, but a condition that can be improved or cured; the success rate is about 50 per cent.

However, the gerontologists note, "the majority of facilities are still unable to provide many of these services." Profit-making homes, like the one Sarah is in, are unwilling to spend the money. Non-profit homes do not always receive enough funding. And, as already indicated, there is a shortage of therapists.

After the operation to remove the blood clot on Sarah's brain, Arthur asked if she would be able to walk again. The doctor held out little hope. "If she were younger, maybe," he said. Arthur proved the medical experts wrong. "It took me two years but I got her to walk."

At the nursing home, he braces himself by planting his feet firmly apart. Then, he pulls Sarah from her chair, grasping her upper arm with both hands. Still holding her, Arthur walks Sarah slowly down the hall. She falters and her backside protrudes. They walk about thirty feet, then return and sit down together. Arthur talks to her and tries to make her comfortable. After about an hour, Sarah is tired and Arthur puts her to bed. "I don't want her sitting. I see them groaning and moaning, and nobody (on the staff) notices anything."

Many nursing homes do not hire enough staff to properly look after the needs of the residents. When they are tired, there is often not enough staff to put them to bed. Those who are in wheelchairs and unable to move are rarely re-positioned. By the end of the day, it is a common sight to see residents, exhausted and in pain, hanging out of their wheelchairs. "I watched fourteen people in a lounge, all restrained, with no one supervising, and all of them agitated and trying to get out, and crying and moaning," recalls Win Lindsay, the former life-enrichment consultant to the Manitoba Health Services Commission.

When Sarah came out of hospital after her operation, she was extremely weak and needed to be watched. But the home is understaffed. So a strap-like restraint was tied around her waist as she sat in her chair. "The nurses would walk by and see her hanging over the side, and sometimes not do anything," Arthur says. When she developed a rash on her sides from the restraint, Arthur demanded that it be removed.

At another nursing home in Winnipeg, the staff insisted that a woman be restrained because she occasionally wanders. "She's quite clear," the woman's daughter says. "She doesn't want it." When the resident's elderly sisters came to visit, they found her tied up in a restraint jacket with her skirt up around her waist. "They were devastated," the daughter says.

A University of Alberta nursing professor says some animals get better treatment in zoos than many elderly residents receive in nursing homes. "If zookeepers tied up animals the way some people are tied up, it wouldn't be tolerated by animal-rights people," Professor Janice Morse says. Morse notes that the most common argument for using restraints is that nurses cannot safely monitor disoriented residents who wander. But she says it is a myth to think a resident is safe under restraint. In Quebec, a psychiatric patient became so angry at being restrained that he had a heart attack and died. Restraints also cause skin breakdown, improper circulation, anxiety and muscle-wasting. An inquest judge in Manitoba called restraints "death traps." Canadians have strangled to death trying to slip out of them. Makeshift restraints like sheets and belts have also killed people.

Morse says the answer is to increase the number of staff, and to provide proper beds, chairs and alarms, so elderly residents will not have to be restrained.

Dr. Colin Powell of St. Boniface General Hospital in Winnipeg conducted a study of the use of restraints in the hospital's geriatric ward. The geriatric ward recognized that the restraints were inhumane, so their use was sharply reduced — with hardly any resultant change in the number of serious falls requiring treatment. Powell concluded that the restraints were unnecessary.

The Manitoba government has not changed its staffing guidelines for nursing homes in the past sixteen years. But the typical person admitted to a nursing home today is older and has more disabilities than the average person admitted sixteen years ago. Home care and medical science have allowed people to stay home longer. The average age of a person entering a nursing home in Manitoba was 80.8 in 1981. By 1986, it had risen to 85.

The Manitoba Health Services Commission assesses residents once a year to see if they have deteriorated and whether staffing levels should be increased to meet government guidelines. But some nursing-home operators report that although commission members are aware that their residents need more care, they do not allocate more staff.

To cut corners on staffing, some nursing homes lean on the families of residents to pay a private attendant to stay with the resident during the day. Attendants feed, dress and take care of the elderly. "It's a great way of not having to staff very high," Patricia Spindel of Concerned Friends says. "That gives nursing homes a lot more money, because then they can cut back on their staffing."

Spindel warns families not to fall prey to nursing-home operators who say that their relative requires too much care and needs a private attendant. She points out that nursing homes are required to give care in accordance with a resident's needs. If the care is not given, a government inspector from the nursing-home branch should assess the situation. If the resident's level of care is within the limits that the nursing home should be providing under provincial guidelines, then the home should be required to provide it.

"A lot of people have been duped out of thousands of dollars paying for private attendants because they don't know they have the right to ask for ministry assessment," Spindel says.

Arthur once wrote to the Minister of Health and asked for a meeting to discuss conditions in the home — including the shortage of staff — but he received only a form letter acknowledging receipt of his letter.

He vents his frustration by going to the YMHA three times a week. "I force myself to go. That's what keeps me going. I beat the hell out of the heavy punching bag there. It doesn't solve my problems, but it helps me." Then he goes home. By three o'clock in the afternoon he is back at the nursing home. He stays until four. "I go through the same routine, day after day. I'm not one of these out-of-sight, out-of-mind guys. I gotta be there. Because if I'm not there, I'm more worried than when I am there."

The anger about Sarah's assault never goes away. "They tried to cover it up. What burns me more than anything was nobody, NOBODY, came to me and said 'We are sorry.'"

"That was horrendous," Dominique recalls with a shudder. "It's just unbelievable that this happened to my beautiful mother Sarah, who was so good to everyone. Even knowing that the inmate who had done this was not in much better mental shape than she was — that didn't help. To me, mercy killings are much more humane than packing them away where someone is going to damage them further."

There are violent residents in every nursing home, staff say. In Selkirk, a town near Winnipeg, an eighty-eight-year-old nursing-home resident terrorizes staff and residents. He hit a nurse across the face with a cane. He pulled a tiny, frail, eighty-year-old woman out of her wheelchair and was choking her when staff pulled him away. "Every night since the attack, our older ladies are ringing and asking, 'Is he asleep? Is he in bed? Is he gone?' These people should be living their golden years in peace, not in fear," a nurse at the Selkirk home said.

"If they're pushed by one of the residents that means there's not sufficient security in the home," Spindel says. "You can't have one group of victims pushing another group of victims around and hurting them. If that's happening, something is wrong in the home. Staffing levels aren't high enough."

Many families get a rude shock when they discover the conditions in some nursing homes.

"My husband was so heavily drugged he was like a zombie," recalls Edie, the wife of a resident of a Winnipeg nursing home.

While there was air conditioning in the public areas of the nursing home, residents' rooms were "hotter than Hades" in the summer, she says. By 11:00 a.m., beds were still unmade. Promised activities, such as visits by local schoolchildren, and animals from the humane society, never materialized. Up to five days' worth of laundry was piled up in her husband's room. "His clothes were constantly lost. When I came in he was wearing somebody else's clothing."

At seventy-four, her husband is completely debilitated by Alzheimer's. He is half his former size, unable to recognize her and dependent on total care. For awhile, she looked after him in their apartment, with the help of about ten hours a week of home-care services. But his deterioration became too extensive for her, and she was forced to put him in a nursing home. "I wish my husband's life was over," Edie says.

The home has a plaque in the front hall that pledges the home's commitment to preserving human dignity. The residents "don't know or care," Edie says. "Preserve it for us, the family."

Like Arthur Wolfe, a Winnipeg woman named Joy also believed that putting her ninety-year-old mother into a nursing home would ease some of the stress and worry of caring for her. Her mother had lived in an apartment with her eighty-eight-year-old husband.

Joy's mother has had several small strokes, and walks with a brace. Home care was successful for about seven months. The three daughters were willing and able to help. But the elderly woman deteriorated rapidly after falling and suffering a cut to her head. While undergoing treatment in hospital, her bowels became blocked. The family decided she was too frail to be safely cared for at home, and she was placed in an attractive nursing home.

"I suppose we were hopelessly naive," Joy sighs. "The workers lead you to believe your parent will receive twenty-four-hour supervision. It's frightening when you discover the reality."

Many residents in the home are incontinent. "The smell of urine is very strong," Joy says. "They're incontinent because no one takes them to the bathroom. There is not enough staff to change them often enough when they're wet." When she raised the matter with administration, she was told the residents are taken to the toilet every two hours. From regular visits, Joy knows this is not the case.

She has hired an attendant to be with her mother on weekends, when the home is extremely short-staffed. "But an attendant can't remove her from that urine smell." Her mother is bathed only once a week. The attendant cannot bathe her, because of the home's legal liability if an accident should occur.

When her mother cracked her pelvis in a fall, some members of the staff tried to force her to walk. "She was screaming in pain." Joy requested a note over her mother's bed to alert staff that she had a cracked pelvis. The administrator refused, saying that it was against the policy of the home to post notes in residents' rooms — and adding that the practice was "too tacky." While her mother's medical chart contained information about her pelvis, the staff were always too busy to look at the records.

Joy's mother never seemed to get enough fluids, and most visits started with her gulping up to three glasses of water. The staff complain that when residents drink too much, they wet their pants. They say they do not have time to take the residents to the toilet, or change their diapers and clothing.

Joy remembers when one confused resident took another, who was in a wheelchair, into a stairwell. The stairwell was supposed to be off limits because of the danger of residents falling. The alarm on the stairwell door was buzzing loudly for ten minutes before someone in authority showed up. "Is that twenty-four-hour care?" Joy asks.

As she walks through the hallways of the nursing home, residents grab her. "I reach out to them. They're desperate for a touch, a few words."

Discussing the situation never fails to bring her to the verge of tears. Her friends have had no contact with a nursing home, and do not understand what she is experiencing. "Friends think it's easier now, but it's not," she says. "Someone (from the family) has to be there every day. There's stress in the family. Everyone has their own idea of what should be done."

Joy despairs at the thought of how much longer her family's suffering will continue. "My mother could be there for ten years," she says. "I'd be happy if my mother died, but I don't want her to have a painful death."

Clara, another Winnipeg woman whose mother is in a nursing home, cried all the way through her tour of the institution where her mother now lives. "There's no way out but feet first," she says. Clara's mother, a high-spirited woman who was still throwing large dinner parties when she was in her late eighties, chose a home that was in her neighbourhood, to make it easier for friends and family to visit.

Although a stroke had paralyzed her on one side, she was in full command of her mental faculties. "They put her in a room with an incompetent, drooling person who was impossible to look at, impossible to communicate with."

Clara protested to management. They moved her in with a woman who could communicate. But her mother's new roommate keeps her radio and lights on twenty-four hours a day.

"My mother would get up at 7:30 a.m. and have to go to the bathroom. But the shift didn't change until 8:00 a.m. and they have a meeting until 8:30 a.m. So she wet the bed. She was absolutely mortified. She was such a meticulous woman."

A rash developed on her eighty-six-year-old mother's right arm. The arm was itching, but she couldn't scratch it because of her paralysis, so she was biting it. "Her arm was black and blue." When Clara called the "house doctor" at the nursing home, she was told that the doctor could not examine her mother unless it was requested by the nursing home. It was five days before her mother received medication for the rash.

Clara rails at a system that lumps together people who need all sorts of physical care, without regard for their mental competency. She wishes there were something different — perhaps a group home for those who are alert but need physical care. Her mother, Clara notes, "looks at these people and says, 'I'm going to be like that.' She didn't want her friends to visit her. She eats her three meals a day surrounded by people wetting themselves and shoving fists down their throats."

One confused resident, a man, periodically enters her room at 3:00 a.m. and tries to get into her bed. "She nearly had a heart attack," Clara says.

She feels her mother's abilities are being wasted. "My mother had a lot to give. She could offer a lot of comfort to people. It's like they shove them away and forget about them."

Clara's mother had open-heart surgery at age eighty. The operation was hailed as a success by the doctors. "Medically, they've given her more years to live, but what the hell for? I would not have open-heart surgery. I would prefer to die. Why risk having this happen to me?"

Clara is anxious about her own impending old age, and is considering contacting an organization that advocates euthanasia. "I'm frightened," she says. "I've got to put things in place so I'm not subjected to that. I don't want to have such loss of dignity. I don't want someone to treat me like a piece of garbage."

Mary believes her ninety-two-year-old mother was sexually assaulted in a Winnipeg nursing home, but her suspicions were pooh-poohed by the administration. She found her mother with bruises between her legs. Although her mother does not always speak coherently, she told Mary: "I don't know why that man goes after me. I'm so afraid." Other incidents in the home trouble Mary as well. Her mother fell, and broke her hip and wrist. "I was told she slipped in her pee." At Halloween, the staff put makeup and costumes on the residents whether they liked it or not. "My mother was so upset about it." She often finds her mother wet with urine. "I say, 'Can't you change her?' and they say, 'No, we have to feed the other patients.'"

When Mrs. Johnson, eighty-two, was moved from the room in which she had lived for five years, and transferred to another floor — once considered a dumping ground for those about to die — the decision was made without consulting her family.

"I don't like it," Mrs. Johnson said. "They just came and said: 'You're going to the third floor.' I wanted to stay where I was. It was my home."

The transfer was for the convenience of the nursing-home administration. Mrs. Johnson was moved onto a heavier-care floor to free up her bed for a prospective resident who needed the lighter level of care available on her floor. At first, the staff said the move was necessary because she was wandering into other people's rooms and becoming incontinent. However, her daughter was paying for a part-time private attendant and had always told the nursing-home administration she was willing to increase the private care as her mother required it. After discussions with the director of nursing, the real agenda emerged.

Mrs. Johnson's new room was inferior to the other. It had no carpeting, no telephone jacks and an immense, unsightly stain on the ceiling. Her eyeglasses disappeared for two days. Furthermore, the floor had a reputation as a dumping ground for hopeless cases. A government official had warned Mrs. Johnson's daughter, Norma, a school counsellor, about the floor. Norma also knew the floor's reputation from experience. Her aunt had deteriorated and died there shortly after a move two years earlier.

Norma tried to make the room look attractive by displaying some of her mother's favorite figurines and photos. But the staff asked her to remove them, because people on the heavy-care floor often wander into other rooms, breaking and stealing things. There was no lounge furniture and no place for families to sit and visit with their relatives.

"There is such a contrast between the floors," Norma said. "It really is saying these people are beyond caring."

"The people are not friendly," Mrs. Johnson said. "The noise drives me up a wall."

When Norma expressed her anger at the disregard shown to their family, she was told that "the staff cannot concern itself with the family — only with the individual and the institution."

"I feel that an institution which fails to consider the emotional impact of its decisions on people lacks humanity," Norma wrote in a letter to the administrator. The administrator did not respond to her letter. On the telephone, he was defensive and rude. "I won't argue this with you," he told her.

Although government officials said they felt the move had been badly handled, there was nothing they could do about it. The institution had the right to forcibly relocate people. Not only did Mrs. Johnson have no rights in the matter, the government — which funds nursing homes — has no right to intervene.

A few weeks after the move, Norma could already see the traumatic effect on her mother. "She certainly has deteriorated."

Family members who complain about the treatment their relatives receive in nursing homes are often branded as troublemakers. Or they are told that they are merely feeling guilty about putting their relatives in a nursing home. A Winnipeg nurse who worked in a nursing home remembers how the staff reacted to a man who fought for his wife when he felt she had been mistreated. The man was labelled "a pain in the ass," the nurse recalls. Yet the nurse admits that the staff were too busy to feed elderly residents who needed help, that bedsores were rife, and that medication was left in hallways where confused residents could easily get their hands on dangerous drugs.

Concerned Friends started as a self-help group for families in Ontario because the families were so often ignored by the nursing homes. "People were feeling so horrendously abused," Spindel says "Every time they raised anything, they were literally told they were wrong; they had no business raising those kinds of things; that they were just feeling guilty. The inference is always that the complainant is irrational or stupid and doesn't understand how things work." Spindel urges individuals who have a complaint to speak to the administrator, but also to contact the provincial nursing homes branch to launch a formal complaint and demand an inspection of the home. The police should be called to handle criminal offences, such as assault or theft.

For many families, their first visit to a nursing home occurs when they are hunting for a place for a relative. Families are under a great deal of stress, and feel intimidated. They often do not know what to look for, what questions to ask and how to assess the answers.

Laurie, thirty-four, felt panic when the social worker at the hospital told her to find a nursing home for her eighty-six-year-old father, who suffers dementia and a heart condition. "I had never been to a personal-care home," she says. "I thought, 'What am I looking for?'"

She picked a home that had a fenced-in area outside, where confused residents were allowed to wander. But that home refused to accept her father because he required too much care. "I was really disappointed. I wanted Daddy to be happy." A social worker told her that her expectations were too high; that it is impossible to find a nursing home where the elderly are happy. Her father ended up in a home she had previously rejected.

Patricia Spindel says hospitals tend to be callous in this regard. "They just simply inform families that they'll have to go to the first bed that becomes available. Or they hand them a list of nursing homes and say, 'Go out and pick one.' They give you a choice of two or three and you take the first bed that becomes available at one of those."

Richard, a Winnipeg businessman, was completely baffled by the system when he went to look for a nursing home for his father. A meeting with hospital professionals to discuss his father's discharge from hospital was little help. "They kept using buzzwords. I had to ask them, 'What does panelling mean?'" (Panelling refers to a panel of professionals who assess an elderly person before the person is admitted to a nursing home.)

Finally, he took a week off work and visited eighteen nursing homes, rating them on factors such as smell, the number of screaming residents, and the number of residents left in wheelchairs in the halls. He was appalled at the conditions. "There are some terrible nursing homes in this town," he said later. Eventually, he found one that seemed bright, clean, spacious and caring. But it took an intensive search to find the home.

In one nursing home, families are asked for donations to the building fund. The relatives of families who make a donation are placed on the "showcase" floors of the home, according to one member of the staff. They get private rooms, are allowed to bring in their own furniture and are treated with more consideration.

Those whose relatives cannot afford to make a donation are stuck on a "horrifying" floor, according to the staffer. It has a stark institutional atmosphere, and fewer staff. The residents' wishes are disregarded. "People would be ringing their call bells for hours and hours."

Concerned Friends receives many telephone calls from people who want to know what to look for in a nursing home. The consumer group suggests random visits to nursing homes, chats with residents and their relatives, and observations of the heavy-care floors. The group recommends looking at government inspection reports. In Ontario, current inspection reports must be displayed in the nursing home, and previous reports are available at the Ministry of Health library. In Manitoba, some inspection reports are available through the Freedom of Information Act. Homes known for numerous problems with food and staffing should be avoided.

The consumer group also says that families should not perceive a nursing home as inevitable for an elderly person. Nor should they underestimate the beneficial effects of remaining at home with support services, such as housekeeping or Meals on Wheels. Above all, a crucial decision about the future of an elderly person should not be made hastily, during a crisis.

On a typical day in Sarah's nursing home, about twenty-five elderly men and women are squeezed into a lounge in front of the nursing station, where they can be overseen by members of the staff. Another six have been assigned a spot directly in front of the station. A dozen more are lined up in the hall. Some are in chairs, others in wheelchairs — heads rolling, bodies twisted. They are strapped in, staring straight down a corridor which has no pictures on the walls. They are sleeping, howling, crying, mumbling, repeating phrases over and over again. One woman is slumped, chin on her chest, clutching a worn blue stuffed animal. Another sleeps, her toothless mouth agape.

"When Sarah first came out of hospital, she couldn't walk, and they used to have her in a wheelchair by the nursing station," Arthur recalls. "She had less than two feet square. I had to pull to get that goddamned chair out. They were so jammed together."

This is a common scene in nursing homes that are understaffed. Residents must sit for hours on end in a spot where overworked staff can keep an eye on them.

Over the past several years, Arthur has noticed more and more younger residents, disabled with multiple sclerosis or paraplegia, brought to Sarah's floor. It is a heavy-care floor for difficult residents who require a great deal of help eating, dressing, washing and going to the toilet. Again, he is struck by how few staff there are. "The young ones need three times more staff. They're taking all the time up and staff are neglecting the other ones." He believes young people should not be mixed with the elderly, because their needs and interests are different.

"It's supposed to be a quiet floor, but these multiple sclerosis types are in there blaring their TVs," he says. "Well, they're young people...They've brought in one young woman who's about thirty-two and her roommate is a woman who's ninety-some years. It must be pretty hard on her. I have to put Sarah in her room because they're playing their TV too loud. I said, 'Why the hell should she have to be barricaded in her room? Why don't you just go and shut the doors or turn the damn thing down a little bit?'"

Adding to the cacophony is a recently admitted demented resident. All day she shouts: "Help, Nurse! Help, Nurse! Help, Nurse!" with military precision; equal emphasis on both words. Or: "Gimme-a-cigarette-gimme-a-cigarette-gimme-a-cigarette."

"She's driving them crazy," Arthur says.

Arthur pays $600 a month for Sarah to stay in the home. The price includes an extra charge of $150 a month for a private room. The majority of rooms in the home are semi-private or four-bed wards.

Margaret, a sixty-five-year-old woman who lives down the hall from Sarah, is confined to a wheelchair because of multiple sclerosis. Margaret has been in institutions for twenty-seven years. "I don't have to be in a nursing home, but my family doesn't want me," she confides to a stranger who is visiting. "That hurts."

Patricia Spindel says residents are rarely asked whether they want to go to a nursing home. Nor are they asked which home they would prefer. "Most people are just told they are going to a nursing home. Many of them cry and they become very very depressed at that point, and they don't want to go. They beg their family member not to put them there. Usually it's all for naught. The doctor or nurse say to the family, 'Oh, she'll get used to it.'"

One Winnipeg study of residents in a nursing home found that 47 per cent of decisions about placement involved the resident's children. One resident in the study described her passive role: "My children felt I was unable to look after things on my own, so I agreed to move in (to the nursing home) when a bed became available."

Some residents are simply abandoned by their families. During an emergency in an Alberta nursing home, families were asked to take their family member home for a few days. More than 10 per cent flatly refused to take any responsibility.

Margaret finds life in a nursing home tedious, particularly on the heavy-care floor, where there are few people who are mentally capable of carrying on a conversation. "I do bugger-all," she says. "There's no one to play cards with, and the activity workers only come up if I go and get them."

Margaret is waiting for lunch, which she says usually arrives cold. The staff first feed people who need help to eat. Then, they serve meals to those — like Margaret — who can feed themselves.

Margaret and other neighbours of Sarah confirm that Arthur's complaints are justified. A few doors down from Margaret lives Roberta, a former nurse who is in a wheelchair, crippled by an unsuccessful hip-replacement operation. She refuses her lunch of corned-beef hash and cabbage. "I'll just have a couple of cups of coffee," she sighs. "The food here is a disgrace. I wouldn't feed this to a dog." The dessert appears to be a little piece of stale cake soaked in fruit juice.

A member of the nursing-home staff comes over to suggest alternatives. "Cottage cheese?" Roberta had that yesterday, and the day before. "How about cold meat?" "By itself?" Roberta shakes her head. The staff member smiles helplessly.

After forty-six years of experience as a nurse, Roberta is especially aware of the shortcomings of the nursing-home staff. There are not enough nurses, she says. "Aides don't know what a nurse knows. They keep me waiting an hour to go to the bathroom when I have to go right away. I get plugged up, and then I have to use suppositories, which I want to avoid."

The problem of constipation is so widespread in nursing homes that the Manitoba Health Services Commission recommends that each institution keep laxatives and stool softeners in stock. Part of the problem is that residents are inactive. But in addition, the regimentation of nursing homes requires that residents go to the toilet when it is convenient for staff. And nursing-home diets tend to contain too little fibre.

A large woman, Roberta is on the heavy-care floor, on which is located the mechanical lift, to get her in and out of bed, and into the bathtub. Like Margaret, she finds there are few residents with whom she can converse. Most of the time she sits and smokes, and reads romance novels.

Sarah's daughter, Dominique, has noticed that there are never any volunteers in the nursing home — which explains the desperation with which the residents reach out to her for a touch, a few words or a smile.

Volunteers can bring pleasure and comfort to residents just by spending time with them. Non-profit homes seem to attract more volunteers than profit-making operations. Many volunteers do not wish to donate their time to homes which make money from their labours. Spindel, of Concerned Friends, says that in some homes, volunteers are not encouraged, because they monitor conditions in the home, and this is not welcomed. A survey of eleven Winnipeg nursing homes found tremendous discrepancies in the amount of time spent in the homes by volunteers. One profit-making home had ten volunteer hours a month. In sharp contrast, a non-profit religious home had 1,500 hours a month.

Despite his dissatisfaction, Arthur refuses to move Sarah to another home. For one thing, it would take about a year, because there are waiting lists. "It would be out of the frying pan into the fire. They're all the same," he says.

He also suspects that, by now, his pit-bull terrier approach is beginning to pay off. By pestering the staff every day, he has forced them to improve the level of care for his wife. "A whole batch of new mattresses came in and I said, 'I think she needs one too.' They didn't have her down for one. And now she's going to get a new bed, because the crank isn't working. At one time, I was putting in six hours a day when I didn't trust any of them. I don't spend all that time any more, because I've got the staff trained."

It's November 1988, and lunch has just been brought up on plastic dishes. They contain tomato soup and crackers, and macaroni and cheese. Dominique takes off her short coat, kisses her mother on the forehead and strokes her cheek. Sarah's mouth begins to twitch. "Ba, ba, ba, teh, teh, teh." A fly buzzes around her face.

"Coming alive, eh?" Dominique says gently.

She used to call her Mum but now she calls her Sarah, hoping to trigger some flash of recognition in her mother's mind. "She was my friend. The person I confided in. There are times when I visit her and I get this eerie feeling. She has these facial expressions that can be read. We were that close. But this person makes no sense. I look at her and think an imposter has taken over my mother's body."

Pulling a chair up beside her mother, she cradles Sarah's head in her left hand and begins to feed her with the right. Occasionally, she uses her left hand to push food out of Sarah's cheek. Sarah closes her eyes and starts to chew. Soup dribbles down under her chin, and Dominique pats it with a white towel from her lap. A few drops trickle between Sarah's breasts and escape the mopping. At one point, Sarah chokes: the coughing goes on and on. Dominique waits until it's over, and resumes feeding her.

At fifty-five, Dominique is youthful and vibrant. She has the figure, striking dark looks and wardrobe of a younger woman. But when she looks at her mother she sees herself. Each day is a struggle to push down the feelings of terror. "I think to myself, how much longer have I got?" Alzheimer's Disease seems to run in their family. Sarah's brother died of it. Her sister has recently been diagnosed with it. Their mother had died of some sort of senility. In each case, the disease started in the person's mid-sixties.

More than 300,000 Canadians over the age of sixty-five are afflicted with Alzheimer's. Some nursing-home operators estimate that up to 50 per cent of their residents suffer from some type of dementia. Alzheimer's is the most common form. This devastating disease is the greatest challenge facing nursing homes today. Decisions made today about the treatment of Alzheimer's patients will shape the nursing home of the future. Will they be warehouses for death? Or can nursing homes become a humane refuge?

Dominique finds it difficult to visit Sarah more than once a week. "It hurts me so much to see my mother the way she is. She's totally unaware of who I am, or if I'm there. I feel anguish when I see her. This disease murdered my mother years ago."

Dominique was not happy when her mother's life was prolonged by a complex brain operation. She has instructed her own husband and daughter to refuse to allow any heroic medical measures if she gets Alzheimer's Disease.

Dominique paints portraits. Her work can be seen in public galleries, in the Manitoba Legislature and in private homes. The one portrait she cannot complete is of Sarah. She started the portrait shortly before her mother was diagnosed with her illness.

"Anything that depresses me affects my work. When she was diagnosed, I went into a real tailspin. At that time, I didn't know there was a familial aspect. And then, of course, the possibility of my getting the disease became apparent."

In the half-finished life-size portrait, Sarah is serious in a dark blue dress and pearls. Dominique recalls Sarah posing for the portrait. "She was so timid and so unlike herself; nervous of not looking quite nice enough, even though I explained to her it really didn't matter."

In her other paintings, the faces of people are serene and the colours soothing. Embroidery or leathercraft are executed in minute detail; books stand upright on a shelf; the canvasses are ordered and harmonious. Artists who know Dominique find it curious that her paintings never express the tragedy and the illness in her family. "One artist said my work is so composed, so controlled. I said, 'Did it ever occur to you that this is the only area in my life that I can exercise complete control over?'"

She worries when she cannot remember something. She reads articles about Alzheimer's. She also takes choline tablets, a B vitamin available at health food stores, thought to have a preventive effect. "I make myself much more alert and aware than I would by nature be. If I went for a CT scan, I could find out real quick if the disease has begun. I'm not that interested." She laughs. "I don't want to screw up the five or six years of lucid thinking I might have left."

When her mother became ill, Dominique turned to a psychiatrist. It helped to talk it out. But her father rejects therapists as phonies, and he shuns self-help groups for relatives of Alzheimer's victims. "I hate this business of misery loves company," Arthur says. "It's a mutual crying society. I know how rotten it is for me, and how rotten it must be for them, so what's the point?"

The Wolfes' living room was once the centrepiece of their house. It had beautiful carved-wood furniture and a red oriental rug. But the couch and easy chair are now draped with white sheets, as if life ended when Sarah entered the nursing home. Several of her fur-collared coats still hang in the front hall closet. "I used to be a good householder," Arthur says. Now the front door sticks.

"I had never heard of this disease, but there were subtle changes to her character," Arthur recalls, sitting at his kitchen table. "She was about sixty-three. She would repeat herself over and over again. She would ask the same questions. All of a sudden she became jealous of me like I was God's gift to women. The only thing I could think of was menopause." One of her elder sisters said, 'She's beginning to remind me of Edith Bunker.'"

Years later, Arthur discovered a fifteen-cent orange notebook in a kitchen drawer. The few words it contained were written in a shaky scrawl that tears at the heart: "Why do I keep repeating myself? I will not keep repeating myself when speaking to other people."

Arthur feels guilty, wondering if perhaps he took Sarah for granted when she was well. "Why didn't I tell her more that I loved her?" he says gruffly. "I was very stupid. She was the only woman I ever loved."

The neurologist told Arthur that Sarah had senile dementia. "I didn't like the term. I was madder than hell. Dementia. She's not insane."

He looked after Sarah at home alone. "She was incontinent. She would get up in the night-time. She still had enough awareness to get out of bed, but she never could find the bathroom. So I put a pail under her. She had a sort of aquaphobia, so I'd have to pick her up and put her in the bathtub. It got to the point where I was afraid I was going to hurt her. Once, I didn't sleep four nights in a row."

After a few months, Dominique arranged to have an employee of the provincial home-care program come to the house to help Arthur look after Sarah. It worked quite well during the day. But the responsibility was still largely his at night. Finally, Arthur told the social worker that it was time to think about a nursing home. He was told to pick two homes: Sarah could go into the first in which a bed became available. But the social worker warned that the process could take up to eighteen months because of the long waiting lists.

Meanwhile, Sarah grew worse and worse, Dominique recalls. "She had to be watched full-time. My father could get away in the day, but he had her all night. He kept saying, 'One of these days I'm going to take her and get in the car and just gas the two of us. I can't live with this anymore.'" Dominique called the nursing-home placement office and said her mother had to go into a nursing home immediately. But it was difficult to deal with the bureaucracy. "I explained that I had this sense of my entire family dying off."

"I'm really sorry," said the woman who answered the phone. "But her social worker is away for two weeks."

"But I could lose my family in three days," Dominique protested.

"I'm really sorry. I'd like to talk to my superior, but my superior isn't here either."

Desperate, Dominique pulled out her only trump card. "Well, you leave me no choice. I'm going to have to contact my friends in the government."

The next day, a bed became available in the nursing home where Sarah now lives. Dominique laughs now as she recalls how flimsy her trump card had been. As an artist, she had been involved in lobbying the government for funds for artistic projects and facilities. Her only contacts were those bureaucrats and politicians connected to arts and culture.

Arthur rapidly made the nursing home part of his routine. "It gives him a place to go," Dominique says. "It gives him a place where he feels he is really needed."

Dominique does not share her father's enthusiasm for fighting the nursing home. "I know it's an institution. There aren't nearly enough people to care for Alzheimer's patients. They really are woefully understaffed. You don't make trouble, because there are at least a couple of people capable of making your life miserable."

After insisting that Sarah have brain surgery, Arthur asked Dominique how she would have handled the situation. "I would have let her go," Dominique told him. "You didn't do her any favours."

But Arthur doesn't want Sarah to die. "I know it's killing me, but I don't care. I don't think I want to live much after she's gone, anyway. Where there's life there's hope."

4

The Nurse

"Nurse! Nurse!" The feeble voice tried again. "Nurse!"

Rosemary blinked back tears as she hurried down the hall of the nursing home, pretending not to hear the voice. It grew fainter. "Nurse!" But Rosemary was too busy to stop.

"Nurses sometimes have to keep walking because otherwise they won't get their work done," she says. "It's an awful feeling."

Rosemary, forty-two, has worked as a registered nurse in a nursing home for seven years. She is also active in the local chapter of her union — the Manitoba Organization of Nurses Associations (MONA). She is an attractive, feisty brunette who cares deeply about the well-being of the residents.

A nurse in a nursing home does not normally provide hands-on care. Rosemary's job is to set up a plan of care for residents and monitor their progress. She administers medication and performs treatments such as dressings for bedsores. She also supervises the health-care aides, who wash and feed residents, and take them to the bathroom.

Rosemary is concerned that the elderly residents are suffering because the nursing home does not hire enough nurses or health-care aides. She paints a frightening picture of older people who are overdrugged, restrained, filthy and ignored — all because there aren't enough employees to look after them properly. And, to cover up the lack of proper care, Rosemary says, some nurses falsify the nursing records of residents.

Rosemary's revelations are all the more disquieting when one realizes that the nursing home in which she works is considered to be one of the better homes in Winnipeg. It is an attractive home in a lovely middle-class neighbourhood. "I wish I had a nickel for every person who said, 'What a wonderful place!' because the floors are shiny," Rosemary says. "Meanwhile, half the residents are wet."

Recently, an elderly male resident was shouting and swearing at another resident, a man who had been innocently standing in the corridor. The head nurse ordered Rosemary to give them both a major tranquillizer. "Instead, I put one in this hallway and one in that hallway, and the problem was solved."

The drug Rosemary was ordered to administer was Haldol (also known by its generic name, haloperidol). It is used daily by about one-third of the residents in the nursing home. Although the drug is intended for psychotic people, Rosemary says none of the users are psychotic.

Instead they are "bad" residents. They are elderly people with aggressive or inappropriate behaviour. "One man might come out of his room, and there's someone in a wheelchair in his way. And he'll say, 'Get the fuck out of my way.' That person is grouchy and an alcoholic, and has been like that his whole life," Rosemary says. "But he gets put on Haldol."

Haldol is a mind-bending drug with a long list of potential adverse effects, including sudden death. "I refuse to give it," Rosemary says. She believes the side effects of major tranquillizers may actually be the cause of many of the problems that plague the elderly in institutions. According to the medical literature, the adverse effects of Haldol can include confusion, incontinence, irrational behaviour, depression and insomnia. All of these are common problems among nursing-home residents.

Haldol may also cause seizures. In addition, it may produce a decreased sensation of thirst, which can lead to dehydration — particularly dangerous in nursing homes, because many elderly people are not given enough to drink. Dehydration can cause death.

The list goes on and on. Another possible side effect of Haldol is shallow breathing, which could result in pneumonia. A side effect that Rosemary often sees is similar to the symptoms of Parkinson's Disease. "Their tongue hangs out, and they develop a funny gait. They get a vacant, blank look on their faces," she says. "But the doctors keep prescribing it, and the nurses keep giving it."

The other drug that Rosemary believes is used too frequently is Halcion (also known by its generic name, triazolam), which is used as a sleeping pill. Although it is only intended for short-term use — up to twenty-one days — Rosemary says some elderly residents have been on it for years. "They may have had trouble sleeping five years ago," she says. Halcion, like Haldol, can cause some people to become excited and act irrationally. They may end up being restrained and labelled mentally incompetent.

Dr. John Morris, professor of neurology at Washington University in St. Louis, says, "People think that any intellectual change in the elderly is the result of Alzheimer's Disease, because it's received so much publicity. But 10 to 20 per cent of the sufferers could be experiencing the side effects of medication which masquerades as Alzheimer's dementia."

Dr. Pat Montgomery, a geriatrician working at St. Boniface General Hospital in Winnipeg, wrote a guidebook for drug use in nursing homes. Dr. Montgomery says that while there has been a significant drop in the use of major tranquillizers in Manitoba nursing homes in the past ten years, they are still used inappropriately.

"The majority of people getting major tranquillizers (in nursing homes) don't have classic psychosis," he says. "There is a tendency and a potential abuse problem where people will use these drugs for a situational reaction; short-term kinds of problems — things that would be better handled by human contact, environmental control and less difficult drugs," he says. "Staff tend to over-use the sedatives and tranquillizers to cover up and manage behaviour problems. We're using them in lieu of appropriately staffed and well-managed wards."

Dr. Montgomery says that in 1985, one-quarter of Manitoba nursing-home residents were receiving a major tranquillizer, while one-quarter were receiving a minor tranquillizer. He believes that drug use by elderly nursing-home residents can be reduced, or eliminated altogether, by hiring more staff, designing better facilities and using behavioural techniques to treat problems. He also says that better diagnosis of physical problems can help reduce behaviour problems.

Rosemary says that nurses sometimes do not take the time to find out the reason that a resident is upset. For example, an elderly person could be crying or lashing out because he or she is anxious, hungry, wet or lonely. Some nurses drug the residents instead of holding their hands for a few minutes, or talking with them. "It boils down to staffing," Rosemary says. "Sometimes people find it easier to medicate somebody than to go through all the right channels. It happens a lot." As a result, she claims, many elderly men and women are over-medicated. They spend their final days in a drug-induced stupor. "People are total zombies."

A report by the Christian Labour Association of Canada on conditions in Alberta nursing homes described a disturbing trend. Nurses were creating "elderly zombies who no longer have a personality of their own" by subduing active residents through medication — sometimes without the consent of a physician. "In an environment where staff is constantly coping with time limitations, and any single incident can throw off the entire day's schedule, the temptation to pacify energetic residents becomes all too strong," the 1988 report concluded.

Not only are residents over-medicated, but sometimes they get medication that is not even prescribed for them. Rosemary says medication errors occur on a daily basis because of understaffing. Nurses are so rushed that it becomes all too easy to make a "med error," as nurses call it. "I hear nurses say there's med errors because they don't have enough time. Med errors probably happen every day. Documented med errors happen four or five times a week. That's where a nurse has actually gone and said, 'I gave this in error.'"

All medication mistakes are serious. "People get another person's medication," Rosemary explains. "If they have one condition, the pill they get might be for something else. They might get someone else's tranquillizer. Maybe they have seizures, and they need their anti-seizure medication. They get drugs that are contra-indicated. I know lots of times people don't get their antibiotics when they have an infection."

Rosemary is allowed fifty-five minutes to give medication to about forty elderly residents. She starts her day at 7:00 a.m. by listening to a twenty-minute tape-recorded report of what happened on the previous shift. Then, she must hand out all the medication before breakfast is served at 8:15 a.m. The rush to distribute the medication makes errors almost inevitable.

"Just about every single resident is on meds, and they're on way too many to begin with," she says."I have forty people who take five pills each. In nursing school, we're taught the five rules — right dose, right time, right patient, right route, right medication. But it's impossible." When Rosemary complained about this to the head nurse, she was told to leave the pills until after breakfast. "When breakfast is over, it's 9:30 a.m., and these are supposed to be 7:30 a.m. pills," Rosemary says in exasperation. When she suggested that the nursing-home hire another nurse, the administrator had another solution. To muffle Rosemary's complaints about short-staffing, she was moved to a floor where the residents do not require as much care and the problem is not as obvious.

Verna Holgate, executive director of the Manitoba Association of Licenced Practical Nurses, says she's heard of health-care aides administering medicine because there aren't enough nurses. "That is a very dangerous practice," she says. Aides are not trained to give drugs.

Most of the elderly residents cannot keep track of their medications. A survey by Winnipeg nurse Cheryl Walker found that 80 per cent of the residents in one nursing home had not received any information from anyone about their medication. "I take three capsules in the evening, and four capsules and one pill in the morning," one elderly resident told Walker. "Nobody has explained to me what this is for. I don't know. The nurse brings it, and I take it."

Rosemary is frustrated that there is never enough time for the things she likes about nursing — things like hugging an elderly resident who is crying. Or sitting down to chat with a lonely older person. "More than anything, those people need emotional and social care."

It was only the elderly man's second day in the nursing home. He was sitting glumly on his bed, dressed in street clothes, when Rosemary started to examine his feet — part of the admission procedure. When she pulled up his pant leg, she groaned in frustration to see that the man was still wearing pyjamas. The nursing-home employees had been so rushed in the morning that they had simply pulled his clothes on top of his sleepwear.

"I could have just cried," she says. To her, the incident sums up how the nursing home operates. Everything is for the sake of superficial appearance. If it looks good, it's good enough for the nursing home.

And — unless you look closely — everything seems reassuring. In the lobby of the nursing home is a framed certificate that lists the many impressive promises to its residents. Another certificate proclaims that the home meets the standards of The Canadian Council on Health Facililties Accreditation. Employees of the nursing home attend training programs, and are showered with thick policy and procedure manuals that beautifully describe how things should be done in the home — in theory. It's the kind of nursing home that makes government inspectors smile, and gives a brief moment of hope to prospective residents and their families.

It bothers Rosemary that the residents of the nursing home do not receive proper care and consideration — yet the home pretends they do.

When residents are admitted to the nursing home, they are asked to describe their likes and dislikes in food. "I don't know why they bother asking," Rosemary says. "They all get the same food. There's no substitutions."

Residents are also asked whether they prefer a bathtub or a shower for their weekly bath. But there is no real choice, Rosemary says. "As many as they can shower, they'll shower. Showers are faster. You stick them in the shower chair and hose them off. It's like going through the car wash. They're sitting there with that hose just squirting up into the hole of the shower chair. It's awful."

Those who are capable of complaining are allowed to bathe. But there is no opportunity to sit back and relax. The nursing-home employees are too busy. It's an assembly line. "Our seniors in long-term care institutions are being treated like army recruits and in some cases like prisoners," said the Christian Labour Association of Canada report. " Our nursing homes resemble assembly plants rather than 'caring' institutions."

Residents at Rosemary's home are only allowed one bath or shower a week, because of understaffing. She says that some people get fungal infections on their feet from bathing too infrequently.

In many nursing homes, appearances are more important than the comfort of residents. An activity worker at one nursing home describes how residents in wheelchairs are not allowed to sit in the main lobby or the auditorium because the administrator does not think it looks good to have old people in wheelchairs congregating in public areas. When the administrator is expecting visitors whom he wants to impress, he rushes about ensuring that all the residents are properly dressed; normally, it is of little concern to him what the residents are wearing, the staff member says.

Often, the elderly residents do not get proper mouth care. Many are not capable of cleaning their teeth and mouths. "When the dentist comes in, he always says this person needs extra mouth care or this person hasn't had mouth care for so long that their gums are bleeding," Rosemary says.

Few of the residents are truly clean. "Go through a home and really look at the (fecal matter) under their fingernails. They don't have their hair combed or their teeth in, or their glasses on. If they do have their glasses on, they can't see through them because there's scum all over them. Their eyes are full of crap. They smell bad."

But a nursing supervisor might come along and be aghast at a resident wearing two slippers that do not match, she says. "Everything is on the surface."

Special diets prescribed by a doctor for medical reasons — such as low-salt, diabetic or weight-loss diets — are almost completely ignored by the nursing-home administration. "It bothers me from a nursing point of view," Rosemary says. "But you can protest, and bring it up at staff-management meetings, and go every route imaginable, and nothing gets changed."

In the dining room, each resident's place at a table is marked with the person's name and kind of diet. The word "diet" is used loosely: a diabetic is simply given a sugar substitute. A low-salt diet means there is no salt shaker on the table. A reducing diet means no dessert.

Rosemary remembers supervising the dining room one day at lunchtime. A resident asked plaintively why he was never given sugar, adding that he had never been diabetic in his life. When Rosemary found the piece of paper on which his name and diet were printed, it was in front of another resident at the same table. The second resident, who was diabetic, had been getting all of the first resident's sugar. And none of the members of the staff had noticed.

"It's a chronic problem. I see it happening all the time with everybody," Rosemary says. But the labels with each resident's diet are impressive to visitors. "It looks like they really know what they're doing."

The food comes in regular, minced or pureed form. Rosemary noticed a resident in the dining room staring morosely at his food — minced meat on a bun. "He could see people at his table having nice lunch meat and a salad," Rosemary says. "I looked and he wasn't supposed to be minced. He was supposed to be regular."

She scoffs at the so-called low-salt diet. "There's so much salt in some of those meals," she says. "And if someone wants salt, all they have to do is ask the guy at the next table, and he'll hand it over."

If the staff do not notice the mixed-up diets, chances are the residents will not either — to the detriment of their health. Cheryl Walker's study of nursing home residents found that elderly people who are on a special diet are often unaware of their dietary needs. Here is a typical conversation between Walker and a resident at a Winnipeg nursing home:

Walker: Do you know what you can eat on your diabetic diet?
Resident: I get a piece of apple pie on my tray.
Walker: Is this on your diet?
Resident: Yes, I guess so. They give it to me.

Different food is served in the two dining rooms of the nursing home where Rosemary works. One dining room serves residents who are able to speak and complain: they get bacon, eggs, porridge and toast for breakfast. The other dining room serves the extremely mentally and physically frail: they get only porridge and toast.

Menus used in the nursing home are prepared by the head office of the corporation that owns the home. These menus, allegedly followed by the cooks, are shown to provincial government inspectors as official records of the meals in the homes.

But the items on the official menu and the food on the plates of residents are two different things, Rosemary says. For example, according to the menu one day, lunch was supposed to be a corned beef sandwich with vegetable sticks and pickles. "All they got was a corned beef sandwich." On two mornings when residents got cereal and toast, the menu said that scrambled eggs and sausage were served.

Rosemary always brings her own lunch. She doesn't trust the nursing-home food. "There have been maggots in the porridge.

There are mice in the kitchen. The kitchenettes (on the wards) are disgusting, dirty." Sinks in the dining room are covered with scum, she says.

Fresh fruit and vegetables are a rarity. "I've seen bananas the odd time, or a bit of lettuce with oil and vinegar," Rosemary says. Many of the foods are now pre-packaged — baked goods like muffins and danish, or chicken pot pie. Drink crystals are used instead of real juice.

Neena Chappell, director of the Centre on Aging at the University of Manitoba, says fresh food in nursing homes may soon be a thing of the past. Chappell once went to a food-industry seminar which was attended by nursing-home administrators. "They wanted better frozen packages so they can cut down on their kitchen staff because they figure they can cut costs," she said. "I said, 'Whatever happened to fresh food?' They looked at me like, 'Who invited her?'"

As a nurse, Rosemary has a bird's-eye view of the kind of treatment elderly residents receive from physicians who visit them in the nursing home. At her home, there are several part-time house doctors, each of whom is responsible for dozens of patients. There are also individual family doctors, who have continued to care for long-time patients after they have moved to nursing homes.

The administration of the nursing home requires the doctors to visit each resident once a month, and make a note on his or her chart. "Towards the end of the month, some doctors will just make notes on all these people's charts who he hasn't physically seen," Rosemary says. "I've seen doctors do it. They write that this patient is still very aggressive, combative, hitting out. And that doctor didn't see the patient. And he bills for it." As a result of a doctor's failure to examine a resident, medical problems can go undetected and drugs can continue to be taken unnecessarily.

Rosemary sometimes tells families to avoid certain doctors. But the nursing-home administrator has scolded her for her bluntness, arguing that, in all fairness, the business in the nursing home should be split among the house doctors.

There are other cover-ups as well. Another nurse in the home suspected that two health-care aides had abused a resident. Because of her union activities, Rosemary was informed of the incident. "The nurse went in one morning to do her rounds and the patient was fine. An hour later, after the patient had been dressed by two health-care aides, she was bruised about the face."

The nurse went to the head nurse and reported what had happened; she also went to the administrator — but nothing was done. "She went the full route within the building, without going to the media or to the police," Rosemary says. "It was all covered up, and we don't know why."

Rosemary also suspects that residents have been abused by other employees than health-care aides, but says her suspicions could only be proved if someone were caught red-handed. "There are some residents who duck when you go to touch them. But they're unable to tell you. I had one lady I know was abused. She came out of her room crying. She was saying something about, 'He hit me, he hit me.'" But the elderly woman was unable to communicate well enough to explain what had happened.

A survey of Ontario doctors working in nursing homes found that 29 per cent of them suspected that a resident had been abused by a staff member. And in Winnipeg, an anonymous letter was published in a local newspaper in early 1989. "Due to my position of authority in a personal care home, I have access to the elderly, many of whom are invalids," the anonymous writer said in a plea for help from an advice columnist at the newspaper. "Initially, I was very caring. However, over the last few years I have systematically abused, both physically and sexually, these elderly residents."

Resident abuse takes many forms; for example, Rosemary says it is common for staff members to steal trays of food that have been sent up by the kitchen for a resident. "In some cases a person has declined a meal. In other cases, the resident waits for a meal that never arrives." Other times, members of the staff remove a dessert from a tray before handing the meal to a resident.

Another problem at Rosemary's nursing home is constant budgetary restraint. Some residents have no towels or pillowcases in their rooms, while nurses are hampered by shortages of dressings, cleansing agents and gloves. "They don't like us to use gloves," Rosemary says. "A nurse was told to do a rectal check without a glove."

Shortages of supplies occur in other nursing homes as well. Dorothy, a licenced practical nurse, worked in a nursing home that refused to buy sterile bandages. Instead, the nurses wrapped strips of old sheets in foil and baked them in an oven to sterilize them.

Other equipment was "just ancient," Dorothy says. The nursing home had an oxygen tank that was so unreliable that "we never knew if it was going to work or not." And suction apparatus, intended for residents who were choking on their food, was a monstrosity that took forever to be lugged from wing to wing. "By the time we got to the wing, the patient would be blue in the face or had already spit up whatever they were choking on," Dorothy says.

Another issue at some nursing homes is the sharp contrast between the treatment of wealthy residents and low-income residents. Financially well-off residents with powerful relatives are treated differently from the rest.

In Rosemary's nursing home, some families are paid for dentures that go missing, while others are not: it all depends on who they are. Some residents can hang pictures on their walls; others are told they cannot. Some can bring furniture from home for their rooms; others are forbidden. And certain people are moved ahead of others on the waiting list for a private room.

One Saturday, the administrator arrived at the nursing home on her day off, and washed the floors of the activity room where residents do crafts. She set the tables with white tablecloths. Then the flowers started arriving — about $200 worth of floral arrangements. It was a lavish anniversary party for a rich man who lived in the home, and his wife, who did not. Four other couples in the nursing home celebrated anniversaries without so much as a greeting from the administration.

"As staff, we don't have the right to go and say, 'Why are you spending your money on this?' We resent it, because there's never enough money for supplies," Rosemary says. "Maybe this family donates things, and the administrator thought it was a politically wise move to make. But why do people donate things to a company that makes millions of dollars of profit? Why do nurses go in on their day off and help with barbecues when the company makes so much money, and none of it goes back to the residents, and none of it goes back to the staff?"

At another nursing home in Winnipeg, the wife of an elderly resident felt so sorry for residents who were in pain because of bedsores that she made a $1,000 donation to buy three air mattresses for them. The nursing home was owned by a huge corporation which could easily have afforded the mattresses; furthermore, the Manitoba Health Services Commission says that the homes should provide them. In this case, the corporation pocketed the money from the elderly wife. A brief letter of acknowledgement was sent to the woman. "In a time of rising costs and cutbacks in government support, many 'little people' could be left out were it not for the basic decency and concern of private individuals such as yourselves," a corporation official told the woman.

On the surface, Rosemary's nursing home puts a great deal of emphasis on staff training. A staff-development co-ordinator is a permanent fixture; head nurses and company officials hold training sessions during working hours, and accreditation officials and government inspectors applaud the sessions. However, some union leaders suspect the training programs are simply a cheap replacement for the measures that should be introduced.

In the past seven years, Rosemary has attended at least fifteen courses on lifting. Proper lifting prevents injury to both staff member and resident; back problems are the most common form of injury to nurses. The courses are useful, but they have become redundant. "I know how to lift," Rosemary says. "I don't need another (training session). I need more mechanical lifting devices or more staff to help me lift."

Unlike Rosemary, other nurses are afraid to tell their head nurse or the nursing-home administrator about poor conditions in the home — even if the residents are harmed as a result. Some nurses who have filled out work-situation reports (provided by the union to identify hazardous working conditions affecting residents or staff) have suffered reprisals and harassment.

One year, Rosemary constantly filled out work-situation reports saying that she could not get her work done on time because of short-staffing; ironically, the nursing home's annual work evaluation criticized her for being unable to get her work done on time. "I'm the one who told them that," she says in disbelief. "I was watched by my head nurse when I went for coffee, and watched when I came back. There were comments made as I left. There were days when I came home and cried."

Rosemary is a self-proclaimed fighter. She wants to correct the injustices she sees. She feels she is getting burned out, but she persists.

"I can fight things in staff-management committee because our collective agreement says we can talk about patient-care issues," she says. "I can go to meetings that have to do with dietary, for example. I can write letters to the administrator. I can put suggestions in the suggestion box. And I do all of those things."

But most of the other nurses cannot be bothered to fight for the residents. "Everybody can't be fighters," Rosemary says. "Things don't get changed."

Sometimes, her actions have an effect. "But the problems surface again, and I start fighting all over again. It's almost like they think I'll forget about it."

Rosemary says she sometimes ignores the problems in order to cope with the many frustrations: the nursing-home system, she says, is ultimately more powerful than the nurses and health-care aides who work in it. "There is a certain kind of person that goes into nursing," she says. "You really believe you're going to help these people. But you can't. Nobody co-operates with you."

Rosemary is in the dining room at 8:15 a.m. to supervise breakfast — make sure that all the residents show up, and help residents who choke on their food. The nursing home has two dining rooms for residents. "It's sort of like the A list and the B list," Rosemary explains. "If you're good, you go in this dining room. If you're bad, you go in the other. If you're really bad — if you spit food all over, and it's distasteful to other residents — you eat on the ward."

Rosemary has recently been supervising the dining room for residents who are confused and disabled, and need to be fed. There aren't nearly enough workers to help them eat — six staff members to feed and assist seventy-five residents. As a result, many elderly residents don't get enough food. "They're eating the cardboard that the butter pat comes on, and nobody's doing anything," Rosemary says.

"Nobody's cutting their meat. People are throwing crackers in their tea instead of in their soup. They're trying to cut their bun, and just getting so totally frustrated that, by the end of the meal, they haven't had anything to eat, because they don't know what to do."

Some residents are too confused to know a meal is being served. But staff members are often too busy to look for them, or to coax them to come to the dining room. "Nobody cares," Rosemary says. "Don't they ever think about the fact that some- day they'll be old and if somebody doesn't take them by the hand they might not eat too?" Moreover, the elderly residents often don't get enough to drink. "Many of our residents go into hospital because they're dehydrated," Rosemary says.

Fluids are served in four-ounce glasses — often only half full. Milk and juice served with meals are frequently left untouched because there aren't enough staff to help mentally-impaired resi- dents drink them. Nursing-home employees sometimes avoid giving residents fluids, because they don't have the time to take elderly people to the bathroom, or to clean them up if they wet themselves, Rosemary says.

As in so many of the homes, residents of Rosemary's nursing home can end up constipated because of the short-staffing. "I had a suppository to do the other day and the health-care aide said, 'No! She had a big bowel movement yesterday — don't give it to her.' I decided to do a rectal check on this lady, and she was full. She had about three big bowel movements that day, after I gave her the suppository. The health-care aide didn't want me to give her the suppository because then she'd have to clean it up." Constipation, she adds, is a serious problem. "I know of a resident who, in my opinion, died of a bowel obstruction."

In the hurly-burly of getting tasks accomplished, the human dignity of elderly people is quickly discarded. Residents who indicate a need to go to the bathroom while they are in the hall or the lounge are hurried into the nearest resident's bedroom to use the bathroom. "Men into ladies' rooms and vice versa," Rosemary says.

By midday, she often sees elderly residents slumped over in their chairs, or hanging over the sides of their wheelchairs, because there are not enough employees available to put them to bed for a nap.

"I have one lady who always comes to me and says, 'I'm really tired today. Can I please go to bed?' If she asks the health-care aides, they won't put her. No time, and too much trouble. It takes two people to put her to bed. Then, they have to re-make the bed when they get her up."

Nurses are supposed to take residents for walks, and help them do exercises prescribed by the occupational therapist who comes once a week. But there is often no time. As a result, residents lose what little mobility they have left. They deteriorate, and lose the ability to do things for themselves. Eventually, they begin to require more and more care. "Walks are really important, so that people don't get contracted, and can still not have to be lifted, and can still get to the toilet," Rosemary explains.

Each nursing-home resident is supposed to have an up-to-date "care plan" among his or her nursing records at the home. This plan is supposed to fully inform staff members about the status of residents: whether the patient is incontinent, and prone to skin breakdown; or unsteady on his or her feet, and prone to injury. There should be a record of the resident's diet, sleep and bowel-movement habits, and conditions such as allergies, hearing difficulties or sight problems.

But nurses do not even have time to read the care plans, let alone update them regularly, as required. "A resident could go to the hospital and have a hernia operation, but there would never be anything on there about their wound," Rosemary says. "One of the problems might be constipation, so the criteria might be that this person have a bowel movement every three days. But we're evaluating the care plan monthly, not every three days."

When government inspectors or accreditation officials visit the nursing home, the care plans are "fixed up," Rosemary says. She remembers being called into work on a day off to update the care plans, because the accreditation officials were expected. Another nurse, who was also called in, was ordered to adjust the care plans to reflect an ideal version of the care the residents theoretically received. "This was the way they were supposed to look for the MHSC (Manitoba Health Services Commission)," Rosemary says.

"Care plans look great," says Donna, a nurse who worked in another Winnipeg nursing home. "Manitoba Health thinks they're terrific. But we don't have time to read them."

Rosemary is responsible for forty residents, and some of her co-workers are responsible for as many as seventy people.

During a typical weekday, there is a head nurse, plus two registered nurses, two licensed practical nurses and five health-care aides — to look after seventy elderly people. The number of workers on each shift fluctuates constantly. "But it never changes in relation to how sick people are, or whether there's diarrhea rampant, or when there's a bunch of deaths and a bunch of admissions," Rosemary says. "It never varies according to resident need." She estimates that, every year, there are two significant outbreaks of diarrhea or flu. Each episode affects at least 50 per cent of the residents and as much as 80 per cent of staff. Scores of elderly Canadians have died of flu or salmonella outbreaks in nursing homes.

Every January and February, officials from the Manitoba Health Services Commission assess the nursing homes in the province to see how much care their residents require, and determine whether their staffing levels are appropriate. The commission, which funds and monitors the homes, decides how much and what kind of staff they should have. The provincial standards represent the absolute minimum. And most nursing homes do not staff more than they must. "We're staffed at the bare minimum that MHSC tell us to be staffed," Rosemary says. "If we're overstaffed, or close to it, they (the nursing home management) start not replacing sick calls. If we're told by MHSC we're understaffed, we'll only start bringing in people before the year-end to make it look like we weren't understaffed when they come in again."

A few weeks before the commission was scheduled to arrive, Rosemary was called in to work extra shifts. Did she spend time with the residents? No. Rosemary's supervisor told her to spend the day putting reinforcements on the holes of the paper on which the care plans are written — for seventeen dollars an hour.

Shortly before the visit by the provincial officials, members of the housekeeping staff were called in to work extra shifts. They were ordered to wash the walls and windows of the nursing home. The administration recorded these shifts as nursing hours so that when the officials examined the records, it would appear that the nursing home had enough nurses to meet the guidelines. "I could have just cried," Rosemary said. "Residents weren't benefitting."

Accreditation is a slightly different process. Inspectors from an independent accrediting agency are sent to assess the nursing home: if the nursing home meets the agency's standards, it receives a certificate declaring that it is an accredited facility.

Nursing homes are very keen on these certificates, because they are a good public-relations gesture. Furthermore, the accreditation process keeps the government inspectors away. In Manitoba, government inspectors do not visit a nursing home in the year that the home is accredited.

The staff realize that the accreditation process is virtually meaningless. The nursing-home administration is informed months in advance about the inspectors' visit, and spends a lot of time and energy preparing for it.

One thing the administration does is hire extra staff. But this is not all. "Everybody goes into high gear," Rosemary says. "Management is in the courtyard raking leaves on Saturday and Sunday. It's a joke — the painting that goes on, the wallpapering and the cleaning. We call it the white-glove test. It's like Queen Elizabeth was going to come to stay at my house. It's totally cosmetic. It's not worth anything. Staff are told to go out and buy new uniforms for that day."

A survey of Ontario nursing-home physicians found that 73 per cent said nursing homes did not have enough nurses to meet the needs of their patients. Sherry Wiebe, former head of the Registered Nurses Association of Manitoba, believes that staff guidelines for nursing homes are outdated. Since the population of nursing homes is getting older and frailer, Wiebe says, more nurses are needed. Vera Chernecki, executive director of the Manitoba Organization of Nurses' Associations (MONA), agrees that the staffing guidelines should be reconsidered. "It's a heavier workload than it used to be," she says.

Chernecki, forty-eight, used to work in a nursing home. At times she would be the only registered nurse on a ward with ninety-nine residents, assisted by one licenced practical nurse and six health care aides. It was not enough. "I would come home frustrated, in tears," she says. "We often compare care given in a nursing home to care given to infants — we have to do everything."

Nurses who work in nursing homes have filed as many as 100 work-situation reports per year to the Manitoba union. These reports — most of which are prompted by understaffing — represent only a fraction of the complaints Chernecki hears on the telephone from nurses who won't bother to put their concerns in writing.

Chernecki says some administrators intimidate nurses who fill out work-situation reports. "They think we're criticizing their management. We say we're alerting them to a potentially dangerous situation."

Donna sums it up: "When you've got a five-minute supper break, no coffee break, and get off an hour late, you've got a staffing problem."

While some provinces, such as Ontario, are experiencing shortages of nurses in nursing homes, Manitoba is still considered to have an adequate number. But Chernecki says the heavier workload, short-staffing and relatively low pay of nurses could produce a shortage in the future. Rosemary says many of her colleagues talk about leaving the profession — or at least leaving nursing homes. "Nurses suffer burnout if they can't do their job properly."

The administrator of Rosemary's nursing home likes to call the home a "restraint-free" institution. It sounds enlightened. But it is not true.

The nursing home has stopped using the most horrible forms of restraints — the restraint jackets and vests that are still used in some other homes. However, some of the elderly residents are still confined to chairs by restraint belts, seat belts or lap boards. A lap board is a piece of plywood that sits on the arms of a wheelchair, and ties around the back of a chair with a piece of cloth.

Typically, the wandering residents are the ones who are restrained; once again, understaffing is the main reason for the restraints: there are not enough staff to watch the wanderers. According to the policies and procedures manual of Rosemary's nursing home, wandering residents are checked every fifteen minutes — which is what administrators tell government inspectors and worried families. But the policy is so unrealistic that it is never observed. "We couldn't possibly get our work done," Rosemary says.

Nurses can be held responsible if a wandering resident is hurt or killed. To protect themselves in case of a lawsuit, some nurses sign the medical records of wandering residents to indicate that they were checked every fifteen minutes even though they were not. "Some nurses go ahead and sign," Rosemary says.

One of the wandering residents at Rosemary's home is an elderly woman with wealthy relatives who are quick to complain when they are unhappy with the care she receives. The nurses feel intimidated: they know that the family would sue if anything happened to the elderly woman. So the woman has been placed in a room directly in front of the nursing station. As the nurses sit in their station, doing the mounds of paperwork they are required to do, they can glance at the resident's room to make sure she has not wandered away. "That's one way of getting around the fact that she can't be checked every fifteen minutes," Rosemary says.

According to the Christian Labour Association's report on conditions in Alberta nursing homes, a common complaint among nurses is the inordinate amount of time spent on record-keeping: nurses who are supposed to provide medical care to residents have become paper-pushers. And health-care aides — who have either minimal training or none at all — end up changing dressings and taking blood pressures, because the nurses are too busy filling in charts, reports and medication sheets. This situation deprives the resident of the trained eye of a nurse who could diagnose problems while doing routine medical checks. Moreover, health-care aides are taken away from their own task of giving direct physical care to the elderly residents.

Many people tell Rosemary that they could never be a nurse like her; they say they could not do some of the things she does. Yet Rosemary loves her job, despite some qualms.

"So many of the things we do — we don't think about them. Like someone's toenails. That's disgusting. I do it at work, but I could never do it for my husband or my kids. Or rectal checks. If

I was going to look in my mirror at 6:00 a.m. and tell myself that in two hours, I'd have my finger up someone's bum, I couldn't come to work."

Each nurse has one task that she really can't stand. With some, the difficulty is teeth: they put the dentures into a resident's mouth with a tissue. For Rosemary, mucus and spit are the problem. "When someone's drooling, and I have to feed them, and it's falling out of their mouth, I find that really gross. I turn myself off lots of times. It's the same with rectal exams. I think that 99 per cent of the time I don't think about what I'm doing. I'm on automatic pilot."

The working days go fast: Rosemary's shift is from 7:00 a.m. to 3:00 p.m. When she first arrives in the morning, the odour of urine and feces is awful. "But your nose becomes accustomed to it after a while."

She listens to tape-recorded messages from previous shifts, then hands out pills and supervises breakfast. After a coffee break, she provides treatments for the residents, including foot-soaks, creams for rashes, and medicated dressings for the sores which result from constantly lying in bed. ("There's lots of those.")

Rosemary's lunch is at 11:00 a.m. Half an hour later, she is back at work, handing out more pills. Then, it is lunchtime for the residents. Rosemary supervises the elderly residents who eat on the ward.

After lunch, she continues attending to residents who need treatment, takes a coffee break at 2:00 p.m., and tidies and leaves at 3:00 p.m.

Abusive residents are a hazard of the job. "You get really good at knowing who to avoid. Or delegating someone else to deal with them." She has been hit but never injured. Other nurses have suffered hairline fractures and concussions.

It can be a stressful job. "Everything falls back on nurses," says Marlene, a nurse who worked in a Winnipeg nursing home. "Half the job is fending off complaints by family and residents. You're always apologizing for the dietary staff serving a lousy meal or for the laundry staff washing a seventy-five-dollar virgin wool sweater."

Rosemary knows her work is special. "I make a big difference in the lives of the residents," she says. "I get so close to them. I really, truly love them. They bring a smile to my face. I resent the fact that society regards them as useless."

Sometimes she wonders whether she will end up in a room in a nursing home — a small, stark room with a few sticks of furniture and hardly any personal possessions. It is a thought that scares her. "I take great pride in my home and the things I collect. To think that I could end up in a room with just a bedside table absolutely terrifies me."

5

The Aide

Hope Kowalski points to a two-inch white scar on her arm. "A little old man lunged at me and scratched all down my arm," she explains. "He didn't want to go to the bathroom."

Hope is a health-care aide at a large suburban Winnipeg nursing home. Among her daily frustrations is the ordeal of putting up with verbal and physical abuse from hostile or mentally-impaired elderly residents. "I've been called a son of a bitch, I've been called a dirty old slut. I've been scratched, bitten and punched."

Hope is fifty-two years old. She sometimes wonders whether she is getting too old for her job. Increasingly, she goes to bed early at night. She is exhausted after she finishes her 3:00 p.m.-to-11:00 p.m. shift; her legs ache, and her back is sore. But then she reminds herself that the real problem is not her age — it is overwork. The nursing home does not hire enough workers to properly meet the needs of the elderly residents. On a typical shift, Hope personally looks after at least eighteen older people.

"It's just crash-bang-boom," she says. "You're rushing. You go from one person to another. You're not giving the proper care. You know inside you're not."

Hope is a solidly-built woman with a hearty laugh and a warm, kind manner. For fourteen years she has been taking the bus or getting a ride with a nurse to her job in the nursing home. But the job is getting harder.

Health-care aides are the backbone of any nursing home. They provide the bulk of the hands-on care for the elderly residents. Their work with the old people includes taking them to the dining room, feeding them, washing them, bathing them, dressing them, taking them to the bathroom, and lifting them in and out of bed or bath. Aides also re-position residents who are confined to their beds or wheelchairs.

"They're always in the ward," says Murray Craddock, a representative of the Canadian Union of Public Employees, which represents health-care aides in Manitoba. "They're always with the residents."

When a nursing home is short-staffed, it usually means there are not enough health-care aides. Aides who call in sick are often not replaced on a shift; sometimes there are fewer people on shift than required by provincial government guidelines. Craddock says this happens more often in the for-profit nursing homes than the non-profit homes. "They don't want to pay a replacement," he says. "It cuts into the profit margin to raise staff."

In the nursing home where Hope Kowalski works, a typical shift consists of two registered nurses, two licenced practical nurses and five aides to look after ninety-nine residents on a floor. A sixth aide comes in for half a shift. There are usually two health-care aides on a wing with thirty-seven elderly residents.

The administration of Hope's nursing home has told health-care aides that they may spend up to twenty minutes putting a resident to bed at night. But twenty minutes is a rare luxury, Hope says; instead, the job usually has to be done in about ten minutes — that includes undressing residents; washing their hands, face, bodies and teeth; taking them to the bathroom; and putting them to bed. "You're not spending as much time as you would like to," Hope says. "You're running."

Because of time pressures and heavy schedules, health-care aides often find it quicker and easier to control a resident's movements rather than encourage a bit of independence. "You're washing their hands and face because it's faster than letting them do it," Hope says. "If someone can unbutton their sweater, we don't let them — because we can do it faster than them fumbling around."

Studies of elderly residents in nursing homes have found that nursing-home staff tend to discourage residents from doing anything for themselves. They tend to promote "learned helplessness" among the elderly residents. Beverley Wilden, director of the psychogeriatric program at a Winnipeg nursing home, conducted an extensive survey of the literature on this subject, and noted that the residents' unhappiness seemed to increase with their level of dependence. Some studies found that the staff tended to praise residents who accepted assistance, and discouraged residents who tried to take care of themselves without help.

The Christian Labour Association of Canada, in its report on conditions in nursing homes in Alberta, observed that the elderly residents deteriorate when they are not given a chance to exert some independence. "Less available staff time for residents means a more rapid mental and physical deterioration of residents, which in turn requires more staff time," the 1988 report said. "It's a vicious circle, with tragic consequences for our seniors."

The Fourth Manitoba Conference on Aging, held in 1985, also noted the terrible spiral of increasing dependence. Said a conference report: "Loss of independence results in loss of self-esteem. This can lead to withdrawal, dissatisfaction, passivity and complete renunciation of personal responsibility."

Elderly nursing-home residents also suffer as a result of staff shortages: calls for assistance are ignored and meals get cold; residents who need help going to the toilet soil themselves, while others are left sitting on toilets or potties for up to an hour; and there is little time for the desperately needed human touch — plumping pillows, comforting someone who is crying, or chatting with a lonely person, even for just a minute.

As indicated, most nursing homes give residents one bath or shower a week. A study of residents in a Winnipeg nursing home showed that some wished to have more baths — but their desires were ignored. "I find it very pleasant to have a bath," an elderly resident told Winnipeg nurse Cheryl Walker, the author of the study. "I would like to have it perhaps two times a week. I did ask the nursing staff when I first came in. They suggested they might be able to change it. But they haven't done so."

Sylvia, a health-care aide who worked in a Winnipeg nursing home for ten years, could see that elderly residents suffered because of short-staffing. "You see lots of people not turned often enough, and they develop bedsores," she says. "When I'm that age I hope no one leaves me lying in poop — which happens lots of times."

A nursing home in Toronto has been taken to the Supreme Court of Ontario over a labour dispute. In this home, cutbacks on health-care aides had led to assembly-line treatment, according to Bruce Land, a representative for Ontario health-care aides in the Canadian Union of Public Employees (CUPE).

Night staff in the Toronto nursing home were instructed to start rousing patients at 5:00 a.m. to get them dressed and ready for breakfast. The staff, who had previously given full sponge baths each morning to all residents who could not walk, were issued new instructions ordering them to wash only the hands and faces of the residents. Genital areas were to be washed "only if required," according to directions from the administration of the nursing home. To save even more time, staff were ordered to reduce the distribution of medication from four times a day to twice a day. As a result, some residents began receiving a double dose of their medication.

The Christian Labour Association report said that employees in some institutions were dressing the elderly residents as early as 5:00 a.m., then putting them back in bed to await breakfast. In most homes, elderly people are roused between 6:00 a.m. and 8:00 a.m. to prepare for the day. Although some homes allow breakfast at a later time for residents wishing to sleep in, the report found that such places were the exception.

It also found that residents who did not arrive on time for breakfast were restricted to a liquid diet until lunchtime. "The rule is, if you're not on time you're out of luck," the report said. "The dining room has to be cleared, floors cleaned, and facilities prepared for lunch. The residents are either taken back to bed, placed in the lounge, or seated in a chair in their room."

Because of the time pressures, residents are expected to answer the call of nature when it fits the rigid work schedule. They are often "assisted" by means of suppositories and enemas. Sometimes residents are put on the toilet with the door open, so the health-care aide can keep an eye on them while performing other duties, the Alberta report concluded. In one Winnipeg nursing home, visitors saw a resident sitting on a potty on her bed. Her bedroom door was wide open.

"Almost universally, the complaint was heard that there was no time to give residents any personal attention," the Alberta report said. "Matters discussed or promises made by employees to residents prior to the 7 a.m. shift change are often unknown to those coming on shift. There is absolutely no time for simple conversations about how the resident has slept, how he or she feels, or whether he or she has physical or medical needs."

The Alberta report concluded that understaffing is caused by inadequacies in the minimum-staffing requirements, the profit motive of private nursing homes, and a shortage of government funding.

Maureen Morrison, a CUPE representative for Manitoba health-care aides, agrees that understaffing is a widespread problem in nursing homes, and that government standards, which dictate staffing levels, should be raised. "Aides would like to do more than the basic physical care," she says. "They would like to have time to interact with patients."

Consultant Win Lindsay recalls one stark example of understaffing. A confused resident was trying to eat by putting her spoon in the steam hole of a plate cover. The spoon would not fit. "No one noticed," Lindsay says. "In due time it was whisked away, and she never had anything."

The authors of a recent book on institutionalization of the elderly in Canada make a frightening suggestion to overcome the problems of short-staffing. William Forbes, Jennifer Jackson and Arthur Kraus suggest that television cameras be used to monitor residents who are at high risk of falling. If this proposal were implemented, it would further erode the little privacy left to nursing-home residents.

In early 1989, a staff shortage at a Regina nursing home forced the relatives of elderly residents to feed and wash their family members. "If I don't come to feed her, I wonder sometimes if the staff would ever get around to it," said the daughter of an eighty-seven-year-old woman — an invalid — living in the nursing home. Union officials agreed that the residents were being neglected. "There just isn't enough staff for the size of our facility," said Tom Crosby, president of local 2569 of the Canadian Union of Public Employees.

Insufficient staffing can lead to tragedies; for example, in a fire. "Between 11:00 p.m. to 7:00 a.m. daily, each nursing home in the province is a potential death trap," the Alberta report said. "Up to about 50 per cent of residents cannot physically help themselves, or cannot mentally comprehend and appropriately respond to a fire hazard."

Short-staffing can be dangerous for members of the staff as well. Hope Kowalski has fallen several times; once, she slipped in a puddle of urine and sprained her ankle: she was off work for two weeks. "The times I've fallen, it's been because we've been working short, and I've been rushing and not looking at the floor," she says. A twenty-one-year-old health-care aide at Hope's nursing home has been absent from work for over a year because of serious injuries suffered during a fall.

When they rush around the home in a futile effort to overcome staff shortages, the employees get irritated — with each other as well as with the residents.

"I myself, who very rarely ever gets snappy, snapped at one of the girls last night," Hope says. "She was a part-time worker, and moving a little slower. I said, 'Pick up speed, we gotta get moving.' She just looked at me. I think she was shocked. She knew I was annoyed, and that's not me."

She adds: "Sometimes I get angry at the residents. I've got so many people to put to bed, and sometimes I don't feel so good myself. I say, 'Just leave me alone.' After I say it I think, 'Oh!' And I go back, and give them a hug and a kiss."

"It isn't that the staff don't care," says Patricia Spindel, of Concerned Friends. "The pressure is such that they can't afford to care. The situation pits staff against residents."

A CUPE survey of workers at three nursing homes in Windsor found that many are victims of health problems caused by over-work. These include fatigue, increased susceptibility to illness, headaches, neck and back pain, anger, feelings of powerlessness, and tensions with people around them.

Hope believes the short-staffing situation is getting worse. "Usually, it's hectic in the summer when people are on holidays," she says. "But this has been going on since summer, right through the winter. It seems like we used to be short on weekends, but now it's short through the week too."

An activity worker, who works in the same nursing home as Hope, recalls conversing with an elderly resident in the hall when a health-care aide appeared. "Without even an, 'Excuse me,' she whisked him around the corner for breakfast. On the way, she was muttering, 'I gotta hurry. I'm late.'"

The nursing home's management, says Hope, is unsympathetic; the attitude seems to be: "You're used to it. You can do it."

Hope lights another cigarette and pours herself a coffee. She always reads her horoscope in the newspaper during her coffee break: "Smile; keep everybody happy," it said one day. That was all she needed: "This is full of bullshit," she told her work-mates; the other health-care aides laughed. "We just complain and go and do it, and that's it," Hope says. "That's our job."

Sometimes, she dreads her daily arrival at the nursing home. "It's not fun any more when we're short-staffed," she says. "But once I get there, I pick up — because one of the residents will say something to me or smile at me and then I know I'm there for a reason." But, by the end of her shift, she is feeling discouraged and frustrated. "It's the same old thing again. I'm pooped and bitchy."

Hope quit school when she was in Grade Nine. She went to the Health Sciences Centre hospital, said she needed a job, and started the same day, as a health-care aide. She was not quite seventeen. Later, she married a tradesman and stayed home to raise a family of four children. But, after sixteen years at home, Hope was ready to return to the work force. "I was losing my self-confidence. I didn't know what was going on in the world."

She found a job at the nursing home — her first experience with geriatrics. "I had seen old people, but only on the street. Nothing like I see here. I was shocked to see how much human beings deteriorate." Work became a necessity a few years later when Hope's husband died of a heart attack at the age of forty-seven.

After deductions, Hope brings home $573.89 every two weeks to support herself and her eighteen-year-old daughter. They also have four cats and a dog. "If I had another paycheque in the home, I'd be all right," she says. "But with just one paycheque, some-times it's awkward. If you want something a little extra you do without, or you save a hell of a lot."

According to her union contract, Hope is categorized as an untrained health-care aide because she does not have a certificate from a community college. She earns $8.79 an hour. A formally-trained aide can make $9.30 an hour. Craddock estimates that about two-thirds of the health-care aides in Manitoba have taken a training course at a community college.

But Hope refuses to take the course: she cannot manage the seventy-five dollars it costs; and after many years of experience, she does not believe that the course could teach her anything. It annoys her that there is little recognition for experience: Hope earns just eighty-eight cents an hour more than an untrained aide, fresh off the street. "They're getting twice as much work out of me," she says. "I think I should be paid to my experience, but they don't see it that way."

Levels of training among aides are extremely variable. Too often, aides are undertrained. According to a 1986 federal study, "staff training for positions in long-term care facilities is often minimal." The lack of training "encourages custodial rather than rehabilitative care." The study also concluded that, "low salaries and lack of opportunities for advancement are a deterrent to attracting and keeping trained personnel."

Consultant Win Lindsay agrees that the staff in nursing homes are frequently undertrained. "There is a tremendous expectation that they will get training on the job," she says. "We know perfectly well that in some facilities we have people who get into positions for which they're not trained."

In Ontario, inquest juries have called for better training of aides. "The over-utilization of undertrained staff results in poor quality care and higher risks to patient safety," the Ontario Association of Registered Nursing Assistants wrote in a brief in 1984.

Hope Kowalski's greatest fear is back injury. When she is working with a health-care aide who is new on the job, she refuses to lift a resident. "It's one of the harder things to learn," Hope says. "There's a certain way of lifting. If you don't lift properly, you put your partner off balance, and that's how you hurt yourself."

Concerned Friends recommends that all aides be required to take a certified health-care aide course, and that aides who are currently working without a certificate get financial assistance from the provincial government to enable them to enrol in courses. The group also recommends that certified aides be licensed, and that a licencing body be established, with the authority to revoke licences in cases of malpractice.

"What concerns us most is whether someone can read prescriptions and medication bottles," says Patricia Spindel. "Can they recognize when someone is in a life-threatening situation? These kinds of things are not being taught in nursing homes."

Hope is worried that new aides at her nursing home do not receive enough training — only a two-day orientation. "I don't think it's enough," she says. "They should work on the buddy system at least four days. It's hard enough to know every resident and put a name to a face, let alone know what to do. The routine is hard to get used to."

Health-care aides are a strange breed. "They are the toughest group of people," says Bruce Land of CUPE. "I tell them to work and leave. But they say, 'What about the poor resident?' They stay late. They run around and do the work of two. Therefore, there's a rise in the number of injuries on the job. Because they're so caring, they're their own worst enemies."

It takes a special kind of person to keep working on the front lines in a nursing home. "Only those with real dedication and a care and concern for the needs of the elderly and enfeebled remain for any period of time," Land says.

Dorothy, the licensed practical nurse whom we have met already, acknowledges that aides are more likely than nurses to be emotionally attached to the residents. "If they have any free time, they'll go in the lounge, and play the piano, and sing or dance with residents," she says. "They invite them to their homes." Often, they give up their coffee breaks in order to sit and talk to residents, or read letters to them. "Sometimes, you find someone crying and you know if you stop and talk, it will put you back fifteen minutes," Hope says. "But you do it."

Most health-care aides in Canada are women; in urban areas, many are immigrant women. Surveys of aides working in Metropolitan Toronto show that many of them began working after their children entered school: typically, they range in age from thirty to sixty. Because of the stress of their jobs, many of them are heavy smokers and drinkers — off the job. Often, tensions at work spill over into family life. "Some women say they don't go home right away," Bruce Land says. "They go for a walk, or else they would take it out on their families."

Some health-care aides hold down two jobs, working two part-time shifts at different places — or even two full-time shifts: they become so exhausted that they go around like automatons. "They're not only working eight hours at one home — they work an eight-hour shift somewhere else," Win Lindsay says.

The work of health-care aides is back-breaking physical labour. CUPE is studying the incidence of hysterectomy, and corrective surgery for stretched bladders, among health-care aides. "We think they're having more than the average for those types of operations," Land says. He believes these conditions are caused by the strain of lifting residents.

There are no rewards of high salaries or prestige for their efforts. "Generally, the work done in nursing homes is considered not very important or valuable," Maureen Morrison of CUPE says. "These residents are just shunted away, and nobody wants to think about it."

But the aides are proud of their role. They see themselves as the true care-givers for the disabled and the elderly. "We do have the closest contact with them," Hope says. "We're dealing with them all the time. Nurses just pop a pill and walk away. The residents talk to the aides more than the nurses. Sometimes their face will light up when they see you. They'll tell us something they won't tell a nurse. They tell us if they ache, or if someone at dinner is slobbering and spitting into their food."

Because aides are on the front lines, they are the first to notice a sudden change in a resident's condition. "We should be paying royal attention to what you girls tell us about the residents, because you see them more often," a nurse said to Hope.

"We make sure the nurses listen," Hope says. "If they're busy, and they don't seem to be paying attention to me, I make a point. My voice goes a little higher, or I'll say, 'Look, she's not well. I don't know what it is but please go and see.' And then she will go."

Hope takes comfort from the knowledge that her work is important, and that she makes a difference. "Not everybody can do it," her sister once told her. "Thank God there are people like you, who do look after the old people."

Despite the poor pay, and the stressful working conditions, she has no intention of abandoning the nursing home. "There are rewards in this job — but they're feelings, not money," she says.

"I never had money all my life. I never had the education. But doing what I'm doing, I'm satisfied with my life. A lot of people say, 'You should do something else.' I don't want to do anything else. These are people that I care for. There's been many times when I've said, 'I'm going to quit, and go work in a hospital.' I come home and I'll think about it. But there's no way. These are people that I love. It gives me satisfaction to help someone. If someone says my name or remembers me, it makes it worthwhile."

Yet she does not want her daughter to follow in her footsteps. "I'd rather my daughter made money," she says. "I don't want her cleaning up somebody else's shit and piss, and taking verbal abuse. You're on the bottom. There's no way up. You have to pretty well enjoy what you're doing, so you don't feel like you're on the bottom rung of the ladder."

Hope still shudders when she thinks about it. She was putting an elderly resident to bed in the nursing home one night when she suddenly heard a commotion in an adjacent room. "Help! Help!" someone was shrieking. She rushed into the nearby room.

"Two aides had this little lady, one on each side, and they were swinging her," she recalls. "I guess they thought it was a joke. I just said, 'Oh, my God,' shut the door and reported it to the nurse right away."

The two aides were fired. Three days later, the elderly woman died. "Deep down in my heart, I think the shock of being swung like that killed her," Hope says. "I think maybe she thought, 'Hell, if I'm going to spend the rest of my life like this, I'm just going to die.'"

Murray Craddock agrees that there are cases of abuse from time to time. One orderly pulled out a catheter that was not completely deflated, causing internal bleeding in an elderly resident. The orderly was fired. Some aides, slapped by confused residents, will slap back at the residents, ripping their paper-thin skin. Craddock says abusive employees are often given the opportunity to resign so that the incidents are not officially listed on their work records.

In Ontario, some nursing home-employees have been charged with physical and sexual assaults on residents.

"That's the problem when you have all these people housed in one place, and you're not screening very well the people you're hiring," Patricia Spindel says. "That's another reason why we want to see these places eliminated. The risk of abuse is so great."

In a sense, many of the staff are victims too. "You have people who are working at two jobs to try and keep body and soul together," Spindel says. "They're dead tired, and then they come to work and they have to deal with very difficult people." Maureen Baker, author of *Aging in Canadian Society*, writes: "The low pay of workers fuels nursing-home profits, but at the same time leads to resentment, and possibly patient abuse by the staff."

At a certain point, some of the workers simply lose patience. They seem to snap. An activity worker in Hope's nursing home recalls a health-care aide mimicking an elderly woman who habitually repeated things in a high-pitched voice. "Apple juice, apple juice!" the aide shrieked into another elderly resident's ear. The resident became agitated: "Get out of here — stop that!" she begged the aide. But the aide kept repeating the phrase.

The aides at Hope's nursing home exchange workloads each month to help prevent burnout. "It gives you a break from certain people," Hope says. "Some of them can be very demanding. Some of them can be very abusive and hard to handle. If you were on a wing forever, you would get very frustrated. You would get to the point where you would work as a machine."

Statistics compiled by CUPE's national health and safety department show that, in a two-year period, 35 per cent of staff at an Ontario home for the aged suffered injuries caused by residents. In another Ontario home, an aide had her head pounded against a wall by an ex-boxer. "The only thing that saved her life was that another employee came into the room by accident and distracted the attacker," says a 1987 CUPE guidebook on violence at work.

Similarly, the study of Alberta nursing homes by the Christian Labour Association reported that a health-care aide was kicked in the chest so hard that she developed an infection in her breast which eventually forced her to stop working. "I've had fire extinguishers thrown at me," says Murray Craddock. Other health-care aides have experienced racist remarks by residents.

According to the CUPE guidebook, injuries are caused by understaffing, and a lack of training in recognizing and defusing violent situations. The latter problem is worsened by a rapid turnover in many institutions. At the same time, says Craddock, nursing-home administrators tend to ignore the abuse. "They say that's part of the job. But our job is not to be a punching bag."

Much of this abuse is "a result of aggression or irritation created when nursing aides rush residents in order to meet work schedules," the Alberta report said. Another contributing factor is that nursing homes have become warehouses for older ex-psychiatric patients. "Because of cuts in health care, fewer institutions exist that have staff or facilities capable of handling such patients," says the CUPE guidebook. "Therefore they are often 'dumped' in nursing homes or homes for the aged where they can't get the necessary special care. Workers in these facilities generally don't have the training to handle these patients and so are put in a potentially dangerous situation."

If a new resident is "a fighter," or aggressive, a nurse or a supervisor will warn Hope to be careful. But a CUPE survey found that many health-care aides are not warned about violent residents.

Moreover, there may be many more injuries than are officially reported, because many require only minimal treatment, and are not reported to the provincial workers' compensation board, or the union. In other cases, workers are reluctant to report incidents, beause they fear ridicule or disbelief. "Would you want to admit that an eighty-year-old woman hit you across the face with a cane?" Craddock asks.

One day, Hope came back from a holiday to discover that the administration of the nursing home had shuffled residents around in the dining room, separating two elderly women friends who had always sat together at a table. "They would eat their meals and talk," Hope recalls.

Under the new arrangement, one of the women had been forced to sit across from a demented woman who plays with her food and slops her tea. There was no conversation between the two. "If I have to stay here any longer I'm going to go crazy," the lucid woman said to Hope.

"She's not eating," Hope says, describing the lucid woman's horror. "She's sitting there looking up at the ceiling because she doesn't want to look across at this lady who's got her tea in her food."

Hope, appalled by the move, still cannot understand why it happened. "I wonder why they do these goddamned things. No wonder we get so bloody frustrated."

Mentally impaired and lucid residents should eat separately, Hope says. "I wouldn't want to be sitting across from someone who's taking their teeth out and putting them on the table. Or blowing their nose on the napkin while I'm trying to eat my supper."

Whenever she returns from a vacation, Hope notices that a number of residents have deteriorated. "You're so used to it that you don't notice the change until you go away," she says. "They start sleeping a bit longer, stop watching TV, stop eating, stop caring. You can just see the deterioration. I feel bad, because I feel we should pick up on these things."

For Hope, a typical shift begins at 3:00 p.m., when she arrives at the nursing home. The first order of the day is to receive a report from the day shift, summarizing the changes in residents' conditions. If a new person has been admitted to the nursing home, Hope reads his or her care plan in the nursing records, to find out more about the newcomer. "I want to know their interests so I can carry on a conversation better," she says.

Then, she starts by waking residents from their afternoon naps. She helps them out of bed, brushes their hair, arranges their clothing, cleans and changes them, and escorts them to the bathroom. Later, she washes them and prepares them for supper.

Supper is served at 5.30 p.m. Hope starts wheeling residents to the elevator at 5:00 p.m., and she parks them outside the dining room until the doors open. Then, she goes back upstairs to get another group. After supper, the migration is reversed: the residents are herded back to their floors, blocking the elevators and the halls. Hope herself beings a lunch to work, but sometimes she eats the nursing-home food. "If it doesn't look good, I won't eat it. Sometimes it's terrible. They don't put any spices or anything in. They overcook the vegetables."

After supper, she takes residents to the bathroom, distributes snacks, answers call bells and prepares residents for bed. At 6:30 p.m., she starts putting the first of the residents to bed.

"Physically and mentally, my job is hard," Hope says. "Not only am I lifting, but I'm convincing people they have to go to bed at 7:00 p.m. because I've got a routine to follow."

The routine sometimes comes before the residents: elderly people who need to go the bathroom in the evening are put to bed instead. "We take them back to their room, put them on the toilet, and then put them to bed," Hope explains. "If we take them back to the lounge, we're wasting time."

Some elderly residents are slumped over in their chairs by 7:00 p.m. "I'm sure they're aching," Hope says. "They're falling asleep. People are just bored with their life. There's no stimulation for them. They're busy in the mornings, but in the afternoons there's nothing. But we can't put everyone to bed in the afternoon. They probably wouldn't sleep at night, and we'd have them wandering around at three o'clock in the morning."

In the evening, Hope is required to push a cart up and down the corridors, distributing juice and tea to the residents. Without the drinks, the elderly residents could become dehydrated, but the health-care aides are on such a tight schedule that the distribution tends to slow them down and halt their momentum. Hope feels constantly pressed by time as she hands out the drinks. "I'm so keyed up. I don't like to slow down," she says.

The juice is an artificial chemical concoction, made from crystals supplied by the nursing home. "Some of the girls in the kitchen don't mix it properly, or they dilute it like you wouldn't believe. The other day, it was just like coloured water."

Most residents are in bed by 10:15 p.m. Hope draws a curtain around their beds and washes their genital areas, keeping up a steady patter as she performs this task. The residents talk about their families, or ask questions. "Why am I here?" inquires one. "Will I ever get better?" asks another. Hope gives them a hug and a kiss, and moves on to the next bed.

She never gave much thought to the intensely personal nature of this nightly ablution until, one evening an eighty-six-year-old woman mentioned it. "I get embarrassed when people have to do things," she said to Hope.

"You shouldn't feel embarrassed," Hope said. "It's just part of the job."

"Well, I do. Even at my age, I do."

"It's just something I do, and I never think of it," Hope said later. "Quite a few of them don't say anything, but they're really embarrassed. There are a few that are sensitive, and don't like to be completely naked."

Hope is offended by the lack of privacy that nursing-home residents must endure. "There's no privacy," she says. "You're living with a total stranger. In some cases, they don't get along." About fifteen per cent of the rooms in the nursing home are private. The rest are semi-private. If the door to a resident's room is open, Hope usually just walks right in. Sometimes, residents are masturbating when she enters. In that case, she turns around and leaves the room. "I wish they all had private rooms," she says. "It would be so much nicer."

Hope says there have been romantic liaisons in the nursing home: one couple met there, and were eventually married. "Their families were fit to be tied," Hope recalls. The couple got a room together — with twin beds.

It bothers Hope that residents must pay extra for some things. If they are moved to a new room because they require more care — or even if the relocation is for the convenience of the administration — they have to pay for their cable and telephone hookup again. "It's a business," Hope sighs.

After the residents are in bed, Hope responds to call bells, helps residents use the telephone at the nursing station, and catches elderly residents who wander into their neighbours' rooms. "By the time 9:30 p.m. comes, my back is aching and my legs are aching."

However, Hope prefers to work evenings, when there is a pronounced spirit of co-operation among aides, licensed practical nurses and registered nurses. Employees avoid pulling rank when there is a skeleton staff — about 30 per cent less than in the daytime — and no administrators in sight. "We're part of a team, and we work together," Hope says. Everybody feeds, and everybody takes someone to the bathroom."

Late in the evening, Hope walks through the corridors, entering rooms to make sure the sleeping residents are still breathing. She must also check on residents who might have accidents because they are incontinent. "I turn on the light, turn back the cover, pat a little bit, and then, if I know they're wet, I have to wake them up."

About twelve of the thirty residents on Hope's wing are incontinent, and require an average of up to six changes of adult diapers and clothing per shift.

"It doesn't bother me to take somebody to the bathroom," Hope says. "Even if they're soaking wet or full of (fecal matter). I don't belittle them. Sometimes you'll get somebody who'll say, 'I'm sorry. I didn't mean to do it.' I just say, 'It's all right. I understand.' I'm not mean to them because they can't help it." The nursing-home administration tells the aides to take residents to the bathroom every two hours. But this is impossible. "We can't do it," Hope says. "We're too busy."

Hope takes pride in being able to handle residents who are considered difficult. She remembers one new admission — an elderly man who was cranky and refusing meals. "You gotta be really firm with him," one of the health-care aides told her.

Hope introduced herself to the new resident, a man of ninety. After she had chatted to him for awhile, he revealed that his wife was in another nursing home, to which he could not be admitted because he needed more care than the home could provide. After decades of marriage, the couple had been forced apart. Hope realized that the man had every reason to be grouchy, and understood that what he really wanted was some kindness and respect.

The man asked Hope her age; when she told him it was fifty-two, he exclaimed: "You're still a young chick!" He didn't want to eat that night, and Hope didn't push him. But the next day, she told him he should go down for supper. He asked why.

"Just to go down and see other people," Hope said. "You can't be stuck in your room all day. It's not healthy. If you don't want to eat supper, go down and have a piece of bread and a cup of coffee. Or have dessert."

Silence. "Will you take me down?"

Hope promised she would. Half an hour later, when she returned to the room, he was ready. "Two other people were in here, and I told them to go to hell," he told her.

As Hope wheeled him past the nursing station, the nurses and health-care aides gaped in astonishment. "How did you convince him?" a nurse asked Hope. "What did you say? And Hope, what did you promise him?" The staff at the nursing station burst into laughter. Hope smiled as she wheeled the elderly man into the elevator and the door closed.

Sometimes, after work, Hope goes out for coffee with some of the other health-care aides. Other nights, she heads straight home, throws her uniform in her washing machine, and gives herself a sponge bath. Even in her pyjamas, she can sometimes smell the nursing-home smell on herself — a strange, pervasive mixture of institutional solvents and body odours.

"You try to get rid of the smell, but sometimes, it seems to linger," she says. "It's in our hair. It's in our clothes."

When an elderly person is dying, health-care aides often dig down inside themselves to tap hidden reserves — even if they are working short-staffed. "Most of the girls will get a little bit more energy and do things for this person, because they don't want to go home at eleven o'clock and feel guilty," Hope says. "All you can do is keep them dry and clean, and keep them as comfortable as possible. To me, that isn't work."

There are stories she cannot tell everyone. Friends and relatives aren't keen on hearing endless stories of life and death in the nursing home. They think the subject is depressing. But Hope doesn't see it that way.

"If someone is dying, I've always gone into the room and held their hand and said a prayer over them," she says. "It bothers me that they're alone. Someone should be there sitting with them."

When a resident dies in the home, it usually takes up to four hours before the funeral home picks up the body. During the wait, the health-care aides go into the person's room, one by one. "We all have our little way of saying goodbye," Hope explains. "I always caress their face, and say what I feel like saying."

Hope has watched some elderly nursing-home residents lose their desire to live and simply will themselves to die. "They stop eating," she says. "They don't converse any more. They don't care what's around them. We have to keep them in bed."

It upsets Hope when someone she has known for years is taken to a hospital and dies there. "We're family. It hurts. We'll miss them for a while. And then we end up forgetting about them. You don't completely forget them, but somebody else takes their place."

Hope believes in God, and wishes the nursing home had a little chapel for the residents and their families. "It would be so nice for families who are losing someone to be able to talk to God without having to go into a coffee bar," she says. "The staff members would go in there too when they have their problems."

One day, one of her favourite elderly residents died. When Hope came home she couldn't sleep, thinking about the woman.

Finally, she sat at the kitchen table while her daughter slept, and wrote a poem on a piece of scrap paper:

The last breathe is taken but you don't see a tear.
We always have them when no-one is near.
We have feelings. They are our loved ones too, for we have taken care of them, loved them, scolded them but always have feelings.
We are not without feelings
But we must go on for there are many coming to take the place of our cherished ones that we have lost.
— From a Nurse's Aide.

Hope showed the poem to the girls at work and they said they completely shared her sentiments.

The administration of the nursing home used to distribute the dead residents' clothing to other residents. "Then, they decided it wasn't quite the thing to do," Hope says. Now, the clothes are thrown out, or given to charity.

Critics have condemned the practice of handing out dead people's clothing as "macabre." But it is still done. "This is where they keep the dead people's clothes," an elderly man whispered to visitors as he pointed to a small, musty room in an old suburban Winnipeg nursing home. In some homes, families who want their relative's possessions returned to them, have been told by the nursing-home staff that the belongings could not be located.

The aides always read the obituaries in the newspaper during their coffee breaks. "You read that there's all these damn grandchildren and you think, 'Where the hell were they?'" Hope says. She tells of times when a dying person's relatives have failed to arrive at the nursing home — even after a call from the nursing-home staff to alert them to the impending death. But they do show up afterwards, to collect the person's belongings.

"Some families only come for half an hour at Christmas. Christmas is a sad time for the residents. It's sad to see them sitting there, day after day, with no one to visit them. I've seen them cry and say, 'Why has my family done this to me?'"

Hope sometimes works on New Year's Eve. "It would be nice if the residents could have a little drink or something before they go to bed," she says. "Something different. But no. It's just another night. When we put them to bed we said, 'Happy New Year. See you in '89.' If we hadn't said anything, they wouldn't have known that there was going to be a new year."

Taped to the bulletin board in Hope's kitchen in her small, bright bungalow is a letter to an advice columnist from an American health-care aide who was exasperated with the poor pay and the lack of prestige.

"Being a nurse's aide is not glamorous. There are many aspects of the daily routine that are demanding and physically difficult," the American aide wrote.

"But I take pride in my work. I try to improve my skills every day. Things do get hectic. Sometimes all the call bells seem to go off at once. My work is the kind that many sons and daughters can't do or won't do, yet somebody must take care of the sick and the old. These elderly people depend on me. Being there for them makes me feel special."

Hope carefully clipped the letter, and brought it to work. "Read it and weep," she told her co-workers during the coffee break. They huddled over the clipping. "Well put," said one. They all agreed.

6

The Priest

Tap. Tap. The priest knocks gently on the bedroom door. It is 6:50 a.m. on Palm Sunday in a nursing home in Kenora, a pulp-and-paper town in northwestern Ontario. Sophie Yanchuk, eighty-six, is still asleep. "Service in ten minutes," the priest whispers to her. The elderly woman hurriedly dresses, and creeps down the quiet hall of the nursing home to the small chapel. She is soon joined by two other elderly residents: one woman arrives by herself, in a wheelchair; the other is wheeled in by the priest.

Rev. Stephan Jarmus is a Ukrainian Orthodox priest who serves a church congregation in Kenora. He also looks after the spiritual needs of elderly Ukrainian people who live in the nursing home.

On Palm Sunday, Jarmus holds a short service for the three elderly women, and administers the rites of confession and communion. Murmuring prayers in the Ukrainian language, he carefully places a mixture of sanctified bread and wine to their lips with a small golden spoon. The following Sunday will be Orthodox Easter: Ukrainians usually go to confession and accept communion during the weeks before Easter — the most important holiday in the Christian calendar.

The previous Palm Sunday, there were seven nursing-home residents at the service, but several of the people have died in the intervening year.

By Ukrainian standards, the chapel at the nursing home is plain, with a brown carpet, office-type chairs and a simple wooden pulpit. But Jarmus recreates the atmosphere of the kind of church to which the older people are accustomed: he covers the altar with a purple and gold cloth; on it he places a candle in a small red holder. Jarmus wears a black cassock with a purple and gold stole, and a large gold cross around his neck; his clothing smells faintly of incense.

"I'm sure that the atmosphere I'm feeling, you're feeling as well," he tells the three women. Their faces light up. During confession and communion, the elderly residents are — for a short while — the focus of attention. "It does wonders," Jarmus says later. "It gives them a sense of something special to be somewhere together. It's only for a short time, but it touches them."

Mrs. Yanchuk later expresses her happy feelings. "I feel better, lighter," she says. "It really makes a difference. Easter is a special time."

The importance of religious and spiritual care in nursing homes is recognized by medical experts as well as clergy. "Any physician is willing and eager for anyone to see patients they're caring for, where that will contribute to the patient's well-being," says Dr. James Kirkland, chief of geriatric services at Queen Elizabeth Hospital in Toronto.

Dr. Harold King, dean of theology at the University of Winnipeg, says churches have always been involved with people who live in institutions. "Pastoral care is important in nursing homes," Dr. King says. "I see spirituality as one of the essential dimensions of human existence. It should be attended to the same as physical care." Many psychological disorders are caused by spiritual problems, he adds. "Before social workers or psychologists were ever heard of, religious leaders were involved in offering care."

The Manitoba Interfaith Council, in a 1984 report on pastoral care in institutions, noted that many more people now live in institutions than at any time in history. "Continued improvements in pastoral care and (spiritual) training for staff will remain a high priority for the forseeable future," the report said.

After the special Palm Sunday service in the nursing-home chapel, Jarmus conducts a service in church for his Kenora congregation.

Following the service, he returns to the nursing home with pussywillows to give to the three parishioners who live there. The pussywillows symbolize the palms used to greet Christ in Jerusalem. Jarmus taps Mrs. Yanchuk gently on the shoulder with a bough. "I'm not hitting you. The branch is hitting you. In a week, it's Easter," he tells her, in a traditional Ukrainian greeting.

Mrs. Yanchuk laughs, responds with another Easter greeting: "Coloured eggs and Easter bread," and places the pussywillow in a vase. She is in a good mood, buoyed by the religious message of the morning — a discussion of the significance of Easter. "This is the highlight of our experience," Jarmus has told the women. "It is a time of reassurance and hope."

To be cut off from the church life they once enjoyed is a difficult loss for residents of a nursing home. "Easter can be very traumatic," Jarmus says. "What they'll miss and cry about is that they won't be able to attend the Easter service. It's a painful thing to be deprived of all that."

On Easter Sunday, he brings them coloured eggs blessed during the church service, "just to see the joy in their faces," he says. "These things nurture them and help them."

Jarmus has been the parish priest of St. Vladimir's Ukrainian Orthodox Church in Kenora since 1971. He also works at the Winnipeg head office of the Ukrainian Orthodox Church of Canada. Chairman of the church's executive committee, Jarmus is also an associate professor of theology at St. Andrew's College at the University of Manitoba, where he teaches students how to provide pastoral care in nursing homes, hospitals and prisons.

Jarmus, sixty-three, has a broad open face with direct blue eyes and a beard. He is short and stocky with a round stomach.

St. Vladimir's is a fading congregation of older people: membership has dropped from a high of about fifty families in the 1950s to about twenty-five regular worshippers today — in a church that can comfortably accommodate 150 people. It is a beautiful church: the morning light shines on its silver onion-shaped domes and illuminates the mauve, green and gold stained glass. The interior is rich with icons, embroidery and vases filled with freshly-cut marigolds. "The people built it with their own hands," Jarmus says admiringly.

Once every two weeks, Jarmus makes the two-and-a-half-hour car trip to Kenora from his home in Winnipeg; during holidays, he comes more frequently; and, as he drives, he sings liturgical songs to himself. The weekend is spent visiting about twenty of the older parishioners, who no longer attend church, mainly because they are too physically frail. Some are still living in their own homes, or in seniors' apartments; others are in the nursing home; still other elderly people are in the acute-care or chronic-care wards of the Kenora hospital.

"Sometimes, I think I have more people in institutions than in the church," Jarmus muses.

Jarmus can see a vast difference between elderly people who live in their own homes, and those who have been relegated to an institution. "While they are at home, the dignity of being human is there," he observes. "There's more life. They're brighter. They look after themselves. In the nursing home, they feel the void."

The nursing home is an old, box-like brick building. Its name is carved into cement over the doorway, giving it an old-fashioned institutional appearance.

It is Sunday afternoon. Emil Bozyk, a ninety-eight-year-old resident of the home, is napping on a twin-size hospital bed in his room, his slippers resting on the pillow beside his head. The door is open. Jarmus walks in and gently wakes the frail old man, who struggles to sit up. His grey slacks have crept up, revealing scabs on his legs. "You're a Cossack," Jarmus compliments him. "A Cossack rides a horse, but you ride this cane," he says, indicating the wooden cane leaning on the bed.

Bozyk smiles broadly; thanks the priest for waking him. "I don't get visitors," he says. Bozyk shares his room: the two beds are partly separated by a partition, but the arrangement hardly ensures privacy — a radio can be heard playing on the other side. Bozyk's side of the room is sparsely furnished with an office

chair, a wall closet, a garbage pail and a fluorescent light over the
bed. Three shelves, which jut out from the partition, hold a tin of
cookies, a clock, a pink towel, an artificial yellow flower in a vase
and a certificate from the premier of Ontario congratulating
Bozyk on his ninety-eighth birthday.

Jarmus asks the elderly man if the nursing-home staff and
administration are treating him well. "Oh yeah, they feed me,"
the old man responds.

"Do they do your laundry?" Jarmus asks.

"Thank you," Bozyk says, misunderstanding the question.
Jarmus sits next to Bozyk on the bed, and repeats the query in a
loud voice, as the older man is hard of hearing. As well, Bozyk
is nearly blind: he pulls an immense magnifying glass from a
drawer to show Jarmus how he reads books.

Jarmus reminds him of a fishing trip they took together many
years ago, and a tear trickles down Bozyk's face. As the visit
draws to a close, the priest promises to return in two weeks: Bozyk
pulls Jarmus into a warm embrace, thanking him for dropping in.

Bozyk is a reminder to Jarmus of another elderly man, who
became a symbol to him of the profound spirituality of the elderly,
and who inspired the priest to increase his contact with institutionalized elderly people.

Wasyl Kowal had been a successful farmer outside Winnipeg.
In his old age, he ended up in a Winnipeg hospital, awaiting a
nursing-home bed. One day, shortly before Easter, Jarmus offered
to come to the hospital to hear the older man's confession and
give him communion. Kowal agreed.

When the appointed morning came, Jarmus rose and gathered
together his supplies — a cross, a Bible, and metal containers of
bread and wine. His seventeen-year-old son, Andrew, awoke and
asked where he was going. "I said I was going to the hospital. I
asked if he would like to come and see life." Andrew quickly
dressed.

Kowal was ninety-five years old. "At first, he didn't know who
I was, and then, after a few exchanges, he remembered why I
came," Jarmus recalls.

The priest laid out the articles he had brought, and began the set of prayers associated with the rite of confessing the sick. First, he invoked the Holy Spirit; then, made a brief prayer to the Holy Trinity; finally, he began to recite the Lord's Prayer. The old man joined him in prayer.

"I began to sense the room was filling with something," Jarmus recalls. "I could feel something happening."

Jarmus offered Kowal some Easter bread that had been blessed in church. "He was really enjoying that morning," he says. Then he looked back at Andrew. "That boy was full of tears. I was rather surprised and I asked him what was the matter," Jarmus says, and remembers Andrew's reply: "I'm seeing Easter in this old man."

"He saw the resurrection in that old man," Jarmus says. "It was a profound thing." He believes the experience inspired Andrew to study theology and decide to become a priest.

And Jarmus himself set out to further his studies in pastoral care for the elderly in institutions.

"Things in this sphere of spirit are real, and they escape conceptualization and explanation," Jarmus says. "To minister to someone, and see that that ministry means something, is very, very rewarding. If the person to whom you are ministering experiences healing and growth, somehow it reflects back to the minister."

It is a Sunday afternoon in September. Sophie Yanchuk sits in a chair in her bedroom at the nursing home, waiting for Jarmus to show up. Her only living relative is a niece in Toronto who telephones each week, and visits Mrs. Yanchuk once a year.

The elderly widow has two crumpled one-dollar bills to pay for the church calendar the priest brought the previous time. "What's this?" Jarmus protests, when he arrives and sees the money. She shoves the bills into his hand.

Mrs. Yanchuk, the widow of a miner, has lived at the nursing home for seven years. It took her a full year to become accustomed to the routine of the nursing home. "Nothing was right," she says. "The food wasn't like the food I used to make for myself.

It's always on my mind: why am I here? I had a home. I had everything."

She used to work at a catering company, and was responsible for parties with up to 250 guests: at the end of the night, she would be led out of the kitchen to applause. Her husband's lunch-box was the envy of his fellow-miners. Now, she lives on a steady diet of macaroni and stew. "It's pathetic," she says.

But Mrs. Yanchuk doesn't complain to the nursing-home staff or the administration. "If I say anything, it won't get fixed, and people will resent me," she says. "I'll make things worse for myself." She says the members of the nursing-home staff compliment her on her attitude.

After her husband had died, Mrs. Yanchuk became a bit confused, because she was grief-stricken. "I'd get up in the middle of the night, and wander the streets, looking for him," she recalls. Her family doctor said she couldn't live alone any more. "I said, 'I want to die in my house.' He said I couldn't do that." She sold her house in the mining town of Red Lake, and moved to Kenora to live in the nursing home.

Several months later, Mrs. Yanchuk began to regain her mental clarity. Today she requires help only with bathing. She even washes her own lingerie, because she's worried about losing it. "If you give the laundry something nice, you won't get it back."

Mrs. Yanchuk has a private room in the new wing of the nursing home — a major improvement from her early days in the home. When she was first admitted, Mrs. Yanchuk lived in a room with three other Ukrainian women, one of whom became her best friend in the home. But the friend deteriorated, and has become mentally confused. "She scoops everything into her suitcase, even her pictures, and announces that she's going home," Mrs. Yanchuk explains.

The mentally-impaired woman was moved to the special-care unit of the nursing home. Sometimes, she asks for Mrs. Yanchuk. "I go to see her. She tells me how busy she's been. She thinks she's been to the forest, picking mushrooms."

Another of Mrs. Yanchuk's roommates was an alcoholic who was constantly screaming and singing. "She continued to drink in the nursing home and that's how she died — drunk," Mrs. Yanchuk says. The third roommate had a relative who would bring sandwiches for all of the elderly women in the room — a pleasant break from the monotony of institutional food. But the third roommate died, and with her, the welcome companionship and special treats.

Mrs. Yanchuk wishes she were not living in the nursing home. In fact, she wishes she were dead. "You'd think I wouldn't be around to suffer all this," Mrs. Yanchuk says to Rev. Jarmus. "I pray and ask God: 'What sins have I committed that I must live so long?'" Nobody in her family lived as long as Mrs. Yanchuk. She has already bought a plot in the cemetery for herself, and erected a monument: she feels ready to die.

Mrs. Yanchuk has always been a religious woman. The rituals of her church are a great comfort, she says. Sometimes, she skips lunch to watch "Meeting Place," a television program that broadcasts religious news and church services from across Canada. Today, she watched a televised service from a Ukrainian church in Edmonton. "When I heard it was a Ukrainian show, I told the staff I didn't feel like eating," she says. As she watched the program, she daydreamed about how she used to attend church every Sunday.

The staff at the nursing home are familiar with Rev. Jarmus. "I ask about the state of my people," he says. Although careful about the way they are being treated, he believes their basic physical needs are being met; the complaints he hears from residents are provoked by emotional and spiritual suffering.

The outskirts of Kenora — a pretty town surrounded by lakes — are marked by clusters of motels. It is Saturday afternoon, and, after his drive from Winnipeg, Jarmus stops for a quick coffee, then drives to a red brick high-rise apartment building, overlooking the railway tracks. Most of the tenants are seniors, and the rent is subsidized.

Jarmus visits a few elderly parishioners who moved into the high-rise after they had been widowed, or had become too frail to maintain their own houses. Most of these parishioners cannot attend church services because of physical disabilities which keep them confined to their apartments. Nevertheless, they are pleased with their quarters; grateful that they can avoid the nursing home.

Katherine Zyla is an eighty-seven-year-old widow. She has high blood pressure and a bad heart, and walks with a cane — but not outside, because she's afraid of falling. As they chat, Jarmus lets the woman do most of the talking. Occasionally he murmurs a response or asks a question. "Who else visits? How do you like the apartment?"

"The apartment is wonderful," Mrs. Zyla gushes. Her suite is at the end of the hall, where it is nice and quiet. She enjoys watching the trains pass: her nephew is a train conductor, and toots the horn whenever she is by the window. Her daughter comes every day to prepare meals, and to help with household chores.

The small apartment has a bedroom, kitchen, living room and balcony. It is immaculate, and has a warm, homey atmosphere, with embroidery, ceramics and pictures of grandchildren. An immense pillow decorates the neatly-made bed.

After fifteen minutes, Jarmus rises from the couch and assures Mrs. Zyla that he will pray for her, even though she cannot be in church on Sunday. The church choir will sing songs for her. He clasps one of her soft, large hands in both of his, and gives her a brief hug and kiss on the cheek. She beams: "Thank you, Father. Thank you. Thank you."

The priest's next visit is to a small woman named Justina Kowalchuk. It was her birthday the previous week: she turned eighty-nine. Jarmus breaks into a booming rendition of "Happy Birthday." She giggles, her nose wrinkling with pleasure. Then she offers Jarmus a drink of brandy from a large, nearly-empty jug. "I've had this bottle for two years," she protests when Jarmus raises his eyebrows in mock horror.

Jarmus tells Mrs. Kowalchuk that a Ukrainian church service is now available on tape. She is interested in obtaining a copy, and says the tape would be the next best thing to actually being in church. "Maybe my son will buy me a tape player."

Mrs. Kowalchuk has lived in the high-rise for about a year, but she is not as satisfied as Mrs. Zyla, and misses her own house terribly. It was at her son's urging that she moved into the apartment, after experiencing difficulty climbing the stairs from the basement, where the washroom was located.

The elderly woman complains that the apartment building is a busy place, with people coming and going, and flushing toilets noisily at 3:00 a.m. The noise makes it hard for her to sleep at night, and her mood is one of dejection. "I never thought I would live this long," she tells Jarmus. "I don't want to live anymore." When she balked at his suggestion that she move, Mrs. Kowalchuk's son did offer to build her a washroom on the main floor of her house, but she thought the renovation would be a waste of space. Now, she deeply regrets her decision. "If I had known what it was like here, I never would have left my house," she says.

Depressed and ill, with plenty of time on their hands, nursing-home residents often think about spiritual matters. They reflect on their lives and prepare themselves spiritually for death. Many elderly people find comfort in religious belief. "It's about the only hope they have left," Jarmus says. "When you're shut up, looking into the eyes of death, you look back on your life and assess it."

For many people, the aging process strengthens their faith. "The fact of God being there or being close is quite often a subject of conversation," Jarmus says. "Some of them speak about death. Some of them look forward to death. They express the wish that they want to die. They express their conviction that there is something like life after death. There is something like heaven. There is the possibility they will rejoin their spouses or children."

While all visitors are important, a pastoral visitor carries special weight. "People do look upon priests as something different,"

Jarmus says. "We are representatives of God. It's up to us to affirm people's convictions."

The Manitoba Association for Institutional Pastoral Care is a professional organization of clergy and lay people involved in pastoral care in institutions. Its literature describes the importance of pastoral care in nursing homes. "In a time of crisis brought on by institutionalization, a person is often vitally concerned with the spiritual dimension of life," the association says. "It is the responsibility of those who care for persons in institutions to include these concerns in their care program."

Jarmus sees the destructive effects of institutionalization on human beings; how separated elderly people feel from their families and friends. "Some of them seem preoccupied with the subject of loneliness," he says. "They feel forgotten; children don't visit them. Or they don't get any visits at all."

For many, a clergyman is the only link with the outside world. "My goal is to bring them some sort of relief and joy," Jarmus says. "To let them know they are not forgotten. I see that they value my visits. In some cases, I am the only person who visits them. They look forward to it."

Lonely people lose the will to live, Jarmus says. A visitor brings hope, and improves their health.

Jarmus has noticed that some priests are afraid to visit the sick or the elderly, because they know that they will be asked difficult questions about life, death and suffering. "Priests think that they have to have the answers," Jarmus says. "They think they have to explain everything. Very often you have to admit you don't know something or you don't understand. It's very difficult to admit you are limited."

Improved pastoral training can help priests learn to provide the spiritual support that the elderly need — and it can help the priests cope with the reality that there are no magic answers for the elderly. "You don't go to perform miracles," Jarmus says. "In many cases, the priest can do nothing but be present. Just a touch or wordless embrace can be so healing."

In his visits with the elderly, Jarmus seldom talks about spiritual matters directly. "I'm not a good seller of religion," he says. "I have no goals to change someone or convert someone. I am oriented to human needs."

Jarmus says schools that train clergy are currently trying to teach them to focus on human needs, moving away from the old style of priest who serves at the altar on Sundays, and does not concern himself with the lives of his parishioners during the week.

The Manitoba Interfaith Council interviewed dozens of residents, staff, and administrators of nursing homes and hospitals to study the issue of pastoral care. Everyone agreed that improved pastoral care and spiritual support are needed in the institutions. "Staff feel that people ... rely upon such guidance and need it," said the 1984 study. "Worship services alone are seen as insufficient."

There is rarely any co-ordination of pastoral care in the institutions: worship services in some nursing homes are arranged by the home; other nursing homes rely on neighbourhood churches to take the initiative to send a clergyman. In the latter cases, it is up to the church to pay the clergyman for conducting services in nursing homes.

During its survey, The Manitoba Interfaith Council heard numerous complaints about a lack of pastoral care in institutions. Residents said there were too few visits by clergy; or, in the case of a particular denomination, no services at all. Some people wanted more mid-week activities — such as Bible studies — while others noted a lack of space for private counselling, or insufficient advance notice to residents of pastors' arrival for visits. There were even institutions that did not encourage pastoral care at all. "Pastoral care in long-term settings means considerably more than visiting and worship services," the report said, adding that some elderly residents of nursing homes had "lost virtually all contact with their families and their original communities."

The council recommended that the Manitoba government establish a co-ordinator of chaplaincy services in institutions, but the recommendation has not been implemented. Although there is a co-ordinator of chaplaincy services for jails and prisons, there is no one to co-ordinate services in institutions such as hospitals or nursing homes. "It's stupid," says Dr. Harold King, chairman of the council committee that wrote the report. "Services are piecemeal. Some homes have good services, but in others, they are uneven and haphazard."

Good pastoral care is almost always the result of the enthusiasm of an individual group or person, the interfaith council says. "Where such a group or person does not exist, persons in facilities are very much at risk of receiving poor or no care."

Ontario is the only province with co-ordinated chaplaincy services in health, corrections and community services. "If you just leave it up to the individual churches, too many people fall between the cracks," says Rev. David Clark, associate co-ordinator of chaplaincy services in Ontario. "Someone has to be responsible for everyone."

Looking after the needs of people in nursing homes can be an onerous task for already overburdened churches, as nursing homes tend to fall to the bottom of the priority list. "Seniors' homes sometimes get the leftovers from churches," Clark says. "There are so many demands on clergy." Moreover, the spiritual needs of the staffs of nursing homes are often overlooked. "Caregivers themselves deserve care in order to nurture and safeguard their capacity to meet the very demanding needs of those whom they serve," as the Manitoba report expressed it.

In Ontario, there are nine regional co-ordinators who help develop committees of local clergy to go into nursing homes and offer a broad range of services. They also provide training programs for the visiting clergy. "We make sure people don't get unwanted visits," Clark says. "Or if they want something, particularly if they're of a non-Christian faith, we try to make sure they get it."

Some churches need government money for pastoral care, because they cannot afford to send clergy to nursing homes, Clark says. The Ontario government helps to pay for full-time chaplains at about fifteen homes for the aged which are run by municipalities or charitable groups. But it is often hard to convince governments to provide money for pastoral services. "Spiritual care tends to be seen as desirable, but only after the basics are looked after," Clark says. "The government is reluctant to pay the church for something the church is supposed to be doing."

However, a growing number of nursing homes are expressing interest in pastoral care because it is a requirement of the Canadian Council on Health Facilities Accreditation. The accreditation council suggests that every institution develop a well-defined plan for providing pastoral services to patients or residents, and their families.

In 1985, the Fourth Manitoba Conference on Aging concluded that older people feel a greater need for belief in God and the afterlife — perhaps to compensate for the loss of friends and family; perhaps because the elderly come from a church-going generation. However, the conference found that the needs of elderly people are sometimes ignored, because our social system "is not adequately prepared to deal with emotional and spiritual needs."

Lillian, a Winnipeg nursing-home resident, belonged to an Anglican church for sixty years, but now refuses to attend the church services in the nursing home. The room in which the services are held is too cold, she says: "It's freezing in there." But her spiritual beliefs have not waned. She keeps a Bible by her bed: "I do a lot of praying," she says. "I was always taught to put myself in God's hands. He looks after me." She points skyward. "There's a place up there for me."

Anna Cook, forty-four, is one of the few full-time chaplains in a Manitoba nursing home. She was a nurse for eight years, but she left the profession to study theology and become a Protestant minister.

"As a nurse, I saw many things I couldn't attend to because I was busy giving out pills," Cook explains. Spiritual well-being, she adds, is crucial to physical health; medical attention alone is inadequate in caring for the elderly and the sick.

"It's a ripple kind of effect," Cook says. "When a person moves into a nursing home, there's a change in their social environment. That is going to affect all other aspects of their being — psychological, physical and spiritual. They may begin to feel they are abandoned by their family, abandoned by God, all alone. Physical and emotional health are tied very closely together."

Anna Cook is a petite, thoughtful-looking woman. The elderly residents of her nursing home are of different faiths: her challenging job is to look after the spiritual needs of each of them. She leads worship and memorial services, prays with the elderly residents and their families, and is available for counselling.

As well, she makes sure that clergy of a variety of denominations come to the nursing home, and reminds congregations and ministers that their parishioners are living in the nursing home. "It's very easy for congregations to forget about a resident who moves to a nursing home," she says. "It's very important to nurture and foster those kinds of relationships, so the residents don't feel abandoned. The congregation had been part of their life for probably sixty years. Why should they drop that now when they really need somebody to walk along with them?"

When a resident is gravely ill, she reminds families to contact their own minister — for their sake, as well as that of the resident. "It's important for the resident to know that all that history, all that community, is behind them. If they're sick, for them to know it's being mentioned on a Sunday morning is important. It's important to keep those connections, so their loss isn't so profound." And when a person is dying, it is Cook who encourages friends and relatives to be present at the bedside. She may offer to read a scripture and pray with them.

Part of Cook's role in being with the dying is just to listen, and be there. "We may not converse much," she says. "We may sit there. I may hold their hand or maybe read scripture. Maybe I will pray with them. A large part of it is for them to know that they are not alone — that I'm willing to walk with them in this last leg of the journey. I'm offering them a compassionate ear."

Simply listening to a suffering person can hasten the healing process. Older people have a need to recount their histories, reflecting on the past to explore the meaning of their lives, while taking care of unfinished agenda — mending relationships or coming to terms with past hurts.

"One of the most important things we can do is to listen to and receive those stories," she says. "It's so often the case that people don't want to receive it, or they've heard the story before. It's a way of emptying out to prepare for dying. A way of letting go of everything experienced here on earth."

Cook believes that it is an advantage to be a female chaplain in a nursing home in which most of the elderly residents are women, some from countries where war and devastation were part of daily life. "Many of these women have been through horrendous times," Cook says. "Many experienced rape. They need to work that stuff through at this time in their life. But they're not going to talk to a man about it."

Although the nursing-home generation grew old with the belief that women should not be in the leadership of the church, Cook has nevertheless been accepted. "These folks have boiled life down to its essentials," she says. "This really is trivia, whether it's a man or woman who's leading in worship."

Cook makes it her job to be an advocate for the elderly residents. They and their families often tell her their wishes and disappointments. Sometimes, families believe that a doctor is not visiting often enough, or that a staff person has offended their relative: Cook is the bridge between residents and their families, and the administration and staff of the nursing home. She passes on the information that both sides need.

Many elderly people feel strongly that they do not want to die in a hospital, and they do not want to be subjected to medical heroics when they are critically ill. Their requests are often passed on to Cook. She makes sure that their wishes are respected. She writes their desires onto the residents' charts at the nursing home, and informs staff of the elderly peoples' decisions.

Cook also helps the nursing home cope with ethical dilemmas, such as the right of residents to refuse treatment, or even food. "They have a right to choose to die," Cook says.

One ninety-six-year-old woman did just that. "She figured God had forgotten her, and she was going to help out a little. She was very clear in her mind, and she decided to stop eating. She died after a few months."

Cook believes that her services are not only for church people raised in a particular religion, but for everyone. So-called religious questions, she says, go to the heart of human nature. Most elderly people feel a need to clean the slate, and assess their lives. "In some way, we all reach out to a force beyond us. The longing is there. It comes not necessarily in religious words."

7

The Advocates

"Help!"

An old, white-haired woman calls out lustily every five minutes from a corner of the nursing-home dining room, where she sits tied in a chair. "Help!"

Anne-Marie Johnston looks up from feeding elderly Mrs. MacDonald and murmurs: "I know what you mean."

And she probably does. As an active member and past president of Concerned Friends of Ontario Citizens in Care Facilities, Canada's only consumer and advocacy group for nursing-home residents, Johnston is no stranger to the harsh realities of some nursing homes.

It is a bone-chilling February afternoon in Toronto, and the fifty-six-year-old housewife is visiting a nursing home after a complaint was made to Concerned Friends by the frantic daughter of a resident. Mrs. Lorenzo, the resident, had been discovered in a neighbour's room with blood streaming down her face, her eye punctured and her vision lost. The hospital had called the family to tell them what had happened. "The nursing home did not inform them. Violation number one," Johnston wrote in her clean, careful notes. Although the incident had occurred at 9:00 a.m., the administrator of the home still knew nothing about the injury by 4:00 p.m.

"Maybe it was self-mutilation," staff suggested to Mrs. Lorenzo's bewildered family. But their mother, although a victim of Alzheimer's Disease, had no history of self-inflicted injury. Furthermore, the home refused to take Mrs. Lorenzo back from hospital unless she hired a private-duty nurse. "Wanders too much," said the administrator. The family could not afford that. Mrs. Lorenzo's daughter took her mother home, and keeps an eye on her in the family's dry-cleaning shop, where she and her husband work.

Johnston suspects that another resident assaulted Mrs. Lorenzo. She also believes that the home is understaffed, and cannot deal with violent or wandering residents. Her mission is to file a complete report on her observations at the home, while visiting another resident, and forward her findings to the inspection branch of the Ontario Ministry of Health, which is responsible for upholding the standards required under the Ontario Nursing Homes Act. She will also put in a call to the provincial Ministry of Community and Social Services, which runs publicly owned homes for the aged, and ask that Mrs. Lorenzo be pushed up the waiting list for a place in a new non-profit home with a unit for Alzheimer's sufferers.

Before she arrives at the home, Johnston has alerted the provincial inspection department by telephone, and once she arrives there, it is clear to her that certain changes have taken place in anticipation of a visit by government inspectors. The floor is freshly washed, but the sharp stench of urine still hits the nostrils immediately upon entering. Visitors are now required to sign in, indicate which resident they are visiting, and wear a pin on their clothing identifying them as a visitor.

Johnston signs in and takes a tiny elevator up to the second floor. Her pretext is a visit to Mrs. MacDonald, whom she knows from a previous visit. "I know damn well Mrs. MacDonald has been moved to the third floor," she confesses. "But I always act so stupid." She blunders from room to room, "looking for Mrs. MacDonald," but her eyes dart about, methodically processing and absorbing each detail of the residents and their environment.

"You start at the top, and just go through the body," she explains later. "Residents were sitting there, slumped over, oily hair, sticky eyes, dirty fingernails, food on mouth, dry skin, one sock on, one bare foot, zippers open, dresses back to front. I can see it all in one go."

She converses easily with residents who invite her into their rooms, speaking in bright tones and skillfully asking questions that draw out information about conditions in the home. "I hate it here. I'm very lonely," confides the woman who is now curled up in Mrs. MacDonald's former room. Johnston observes that she has no dresser or easy chair, only a grey metal hospital bed, bedside table and wheelchair. The woman shares a two-foot-wide closet with her roommate. Her bare legs are covered in sores. "I didn't think my daughter would do this to me," she says. "I did quite a lot for her." She doesn't elaborate. Johnston offers her a drink of water, and the woman thirstily gulps two full styrofoam cups.

She tells Johnston that she likes music, but her tapes and tape player are at her daughter's. Her daughter has been urging her to attend activities at the home, but she does not like them. She loves to read, but her eyes are bad and it never occurred to her to ask for large-print books. Johnston promises to visit again, making a mental note to include in her report a suggestion that government inspectors offer the nursing-home staff advice on how to bring some pleasure and recreation into this woman's life.

It is nearly lunchtime, and half-a-dozen residents have congregated in the lounge by the dining room. Several are wearing two different socks. One barefoot woman wanders by in a nightgown. The men are unshaven. Two women have their pant legs rolled up above their knees. One woman's slippers appear to be smeared in feces. On the floor is a spilled cup of what might be either vomit or pureed food.

The scene in the dining room is worthy of Dante's descriptions of hell. Faces are twisted with distress. One woman sobs bitterly, to the utter oblivion of staff and fellow-diners. About two-thirds of the residents are in wheelchairs, jammed around tables for four. Some are asleep. There is no laughter or conversation, only the sound of clanking metal food containers.

A sign at the dining-room entrance promises cream of mushroom soup for lunch, along with stuffed green pepper, creamed corn and creamy cheesecake. As the food arrives, people start to babble and attempt to eat. One woman's green pepper lands on her chest. Others drop food and cutlery on the floor. Heads roll back, faces encrusted with food. There are far too few staff — about five staffers for fifty severely disabled residents. The staff are shouting over the heads of the residents, trying to figure out which meal to bring to whom. No one seems sure who gets regular, minced or pureed, although each setting is marked by the resident's name and the type of diet he or she takes.

The staff try to feed some people. "C'mon, sweetheart. Wake up. Anybody home?" One aide pours milk into the soup before feeding it to a confused woman. "Tastes good, eh?" she encourages. She stands over the woman, and after a few spoonfuls, moves on to the next person. A teenage girl, holding a plastic pot of coffee in one hand and a sugar dispenser in the other, pours coffee into brown plastic cups, adds sugar without asking, and slops milk from resident's glasses into the coffee.

Although Mrs. MacDonald is blind, no one has come to help her eat, until Johnston arrives. Another woman at the same table shakes uncontrollably, and spills more soup than she can raise to her lips. Mrs. MacDonald's head is drooping with fatigue; she has a black eye, and an oozing wound on her hand. "We're all getting old," she remarks.

She is too tired for dessert, and wants to go to bed. But the staff are too busy to help her: the residents must stay in the dining room until the meal is over. As Johnston begins to wheel Mrs. MacDonald out of the room, an aide rushes over. "You haven't had coffee."

"I'm tired. I don't want any."

"But you would like some coffee."

"But I'm tired."

"Oh, I know you would like some coffee."

A reluctant Mrs. MacDonald ends up being wheeled back to the table.

Back in her car, Johnston sighs. A staunch Roman Catholic, she attends mass each morning to bolster her inner resources, but these visits drain her. "Sometimes I just sit in the car and cry, and say, 'Oh God, when will it ever end?'"

Concerned Friends is a volunteer citizen's group founded in 1980 by Betty Hatt, a filing clerk for a Toronto oil company. Hatt was perturbed about the quality of care her mother was receiving in a nursing home, and *Toronto Star* columnist Lotta Dempsey wrote about her concerns. On the day the column appeared, Hatt received forty calls from people who were also outraged by conditions in nursing homes. The current membership of Concerned Friends is about 700 — mainly in Toronto, Windsor and Ottawa. About 75 per cent are women and 50 per cent are over the age of sixty-five. Originally a handful of angry relatives, the organization grew to an extensive network of residents, family, professionals and academics. Membership is not open to staff or owners of nursing homes.

Concerned Friends took on a problem of massive proportions: about 30,000 Ontario residents live in about 339 nursing homes, and another 29,000 live in 180 non-profit homes for the aged. But the group's determination has never wavered. "We're fairly small, but mighty," says member and past president Patricia Spindel, a teacher of community activism and social advocacy at Toronto's Humber College.

Spindel, forty, is one of those who read Dempsey's column and got involved because she was horrified at her grandmother's six-year experience at a nursing home. "She was on a salt-free diet, but they loaded her food with salt. She was losing weight horribly. They were forcibly relocating her to different floors and when they did she became very depressed, and they put her on anti-depressants. She was just drugged to the gills and crying all the time." The home refused to pay for a food supplement, so it was up to Spindel to buy a case of the expensive product every other week.

The position of Concerned Friends is that non-profit facilities are best; smaller facilities tend to have a better quality of life; and profit-making facilities should fully disclose how they spend public money. "We thought if we can't get rid of commercial operators overnight, we're at least going to make them accountable for the dollars they get," Spindel says.

The group has achieved some remarkable successes. Its members are responsible for bringing in legislative reforms that are unique in the country. These include a nineteen-point legislated bill of rights for nursing-home residents that spells out what these residents may expect in terms of care, treatment, privacy, decision-making and information. There are now also requirements that nursing homes post financial statements of revenue and expenditures in prominent locations in their homes, and that annual licence-renewal inspection reports be posted in nursing homes and be freely accessible to the public. (The exact wording of a financial disclosure rule has been on the drafting table for two years, as of May 1989.)

Concerned Friends was also successful in establishing a written contract between nursing home and resident that sets out the rights of the resident, provides information necessary to enable the resident to make a complaint regarding the nursing home, and specifies any agreement for additional services and charges. Most nursing homes have set up their own contracts, although Concerned Friends had asked for a universal contract. The group says that in some contracts, the residents end up signing away their rights.

A 1987 study of commercial nursing homes in Ontario notes that Concerned Friends and other consumer groups have "indeed led government to play a greater role in the field of nursing home care, even to the point of challenging the business orientation of nursing homes." Since Concerned Friends came on the scene, charges have been laid, prosecutions carried out, homes closed, and administrators and staff fired. Residents' councils — which give residents a say in how nursing homes are run — are now mandatory. Leaves of absence for residents have been increased from three days to fourteen days, and government inspections have improved.

The group was also instrumental in the development of the Advocacy Centre for the Elderly, a clinic under the Ontario Legal Aid Plan. Its members have sometimes forced inquests to be called when a nursing-home resident dies, and they have assisted at the inquests. And they were successful in halting a proposed drug experiment on incompetent residents in homes for the aged.

Under the 1987 Nursing Homes Amendment Act — which addressed some issues brought forth by Concerned Friends — it is mandatory for staff and visitors to report any abuse or neglect they see in the nursing home. An anti-reprisal clause in the legislation prevents nursing homes from retaliating against those who report such incidents.

"It has been a very hard struggle, but we have made considerable progress, and we've changed a lot of things," Johnston says.

The secrets to their success are superb organization, a flair for publicity, and the ability to attract talented leadership and behind-the-scenes consulting expertise from lawyers, accountants, physicians and academics. For example, drawing on her work in the mental-retardation field, Spindel taught the group how to lobby. A research committee scans all journals and research papers, and keeps files on every nursing home in the province. The newsletter committee educates the membership. The phone committee can mobilize up to 600 members within twenty-four hours, to descend upon the legislature or telephone a politician to express their views on a current issue. The advocacy committee investigates complaints about nursing homes. Members of Concerned Friends speak to numerous groups and organizations across the province.

They meet with health ministry staff, and invite government officials, such as the minister of health, to speak at public meetings sponsored by Concerned Friends. They have established contacts with groups such as the Canadian Pensioners Concerned, United Senior Citizens of Ontario, Registered Nurses Association of Ontario, Alzheimer's Society, Social Planning Council, the

National Council of Aging and the Coalition of Senior Citizens. Most recently, they have joined a powerful American lobby, the National Citizens Coalition for Nursing Home Reform. This organization, based in Washington D.C., comprises 300 member groups, which mounted a successful campaign in 1987 to achieve the most comprehensive federal nursing-home reforms in the United States in over a decade.

The success of Concerned Friends is also due to a hard-nosed attitude towards politicians. "Many of our members have been through some very hard times, and they don't take kindly to platitudes," Spindel says. "They know what's true, and what's happened to their relatives. No one is going to convince them it's their imagination, or that things are okay. When our members speak to politicians, they really speak from direct experience."

"We have pictures. We have documented evidence. We document every call that comes into our organization. We never say anything publicly that we can't absolutely back up, or that we've run by our lawyer. When politicians ask us policy questions, we can give them specific examples about what's going wrong. Of course, those examples are good examples to give to the press in the event the politicians don't do what they're supposed to do."

In 1985, when the newly elected Liberal government approved the takeover of two nursing homes by Carewell Corporation — a nursing-home chain that had been charged with eighty-eight violations of the Nursing Homes Act at its Elm Tree Nursing Home in Downsview — Concerned Friends swung into action to publicize how easily nursing-home licences could be obtained. One day, at lunch hour, clusters of elderly men and women positioned themselves at each exit at Queen's Park, and handed out "nursing-home licences" which read: "This is a Licence to Print Money." The "licence" entitled the bearer to open as many nursing-home beds as he liked. It noted that compliance with the nursing-home act was not a prerequisite. "Multi-national corporations preferred.... Non-profit organizations wishing to provide innovative housing alternatives which prevent elderly people from being forced into institutions like nursing homes NEED

NOT APPLY." A copy of the sham document was delivered to the office of the health minister, to the delighted giggling of staff there. "Can you give me ten?" one man whispered. "Take a few to the office down the hall," chuckled another.

Embarrassed officials snuck out the back doors, but there was no escape. Elderly people were standing there, leaflets in hand. Soon, curious students from nearby University of Toronto gathered. Meanwhile, the TV cameras rolled, and newspaper reporters interviewed everyone in sight.

Today, public hearings are required for a licence to be granted.

The activities of Concerned Friends have won the approval of gerontologists and other experts. "They go too far," laughs Dr. Cope Schwenger, professor of community health at the University of Toronto. "But somebody has to."

When residents of a Toronto nursing home were served a lunch of some sort of burnt crust filled with the previous day's leftovers, a staffer tipped off Spindel, and delivered a sample lunch to her home. Spindel slipped the meal on a plate, photographed it for her records, and plunked it on the inspection director's desk, with a note: "Bon Appetit. With the compliments of Concerned Friends."

When a rural Conservative MPP called for more nursing-home beds instead of alternatives to institutionalization, Concerned Friends peppered his riding with thousands of flyers telling constituents that their representative wanted to slap them into a nursing home once they were old.

When an elderly woman was forcibly moved from a non-profit home for the aged into a for-profit nursing home, Johnston and Spindel rushed over to find the woman already standing outside, holding a small suitcase. A taxi was waiting. While Spindel called a lawyer, Johnston blocked the cab's only exit by sitting on the ground directly in front of the vehicle.

"Many of the older people are not comfortable with public disobedience or demonstration," Johnston says. "They have never done it in their life. I find them very courageous to stand up for their convictions. It shows people really have power if they would only use it."

Concerned Friends received 1,736 complaints in the year ending October 31, 1988. Of those complaints, 1,104 were from profit-making nursing homes, 147 were from non-profit homes for the aged, 336 from retirement homes, 46 from acute-care hospitals, 56 from chronic-care hospitals, 35 from boarding houses and 12 from group homes. Each complaint is followed up by members of the organization.

Johnston, a member of the advocacy committee, gets about fifteen calls a day from families and residents seeking the group's help in dealing with a problem. "I let them talk and let it all out of their system. They need to feel that they are understood. A feeling they are not crazy — as they are very often made out to be by the nursing-home administration. You learn how to inter-rogate people but you do it very gently. I say, 'Yes, I believe you implicitly. But give me the proof.'"

She takes notes, and reads them back to the caller. She looks at the institution's file to see if there is a history of similar trouble. "I say, 'What is it you want me to do? These are the options. I will pursue them all.' Then you try to do exactly what they tell you to do. If you are a good advocate, you really do what your client asks you to do even if you think it's not right, and in the long run, things may go really wrong for that person. Otherwise, you become very paternal and think you know best."

She gets written authorization from the caller to act on behalf of the residents, to visit them or obtain information about them. Strictest confidence is promised, and requests for anonymity are respected. If people do not want their names used, a report to the government inspections branch will indicate only what general area to investigate.

After a complainant authorizes Johnston to investigate his or her situation, any number of things occur. For example, Johnston calls or writes to the inspection service, and follows up the complaint to find out what action has been taken. As well, two

members of Concerned Friends visit the home — usually together
— and write notes on their observations, forwarding these to the
ministry of health.

Johnston educates callers about all their recourses: the bill of
rights, the Nursing Homes Act, community resources. "You give
them a little boost for their morale, and you give them the tools
to do something about this the next time." She might advise the
distraught caller to ask for a meeting with the health ministry or
nursing-home administration, and offer to have a member of
Concerned Friends attend the meeting. "Never go alone," she
advises. "One has to ask questions, and the other has to write
down the answers. You keep pushing. Asking why, why, why. If
they tell you you won't understand, say, 'Try me.' And then they
get very angry. And when they get angry, they start to contradict
themselves." And that is when Concerned Friends scores points
and wins concessions.

In pursuing complaints, it is important to document every
observation and every attempt to resolve the complaint with staff
and administration, she adds. Documentation makes it easier to
resist intimidation from the nursing home.

Johnston tries to build morale among the overworked staff of
the nursing homes. She encourages complainants to praise the
employees who seem to be doing a good job. This approach also
helps the relatives gain allies in the homes. "The staff are mud-
dling all day in shit, and it's nice when someone comes and pats
you on the back. It builds up relationships. It's not us and them."

The phone rings at Johnston's beautiful Willowdale home, and
she scrambles for her cigarettes. The German shepherd watchdog
puts his head on her lap. She listens intently and begins to
scribble.

"Did they discuss it with her?," she asks. "Did they discuss it
with you? Did they ask her permission?" She listens some more.
"So what has happened is her rights have been violated.
Everybody has the right to refuse treatment or medication."

The caller is an elderly man whose wife is in a chronic-care hospital. After weeks of looking forward to a weekend at home, she was refused, because there are three stairs into the house and staff said they were concerned that she could not mount them. Horribly disappointed, she began to shout in frustration, and was given a heavy sedative. When her husband protested, he was informed that the hospital wanted to put his wife on the psychiatric ward. She had never before acted this way.

Johnston coaches him on how to approach the hospital staff.

"You say you want to have an independent assessment done. Everyone has the right to an independent opinion and they cannot object to that. They will try. First, they will start nicely, and when they see you won't budge, then they will start to be a bit more threatening and say, 'Well, then you have to take your wife home.'"

"That's when you look them straight in the face and say, 'Are you threatening me?' Then they will start blustering and saying you are not very co-operative. Then you say, 'Hold it right there.' Then you explain your wife's expectations, how that was handled, how they drugged her, which made it worse. And now she is considered the villain. It won't be easy, sir. They will treat you like something that crawled out from under a stone. Just remember: but for people like your wife, all those people would not have a job. Just keep your cool."

Johnston adds: "We are not always heard the way we think we should be heard, but sometimes something happens even better than what we asked for." Her face softens at the man's fervent thanks.

One case in particular still troubles her: a woman whom she had been visiting in a nursing home for years had been given medication that made her mentally incompetent. Johnston had earlier drafted a document saying that the woman could not be removed from the home without Johnston knowing about it, and giving Johnston the authority to act on her behalf. But before the woman could sign the document, she was removed to a psychiatric facility, where she received shock treatment — "the one thing she feared most," Johnston recalls. "I felt like a heel. I felt like a traitor. I thought, 'Now they can do what they want with her.'"

The phone rings again: another Concerned Friends member is going to visit the nursing home where Mrs. Lorenzo lost her eye. Johnston informs her that the police have refused to investigate. "This is all a cover-up," she says, adding that Spindel will speak to the police and remind them of the attorney-general's statement that complaints in nursing homes are to be taken seriously. In the meantime, as part of Concerned Friends investigation, the group's geriatric consultant has compiled a list of questions to ask the inspection department. Did Mrs. Lorenzo have a history of self-mutilation? Is she right-handed or left-handed? What was the angle into the eye?

Johnston tells the fellow-member that if she visits the home after the change of shift at 3:00 p.m., she will see how few staff there are. "Then they have five staff for ninety-two people," she says. "Take a clothes-peg with you; you might have to put it on your nose. If it stinks, show off. Have a big handkerchief in front of your nose. Have you got a big can of Lysol? Pop it quickly in front of you and pretend you are gasping for air. Have a good afternoon. And don't choke."

Johnston is a passionate red-haired woman who was born in the Netherlands: her fluent English is underscored by a definite Dutch accent. She has worked as a midwife in Africa, and a lay missionary in Malaysia and Hong Kong. Her husband is a senior executive with a chartered bank.

Johnston first became involved with nursing homes as a volunteer at a neighbourhood facility. In 1981, she was taking some residents to their rooms when a meticulous elderly woman she describes as "a little china doll" said she had to go to the bathroom. As a volunteer, Johnston could not take her: if something happened, she could be sued. But Johnston offered to fetch a staff person, found three employees chatting in a bedroom, and asked for someone to come.

Meanwhile, the woman was holding onto the hand-rail along the wall, and painstakingly inching her way to the bathroom. Twenty minutes later, no staff had come. The woman finally released her bladder with a horrified gasp. Johnston went back and informed the staff what had happened.

A big, hefty staffer took the resident by the scruff of her neck and said, "You naughty girl, now you have pissed yourself."

Enraged, Johnston reported the incident to the administrator and the director of nursing of the nursing home, both of whom said there was nothing they could do. "Then and there, I vowed I would do everything in my power that that would never happen again. Very naive, of course."

The next month, she attended her first meeting of Concerned Friends, and six months later, she started handling complaints.

It was the beginning of the end of her volunteer career. A newspaper reporter attended a meeting of Concerned Friends, and asked about security. "The place I work in is just terrible," offered Johnston. "In the evening, anybody could come in and murder six people, and nobody would know it." It was true. Only the week before, plainclothes detectives had visited the home to find out how four paintings and three wheelchairs had disappeared from the front hall. When the newspaper article appeared, the administrator was livid, and Johnston knew she was targetted.

Some months later, a television station called her, asking to interview some nursing-home residents. Johnston polled the residents, and found that they were pleased at the idea. "Bloody marvelous," crowed one ninety-six-year-old woman.

At 10:00 a.m., the TV crew trooped in with yards of cable, a huge camera and large lamp-stands. Nobody was at the front desk, so Johnston led them up to a resident's room. Suddenly, the director of nursing flew in. "What's going on?" she demanded. "Oh, that's Global TV. They just want to interview some residents," Johnston replied.

The director of nursing disappeared, and returned with the administrator, who announced that she forbade the interviews. "Are you saying this woman cannot see and speak to whoever she wants?" demanded the reporter. The officials were forced to say that she could; however, they insisted on staying in the room during the interview. "When you have visitors, is it the habit of the administrator and the director of nursing to stay in your room?" the reporter asked the elderly woman. "They don't even know my name," the woman squeaked. The reporter turned back to the administrator: "Are you saying then that you will invade the privacy of the resident, and will not leave the room and give the resident the chance to associate with whomever she wants?" The camera was rolling. The officials left.

A few minutes later, the cameraman pointed his camera at the door, and Johnston quickly opened it. "These two administrators literally fell in, because they had their ear to the door, listening." It was all on the 6:00 o'clock news, and Johnston was discharged as a volunteer. "It really was a big traumatic thing for me."

By dismissing Johnston, the home unleashed a formidable opponent, who will do anything legal to expose the plight of nursing-home residents.

In one experiment, Johnston asked her daughter to tie her to a kitchen chair with nylon fabric to see what it is like to be restrained. Thousands of elderly people in nursing homes are locked into geriatric chairs — a chair on wheels with a tray that goes across a person's abdomen and acts as a restraint — or tied to chairs or beds with belts, bars or vests.

"After three hours, I was begging to be freed," she says. "I couldn't move my knees, I had no feeling in my feet and my back was sore. My bones were hurting. The pressure and the burning were unbelievable."

Johnston notes that many restrained residents sit for hours, often wet with their own urine, without being re-positioned — because nursing homes are short-staffed. As a result, many suffer pressure sores, skeletal deformities and contracted muscles.

To prove to the provincial inspection branch that the situation was so extreme, Johnston went to a local nursing home at 5:00 a.m. and peered in the window. She could see six residents already sitting up, restrained in wheelchairs. She measured their position by counting the floor tiles, and returned at 1:00 p.m. They were in exactly the same spot. And at 8:00 p.m., the residents were still sitting there. "It makes you wonder whether they are being taken to the bathroom, fed or re-positioned," she says.

The next day at 7:15 a.m., Johnston called the provincial inspections director to report her findings. He had given his direct line to the group, so that they could contact him on urgent matters before the business of the day got underway. The director sent an inspector to the home.

Today, Johnston is trying to ease her responsibilities. She suffers from severe arthritis and migraines, and doesn't feel she can continue at the same pace. "I have been very unwell for the past year. I'm tired. Really tired."

Concerned Friends burst onto the public stage in September 1982, with its first report to the minister of health. "At present," the report said, "nursing homes are not homes, but institutions — sterile, friendless, and lacking humanness and warmth, where old people sit and rock, stare at the walls for most of their day or are led around by the hand like small children by inadequately enlightened staff who refer to them as 'dear'. Their days are regimented. They are told when to get up, when to lie down, when to eat, when to bathe and when to go to the bathroom. This (is a) lack of respect for the privacy and dignity of people who have lived their whole lives as independent, contributing members of society. Many are not even dressed and live their lives in bedclothes and slippers. If they protest at the treatment they are receiving, they are considered 'difficult' and may be restrained or medicated for their ill-conceived attempts to regain some of their lost dignity. If friends or relatives protest on their behalf, they are often considered to be troublemakers. All of this has contributed to nursing homes being seen by the public as inadequate, hopeless places where old people 'go to die'. Even officials of the Ministry of Health have commented that they hope never to end up in one."

The report noted that Concerned Friends does not suggest that every home neglects and dehumanizes residents. "Evidence is mounting, however, that an uncomfortably large number of the homes conform to some or all of the previous descriptions...."

Concerned Friends found that residents were being charged extra for plugging in radios, or using incontinence supplies. They were left in the lounge with their genitals exposed, unable to cover themselves because of paralysis. "Specific examples of poor conditions have too long been viewed as exceptions or isolated situations. Unfortunately these isolated incidents have, according to our experience, become more of the norm...."

Concerned Friends noted in its report that minimum staffing guidelines, issued by the government, constituted the maximum in many homes. Nursing homes resisted taking residents who required total bed care, preferring ambulatory residents with limited needs. "Since nursing homes tend to be private, profit-making ventures, there are diminishing returns in keeping residents as their care requirements slip over the minimum level required under the Nursing Homes Act and Regulations."

The reluctance of nursing homes to accept difficult residents had caused an excessive demand for chronic-care hospital beds, because there was nowhere else to put such individuals. This situation in turn, created a shortage of acute-care hospital beds, causing the public, who did not understand what was behind these so-called "shortages," to demand more nursing-home and hospital beds.

Since the report was released, not much has changed, in terms of conditions in the homes. The 1,736 complaints documented by Concerned Friends in 1987-1988 ran the gamut of horror stories.

The organization heard about and saw dehydration, malnutrition and injuries; vermin and cockroaches; staff shortages and doctors who do not come; over-medication and medication errors; over-use of restraints; no rehabiliation; pervasive dirt; verbal and physical abuse; staff who were rude, indifferent, uncaring, hostile and threatening; lack of activities other than child-like crafts and TV; denial of privacy and dignity; and forced relocations within a nursing home.

They documented residents with oily, smelly hair; dirty fingernails; dry skin; and mouths encrusted with food, and cracked at the sides from being pried open with oversized spoons at mealtimes. The homes they visited often had sticky floors and furniture, dustballs, stained walls and ceilings, ripped carpets and loose ceiling tiles. They discovered poor quality food of insufficient quantity, therapeutic diets that only existed on paper, conveyer-belt feeding of residents, and a lack of fluids for residents. In a 1987 brief to the province, Concerned Friends pointed out that facilities with fire hazards were continuing to operate. In some homes, wheelchair-bound residents were housed on upper floors although there were no elevators in the building.

These endless revelations forced the group to dig for the root of the problem, which led to an inescapable conclusion: there should be no institutions for the elderly at all. Or, if it were not possible to abolish them, then all facilities should be non-profit, since the profit motive is incompatible with providing high-quality nursing-home services.

Concerned Friends favours keeping people in the community, in small group homes, or apartments with nursing staff and meals. The group also approves of keeping people in their own homes, with home nursing and housekeeping services.

"When they say there will always be people who need to be in an institution because of heavy care, why do we have to put 200 together?" Johnston asks.

The group's anti-profit stance disturbs the nursing-home industry. When Concerned Friends condemned conditions in nursing homes, the industry used the group's frightening revelations to demand more money to carry out improvements. Ontario Nursing Home Association president Harvey Nightingale called the group an "ally," in that respect. But to challenge the essence of the industry — the profit motive — was going too far. The industry declared that Concerned Friends had lost credibility.

"They served a useful purpose, and then they got lost," says Nightingale. "It was great to have them as a critic of nursing-home services. By attacking us they allowed us to respond. But they went on in a blind philosophical way — saying that the private sector is no good. If the only solution is to get rid of the private sector, that's not a solution. You can't dismiss 330 nursing homes. What are we going to do? Throw these people in the street?" Nightingale claims the group lost credibility with "too many outlandish charges without the facts to substantiate them."

But Spindel believes that these are the cries of a panicked industry. Since the Liberal government took power in 1985, it has expressed a preference for the non-profit sector in granting new licences. Non-profit operators currently control about 13 per cent of nursing-home beds in Ontario.

"The nursing-home industry knows the writing is on the wall," Spindel says. "Large institutions operated for profit are no longer considered to be viable by the government. They just haven't figured out yet how to get rid of them."

It is Spindel's conviction that one reason the Conservatives lost the 1985 provincial election, after decades in power, was that they promised to create another 4,500 nursing-home beds. Concerned Friends and other seniors' organizations held a press conference during the election campaign, saying it was an insult to seniors to bring in more nursing-home beds. They called on seniors to vote against the Conservatives. "I've talked to hundreds of senior citizens who voted Liberal for first time in their life," Spindel says. "Seniors were very angry and upset that the Conservatives were — in their view — betraying them."

Nightingale's criticism of Concerned Friends is backed by the biggest operator of nursing homes in Canada — Extendicare Health Services Inc.

"It's too bad they got so badly off the track," says Margaret Bouillon, director of standards for Extendicare.

"Some of the administrators get very disturbed about some of the things that happen in their homes," she says. "I hear about people, who may or may not be part of the organization, going into a nursing home, not telling the administrator who they are, invading the privacy of the residents, taking their bedclothes down and looking at them to see if they're wet, asking residents questions and taking the responses they get from those residents, who may be very confused, and misconstruing that information."

When Concerned Friends first heard these allegations nearly three years ago, they wrote to Extendicare asking for details and names. "We wanted to investigate immediately, because we don't do that," Johnston says. She says the organization is still awaiting a reply. The industry is just trying to save face, Johnston says. "Millions are at stake. Once the reputation is gone, it's very difficult to recoup it."

Margaret Bouillon says the group's tactics are unfair. "They use an example of something, and the way it's presented in the media is that this is the way all nursing homes are. Maybe they have encountered one incident of that. It's an insult to professional staff. I consider it a personal insult. I pay no attention, unless someone says Mrs. So-and-So, or Nurse X, or Home Y. Something that can be dealt with."

Spindel acknowledges that some homes are better than others. "But the real question is: do you want to live in an institution? Do you want to live in a place where your whole daily routine is regulated for you? Where you don't have any choice, where in many cases you're not taken seriously? Where you literally leave your rights at the door, because someone decides for you what you're going to have for breakfast, when you're going to get up, when you're going to go to the bathroom? We're not opposed to every institution. What we're saying is people who don't want to live in one shouldn't be forced to. We've hardly ever found anyone who really wants to live there."

The latest battle between Concerned Friends and the nursing-home industry was sparked by a series of thirty-two deaths at an Extendicare nursing home in Toronto between October 1987 and January 1988. (Another disturbing death followed, in April 1988, when an eighty-seven-year-old resident of the home died in a hospital rape-crisis centre after an apparent sexual attack. She was found in her room at about 1:00 a.m., bruised and bleeding, with her clothing in disarray.) Spindel says that neither the coroner's office nor the ministry of health was aware of the high death rate until Concerned Friends raised the red flag. The group was alerted after it received seventy-six complaints from residents' relatives and nursing home staff, citing verbal abuse, rough handling of residents, and falsification of medical records.

Through the provincial freedom of information act, Concerned Friends requested information on the thirty-two deaths to determine the causes. "For a lot of them, they couldn't even say. It said possible pneumonia, probable cardiac arrest," Spindel says. Only a few autopsies were performed, but the coroner decided that they all died of natural causes. "Autopsies are expensive," explained Dr. James Young of the Coroner's Office. The coroner's report said complaints that the deaths may have been linked to poor care at the home were unjustified.

In Spindel's opinion, the investigations by the coroner's office were superficial. "They often go and look at just the nursing notes or the doctor's notes when someone has died, and of course, that's in essence doctors and nurses investigating themselves."

The thirty-two deaths were reviewed by a medical advisory committee of doctors at the home, the Ministry of Health and the Coroner's Office. "The results of all these investigations confirmed that the residents were very old and died of causes attributed to their medical conditions," Extendicare executive vice-president Carl Hunt wrote in a letter to a Toronto newspaper.

Concerned Friends is demanding another investigation in the deaths. To this demand Extendicare has reacted angrily. Carl Hunt wrote to another newspaper: "It is destructive and self-serving that Anne-Marie Johnston of Concerned Friends of Ontario Citizens in Care Facilities persists in questioning the findings of legal and medical experts from the Ministry of Health and from the Coroner's Office into the deaths by natural causes at Bayview Villa Nursing Home.

"The self-righteous arrogance that propels Anne-Marie Johnston to believe that she knows more than the residents' physicians, the Ministry of Health's inspectors, the police investigators and the pathologists of the Coroner's Office is staggering," the letter said.

Johnston thought about this for a while. Then she decided: "Self-serving I'm not. But if questioning the experts makes me arrogant, then yes, I am arrogant."

Both Spindel and Johnston have been the objects of anonymous threats which they believe come from nursing-home operators. A telephone caller told Spindel's mother: "Your daughter better be careful, because not everyone agrees with her."

In Johnston's case, a caller asked whether she knew what happened to people who did not co-operate. "He said heaters blow up, and cars have mysterious accidents, and people have been found hanging in their bathrooms," she recalls.

The threats do not deter the women. "But it's disconcerting to think it's people like that who are running nursing homes," Spindel says. She points out that Helmuth Buxbaum — who was convicted for arranging to have his wife murdered in 1984 — was a millionaire nursing-home operator in Ontario. "It becomes a little unnerving to think they have these contacts."

One of Spindel's favourite stories involves Buxbaum. When she told a health-ministry official she was appalled that someone like Buxbaum could run a nursing home in Ontario, his response was: "You're assuming that just because he killed his wife, he wasn't a good nursing home-operator."

While Concerned Friends has succeeded in changing legislation, and getting new policies and guidelines in place, they are now concentrating on the implementation and enforcement of these improvements. "That's where things fall down," Johnston says.

Despite improvements in staffing levels and frequency of inspections, Concerned Friends remains unimpressed with the government-inspection process. Johnston says the wool is constantly being pulled over the eyes of inspectors, who sometimes seem wilfully blind.

The first problem, she says, is that inspectors rely on paper evidence: if a home records an expenditure of $3,000 on activities, the inspectors nod approvingly — but they don't examine what activities are actually available.

The same situation occurs with the food issue. "We tell them we have been getting complaints about horrible food, not well cooked, not enough, same thing three days in a row," Johnston says. "The inspectors go and look at the menu sheet." But what food the residents actually get is often quite different from what is printed on the menu, she says.

During their visits, inspectors will often note that the staff are responding immediately to call bells from the residents. But the employees are not stupid enough to neglect the residents in front of the inspectors, Johnston says.

During complaint investigations, she adds, the explanations provided by the nursing home are often accepted at face value, without the complainant having been interviewed. Nursing-home staff are sometimes interviewed in the presence of nursing-home officials.

These days, Concerned Friends is also dedicated to preserving its hard-won amendments to the Nursing Homes Act, now that the government is drafting an omnibus Extended Care Act, which is expected to replace the Nursing Homes Act of 1972 and the Nursing Homes Amendment Act of 1987. The group has also helped the government with a plan to set up a system of full-time paid advocates for people in long-term care institutions.

For friends and families who want to do what Concerned Friends has done, Johnston offers the following pointers:

Start with a core group of people who are angered by what is happening. Talk to other relatives visiting in the nursing home, and find out what they think.

Familiarize yourself with the act that governs nursing homes and the inspection process.

Get incorporated, so that a member cannot be sued as an individual. Try to find a lawyer to do this for you for free.

Set your goals; determine what direction you want to pursue.

Set up an internal structure and committees: these can include research, policy, advocacy, liaison, reception, phone, newsletter.

Decide who can be a member. Concerned Friends does not allow nursing-home owners and staff to join.

Organize a financial structure: how much will it cost to belong? What will that money be used for? Concerned Friends has never had more than $9,000 in the bank, and each year, it tables public financial statements at the general membership meeting.

Recruit people with expertise. It is useful to have members who can analyze a legislative act or a financial report.

Organize a process for handling complaints. Always follow up with a phone call or a letter. Ask for inspection reports, findings of complaint investigations, and fire-inspection reports.

Be prepared to drop everything to check out a problem. Staff and families who report problems want to see action. Without it, they'll stop calling.

Appoint an official spokesperson. An organization can stand or fall on this choice: the person must be articulate and knowledgeable about the issues.

Keep files as you begin to collect information.

Hold regular meetings. Hold press conferences to publicize an issue.

Establish relationships with the media, nursing-home staff, unions, and groups concerned with seniors' issues.

Spindel believes that society's negative attitude towards the elderly is the fundamental reason that so many are shipped to institutions.

"There really is an underlying feeling that when people have outlived their usefulness, they should just die and get out of the way, so the rest of us don't have to look at them. Instead of seeing older people in our society as a wealth of knowledge and compassion, we tend to see them just as people who are in the way. They're the ones who slow us down when we're in the lineup in the grocery store."

Ever since Johnston starting working with older people, she has had a recurring dream. "I dream that when you are sixty-five, some civil servant comes to the house with a beautiful birthday cake and little blue pill. I even see the guy who brings it. When you swallow it, you die. This must be the logical outcome of a society that cannot be bothered with old people."

During the war, Johnston lived in Holland, near the German border. At the end of the war, she saw people emerging from concentration camps — a sight that has haunted her ever since, and filled her with a sense of people's inhumanity. The sights in nursing homes in Canada remind her of the concentration camps. "There are people who were in concentration camps during the war. And now they are in the same situation at the end of their life. It's frightening."

8

The Homes

Manitoba is considered to have one of the better nursing-home systems in Canada. Admirers cite the single point of entry for both nursing homes and home care; the assessment for nursing-home care by a multi-disciplinary team of experts; and the absence of a medical requirement for placement. Unfortunately, a model bureaucratic system does not guarantee that actual conditions in nursing homes will be good.

"Wheeled to dining room in silence. Food placed in front of resident in silence. Eyebrows trimmed with no warning." These are the terse observations of a Manitoba government inspector after visiting a Winnipeg nursing home and studying the treatment of the elderly residents.

The inspection report's dry but compelling statements capture the stark, impersonal atmosphere of many nursing homes. "Moved without explanation of why. Hands and face washed in silence. Walking resident from dining room to own room in silence. Staff member stood directly in front of a resident but did not acknowledge her."

The Manitoba Health Services Commmission, which funds nursing homes, inspects them at least every two years to make sure that they are observing provincial standards of care. But a random sample of inspection reports on seventeen Winnipeg nursing homes between 1986 and 1988, obtained through the Manitoba Freedom of Information Act, shows that the homes usually fall short of these standards. The reports reveal homes that are dangerous, dirty, depressing and de-personalized.

The conditions described by inspectors substantiate thousands of anecdotal reports by families, nursing-home residents and staff, throughout Manitoba and in other provinces. These are issues that transcend the individual nursing home. The root causes of the problems are found in all nursing homes. Profit-making homes are motivated by profit; non-profit homes are frequently underfunded; and the realities of institutional life affect all homes. The inspection reports suggest that the most serious problems were more common in the profit-making homes than the non-profit homes. However, each of the inspected homes had deficiencies.

In one home, breakfast trays were brought to the bedrooms of some residents as early as 6:30 a.m. The early breakfasts were apparently scheduled for the convenience of the overworked staff, who opposed an inspector's suggestion that the meals be served at a later time.

In several nursing homes, strong body odours lingered in the air, both in residents' rooms and in public areas. Carts full of medications were left unlocked and unattended in corridors and lounges, where residents had access to them. A bedridden elderly resident was not given skin care, although the person was at risk of developing bedsores. Pork sausage was served to a resident who was supposed to be on a bland diet.

The dehumanizing effects of institutional life are well illustrated by the inspection reports. Inspectors noted that residents were ignored while staff chatted to each other; even when they did address the residents, some staff used patronizing terms such as "dear," "honey" and "sweetie." They called the elderly residents "good boy" and "good girl." The staff selected clothes for the residents without asking them what they wanted to wear. Staff entered residents' rooms without knocking, making eye contact or uttering a word. The inspectors and nursing-home staff used the term "feeders" when they talked about residents who needed help eating.

The inspection reports confirmed the shocking lack of privacy in the nursing homes; for example, two residents were bathed in

the same room at the same time, with the dividing curtain left
open. In one home, confidential nursing documents, containing
information about the residents, were kept in an open shelf in a
crafts room, where other residents and staff could easily read
them. In another home, a resident received a treatment in a central
public lounge.

The nursing homes were sometimes dingy and decrepit, and in
desperate need of repair and renovation. Inspectors noted that
some homes needed painting and their furniture replaced, because
it was falling apart after decades of use. Lighting in some dining
rooms and corridors was described as inadequate or very dark.

"The facility looks shabby," one report said. "It has not been
painted for several years and it is hard to tell if a surface has been
cleaned. Walls have been damaged by equipment and furniture.
The corridor walls down the stairs and in the hallway are badly
damaged. The condition of the laundry is poor... Nameplates on
the resident room doors are handwritten and the handwriting is
difficult for the residents to see." Like many of the reports, it noted
an inadequate supply of linen. "The linen which is supposed to
be white has a beige cast." There were holes in the fabric of
bedside curtains. And the inspector found more problems in the
dining room. "The environment is not pleasant for dining." The
dishes were a mix of institutional china and institutional plastic
ware. "Much of this china is well worn and unsightly." The tops
of dining room tables were broken. "This is unsanitary."

In another home: "Sofas were sagging and thus made it difficult
for residents/visitors to get out of." Floor tiles were loose. The
inspector noted badly stained flooring in the washrooms of the
home and brownish stains around the bases of some of its toilets.

Although meals are often the only highlight of the day for a
nursing-home resident, the inspectors witnessed some disturbing
incidents at mealtimes. "Noise resulting from the renovations
being made in the resident care centre and the crushing of pills
with a hammer on the third floor did nothing to provide a relaxed
mealtime environment for the residents," one inspector noted.

At another home, an inspector found that dirty dishes were often placed in front of residents who were still eating. "When dirty dishes are removed, the tote box with soiled dishes collected from other residents should not be placed on the table in front of the residents still at the table, especially if they are still eating." The dining room had an inadequate window covering, leaving the residents blinded by the sun.

In one home, undignified bibs were used instead of table napkins. In another, residents were not asked their choice of beverage. "There was very little interaction with the residents," the inspector wrote.

In another home, the meal service was so disorganized that the inspector saw residents waiting for meals while the nurse walked around the dining room at least twice, looking for residents who had not received their meal. "It is uncomfortable for residents to have to sit and wait while others at the same table are almost finished eating before the other plates had arrived," the inspector wrote.

In that same home, inspectors received a complaint about the meals from a visitor who called the food "atrocious." A copy of the complaint report showed the following meals were served: Monday noon meal: one piece of sausage, greasy fried potatoes, no vegetables, weak coffee, skim milk and pudding. The following week, Tuesday lunch consisted of half a piece of fried bologna, greasy fried potatoes, no vegetables and pudding. The visitor was concerned that the resident was losing weight. "His condition seemed to be deteriorating rapidly," the complaint report states. When an inspector visited, she found that the home had a nutritionally balanced menu. The problem was that it was not followed. "The only similarity between what was on the menu and what was served was one of the desserts," the inspector wrote. Other relatives had also questioned the heavy use of wieners, bologna and garlic sausage, she noted.

In many homes, staff fed residents while standing over them. "Staff should be seated in a relaxed, comfortable position so that the resident does not feel rushed and to provide the resident with a more normal social environment in which to eat his meal," an inspector said.

In one home, there were no nursing staff in the dining room at mealtimes: the staff had been replaced by volunteers — a dangerous practice, as elderly people often choke, and need a nurse's assistance. In another home, staff were so busy and disorganized that two different workers put sugar in a resident's cup of tea. And they seemed oblivious when one resident left the dining room without having breakfast.

One home was so short-staffed that two health-care aides had to serve a meal to ninety residents. Another inspection report noted that food was cold because there was no cover for the portable hot-food table from which meals were served in the dining room. Endless use of the same cheap foodstuffs is a common complaint: one inspector had to tell a nursing home that when the kitchen serves spaghetti for lunch, there should not be macaroni in the soup.

In at least one home, some residents did not receive fluids in the morning, between meals — against government guidelines that drinks be offered between meals to prevent dehydration.

Over and over again, inspectors found that medications were served with meals. This practice is convenient for staff, because the residents are all in one place, but unpleasant for the residents — and sometimes counter-productive. "Some medications such as antacids are inactivated by the presence of food in the stomach," an inspector wrote. "Mealtime enjoyment can be destroyed if the meal is interrupted or swallowing medication is particularly difficult." Other medications "have an unpleasant taste that can ruin the taste of the meal," another inspection report said.

In some nursing homes, the medication cart was wheeled right into the dining room. In one home, residents arrived for their noon meal to find their medications sitting beside the plates. Medication at mealtimes "compromises the home-like quality we are striving to achieve in personal care homes," an inspector wrote.

Inspectors discovered that some elderly residents were over-medicated. In some homes, residents were taking three or four different kinds of laxatives. "The greater the number of medications prescribed, the greater the opportunity of a drug interaction or adverse drug reaction," one inspector said.

In one home, medications were left at residents' bedsides, and unlabelled bottles were found in the room where the residents were bathed. "Is safe resident care being provided?" an inspector wondered, also noting that there was no system to keep track of the use of narcotic and controlled drugs. In another home, a resident was given four medications to swallow while lying flat in bed. "This particular situation could have led to the patient choking on her pills," an inspector wrote.

Inspectors frequently found medications that were being used past their expiry date, or had no expiry date listed on them. Medications were not checked often enough to see if they were still necessary. In one home, a resident received Tylenol without asking for it. "He always asks for Tylenol at lunch, so I just give it to him even before he asks," a nurse told the inspector.

A staff member at one nursing home was seen measuring a dose of medication without shaking the bottle, although its label indicated it had to be well shaken. "This could cause serious complications," the inspector wrote, noting that a toxic dose of the drug in question would be fairly easy to give. In another report, an inspector observed medication being administered without water; as a result, it was spit out by the resident.

Many residents were restrained in geriatric chairs, wheelchairs or straight chairs. "The adage of restraining to prevent falls is not acceptable," one inspector said. "Alternatives to the use of restraints for the resident behaving aggressively are also required." Residents who were restrained were not checked frequently enough to make sure they were safe and comfortable, the inspection reports show.

In numerous homes, inspectors found that the health records of residents were incomplete. One person's care plan made no mention of his leg contractures or leg brace. Sometimes, injuries were unaccounted for. One chart referred to a "large bruise noted to right arm, cause unknown." Records in one location contained information about a resident that contradicted information in other records. There was no record of the medications given to residents in one home.

Inspectors found unsanitary practices among many nursing-home employees. They did not always wash their hands after handling soiled laundry, or between caring for different residents. In one home, the same comb was used for a number of different residents. A communal basin was used to clean residents, hands, faces, and even the tables that held their food trays. Residents' genitals were left unwashed.

In another home, clean dishes became contaminated because dishwashing staff handled dirty and clean dishes without washing their hands. Staff lunches were stored next to medications requiring refrigeration, risking contamination of the drugs. A maintenance room was located behind a nursing-home kitchen, and physical-plant staff were constantly parading through the kitchen.

In another home, soiled laundry was left in residents' washrooms. Urine was allowed to dry on the floor of a resident's room. Inspectors noted that kitchenettes, cupboards and cutlery containers were dirty. In another home, soiled laundry was left in the middle of residents' rooms.

"The noise level in the centre lounge was of concern i.e. radio, TV and activities vying simultaneously for residents' attention," a report said of yet another home. Other irritating sounds noted by the inspectors included the public-address system cutting in and out, two televisions blaring at the same time, and noisy dishwashing.

Many nursing homes herded residents together for activities that were not appropriate to them all. "Taken to unsuitable activities," one inspector noted. "Not mentally able to play Bingo." Another report found that the "excessive stimulation and distraction" of the large groups of residents were causing the frail or confused elderly people "to withdraw from meaningful participation."

What is clear from these reports is that some nursing homes are unfit to look after frail, elderly people. The government inspectors are forced to educate the nursing-home administrators on the basic rules of sanitation. In some cases, these are homes that have been operating for decades, yet the inspectors actually have to suggest that nursing-home staff receive training in such basics as the proper handling of soiled laundry, and the correct way to wash their hands to prevent the spread of infection.

Some nursing-home administrators blatantly ignore inspectors' suggestions which would bring them up to the minimum standards required by the government. Inspectors often noted that their advice from previous visits was not followed. A cook was told to upgrade her qualifications, but she didn't. Homes with foul odours on one visit still smelled bad a year or two later.

A 1987 inspection report noted that one nursing home took no steps to implement recommendations dating back to 1982, even though many of the recommendations "relate to unsafe conditions and practices.... Many issues relate directly to the quality of life of the residents."

One reason that nursing homes continue to scorn government guidelines with impunity is the lack of strong enforcement procedures. Instead of prosecuting or closing a home that does not comply with government guidelines, the Manitoba Health Services Commission gently suggests that the administrators and staff need more education — at taxpayers' expense, of course, with the use of government consultants. This approach does not make sense. A major two-year review of the regulatory system for nursing homes in the United States published a report in 1986. The report, "Improving the Quality of Care in Nursing Homes," concluded that education and consultation in profit-making homes should be the responsibility of the industry, not government.

Very few nursing homes are ever closed. In Ontario, between 1984 and 1988, 684 charges were sworn against 58 nursing homes. Of these, 29 homes were convicted of 146 charges. Total fines against the licence holders and administrators ranged from zero to $12,000. The majority of the fines were under $2,000, six nursing-home officials received suspended sentences, and the rest of the charges were withdrawn or dismissed. The Ontario nursing homes branch has closed three homes. In Manitoba, no home has ever been closed, or even prosecuted.

The Manitoba government's nursing homes branch has a policy of being co-operative and friendly with nursing-home operators. In their effort to be non-confrontational, the behaviour of the bureaucrats sometimes borders on silliness. "Your plan to purchase three-ring binders for the health records is encouraged," one inspector wrote in a report on a home which had far more serious concerns, such as dirty and unsanitary conditions, unsafe medication practices, and a foul odour.

In Ontario, nursing-home operators are given no advance warning of enforcement-style government inspections. But in Manitoba, nursing-home administrators are informed well in advance of an inspector's visit. Manitoba Liberal Leader Sharon Carstairs criticizes this policy. "What's the point, if you're telling them you're coming?" she says. "The (nursing home) population are like infants in terms of their ability to speak out. Constant checks are required."

Win Lindsay, a former Manitoba nursing-home inspector, noticed that nursing-home administrators would make an effort to create a good impression when they knew in advance that an inspector was coming. "Residents would say to me: 'Oh, are you the reason we're up so early and dressed so nice?'"

During any year when a nursing home is assessed by the Canadian Council on Health Facilities Accreditation, partly funded by the nursing-home industry, Manitoba does not send inspectors to look at the home. The nursing homes branch is satisfied that the agency can do the work of the government. "We don't repeat work that's already been done," says Kay Thomson, the provincial director of long-term care. Even the executive director of the council says accreditation is a horse of another colour. "It's a different process from an inspection process," says Ambrose Hearn, former deputy minister of health in Newfoundland. "An accreditation program should not be viewed as an inspection program. (During accreditation) the facility wishes to improve, and invites colleagues to assess it against national standards. The CCHFA comes by invitation." A study of the Ontario inspection system — written by consultants from the firm of Woods Gordon — concluded that government inspections are essential. "Accreditation is not a viable substitute," the 1986 report said. Unlike Manitoba, Ontario does not substitute accreditation for inspections. "Our inspections serve as a way of assuring the public that taxpayers' money is being spent appropriately," says the acting director of the nursing-homes branch.

In Ontario, the Ministry of Health's nursing-homes branch is responsible for monitoring compliance with nursing-home legislation and collecting evidence for prosecution. In Manitoba, by contrast, the nursing homes branch believes that its job is to consult, advise and educate. The very word "inspections" is poison in Manitoba. "We don't call them inspections," Thomson chides. Instead, the branch merely tries to encourage nursing homes to do the right thing. Its assumption is that nursing home abuses are just a result of insufficient knowledge among the nursing-home operators.

According to the Woods Gordon study in Ontario, other provinces tend to combine both consultation and enforcement, although each system tends to emphasize one or the other. For example, New Brunswick and British Columbia emphasize compliance while Manitoba, Saskatchewan and Alberta emphasize consultation. Since the report, Ontario has moved from compliance to consultation in its emphasis. At the same time it has strengthened penalties for non-compliance.

The Woods Gordon study in Ontario suggests that the consultation approach is problematic. When a nursing-home operator fails to comply with regulations, it is not necessarily because of ignorance or a lack of education, the study said: the failure to comply is sometimes the result of a reluctance to spend the necessary money.

Staff, residents or visitors who have a complaint about a nursing home sometimes believe they will get a sympathetic hearing from the nursing homes branch. But this is not always the case. The officials often side with the nursing-home administration, downplay the complaint, or claim they can do nothing about it.

Thomson says the Manitoba branch does not keep records of complaints about nursing homes; she estimates there are about thirty a year. Moreover, when the branch receives a complaint about a nursing home, it does not necessarily visit the home. "We may phone," Thomson says.

The Woods Gordon study in Ontario found that inspectors spent most of their time looking at buildings and paperwork, rather than residents and the care they are receiving. The study said there is little enforcement of regulations for homes with serious, recurring problems.

According to a report by the Christian Labour Association of Canada on conditions in Alberta nursing homes, inspectors tend to focus their attention on the cleanliness and general appearance of a facility. They make little effort to talk to employees or residents. Inspectors tend to judge a home on the basis of its nursing charts and its physical appearance. "Yet these two elements tell only a small part of the story," the 1988 report said.

The attitude of some nursing-home operators towards inspections is curious. Although nursing homes receive public funds, some nursing-home owners and administrators told Woods Gordon that "they perceive the nursing home inspection system to be an unusual and unwarranted form of government involvement."

The Ontario study found that most violations in nursing homes are not merely minor infractions. In most cases, the violations are a result of conditions that are unsanitary and hazardous to the health and safety of residents. The study concluded that decreasing the frequency of inspections would result in more violations.

As a result of the Woods Gordon study, the Ontario nursing homes branch has introduced tougher penalties. If prosecuted, Ontario nursing homes face fines of up to $5,000 for each first-offence violation of the Nursing Homes Act and regulations, and fines of up to $10,000 for subsequent offences. There are also interim measures, such as a ban on new admissions to troublesome nursing homes. If the health and safety of residents is in jeopardy, the director of the nursing homes branch may threaten to revoke the licence. In such a case, a home may appeal to the Nursing Homes Review Board, and is usually given six months to meet provincial requirements. In case of emergency, the health minister can revoke a home's licence.

Inspection reports can be invaluable to elderly people and their families, when they are choosing a nursing home. Yet they are not easily available to the public in Manitoba. They must be requested from the government through freedom-of-information legislation, which can involve a lengthy waiting period and the payment of fees to the government.

In Ontario, annual re-licensing inspection reports are freely available at government libraries. Furthermore, it is required that each home's most recent annual report be posted in a prominent place in the home. These reports include facts about the home, such as ownership, accreditation status, recent violations, and the operator's plan for improvement.

In 1987, there were 2,627 special-care facilities for the aged in Canada, containing 168,447 beds. Less than half of them (about 74,264 beds) were officially accredited by the Canadian Council on Health Facilities Accredition. Governments do not require that nursing homes be accredited.

Concerned Friends calls accreditation a farce. The accreditation visits (officially described as "surveys") are scheduled in advance, with the knowledge of the nursing homes. Manuals are provided to help the nursing homes prepare for the surveys, which are typically completed in thirty-six to forty-eight hours by a couple of surveyors, often nurses or adminstrators from other nursing homes. The council's objective is to encourage all long-term care facilities to apply for accreditation. For this reason, surveyers usually grant a minimum accreditation status — one year — to encourage marginal homes to keep trying for accreditation. About 90 per cent of homes that are surveyed are accredited. "Then it goes right back to the way it was," says Patricia Spindel of Concerned Friends.

Despite an appalling number of violations of nursing-home regulations and guidelines, the homes continue to be accredited by the council. A home in St. Catharines, Ontario, for example, was accredited for a two-year period in July 1985. Eight months later, it was inspected by the Ontario government for its 1986 annual licence renewal. Government inspectors found twenty-two violations of the Nursing Homes Act.

The inspectors noted that the residents of the St. Catharines home were not provided with comfortable chairs in their rooms. Call bells were not in working order. A resident was restrained without a doctor's order. The elderly residents were poorly groomed, wearing clothing that was torn, unhemmed, soiled, worn and ragged. The nursing-home staff were administering medications without doctor's orders. The kitchen and bedrooms were filthy, with soiled walls and an "excessive amount of dust, dirt and debris." Supplies were in poor condition. "Plastic dishes in use for residents were stained, scratched and had no glaze remaining." Therapeutic diets ordered in writing by doctors were not being followed.

When government inspectors returned a year later, in 1987, they found even more violations — thirty-one. Many problems, noted during the previous visit, were still uncorrected. In addition, inspectors found that residents lacked pillowcases and towels. "Washcloths in use were frayed and sheets very thin," the report said. In one case, a physician had prescribed special mouth care for a resident, but the care was not provided. Residents' nails were cut so short that they were inflamed. Toilet seats were soiled, and privacy curtains stained. Residents were walking around in stocking feet. There were not enough workers to meet the needs of the elderly residents. The administrator's qualifications did not meet the requirements of the Nursing Homes Act.

"A staff member was observed lighting a cigarette for a resident by putting the cigarette into her own mouth first, lighting it, then putting it into the resident's mouth," an inspector noted. Food was prepared too far ahead of time, risking contamination. People on pureed diets were given the wrong kind of food.

Amazingly, the nursing home was accredited again, for a further two years, in 1987. The two-year accreditation is supposed to be reserved for homes that show average or above-average compliance with most of the council's standards.

The nursing home just kept getting worse. In 1988, government inspectors noted forty-eight violations. The home was even dirtier than before. Floors, walls, furniture, washrooms, bathmats and cupboards were all dirty, sticky and dusty. Chairs were torn and broken, and the lighting was poor. Residents were not receiving attention during meals, and the staff didn't check to see if the residents were eating their meals. "There was weight loss for some of the residents," the 1988 inspection report noted.

The story is the same in other nursing homes. A home in Toronto was accredited in 1985 for two years, yet government inspectors found thirteen violations in 1986, including strong urine and fecal odour, cold food and live cockroaches. In 1987, there were a further seventeen violations; for example, residents were being prevented from resting in the afternoon because their beds were unmade. Kitchen utensils and work areas were dirty.

Another Toronto home was accredited for three years — the highest level of accreditation — in May 1985. Three-year accreditation is supposed to be reserved for full compliance with standards. Yet in that same year, government inspectors found nineteen violations of the Nursing Homes Act at the home in question. Residents' call bells were not working; they had no towels or washcloths; and they had access to drugs, which were left in easy reach. Some residents were being charged extra for special services, even though there was no indication in writing that they had agreed to such charges. The food was cold, and therapeutic diets were not followed. Fluids, which are important to prevent dehydration, were not served between meals.

In each of these cases, the nursing homes were not only accredited, but they were re-licensed by the government.

The Woods Gordon study in Ontario found that government inspectors doubt there is any relationship between accreditation, and compliance with the Nursing Homes Act and its regulations. "Accreditation status appears to have considerable 'image' value among nursing homes," the report said. "Nursing home administrators believe that families of potential residents view accreditation as an important factor in choosing a nursing home."

Nursing homes have a financial incentive to get accredited. In Ontario, they get a daily thirty cents more per resident if they are accredited. But staff and critics of nursing homes say the changes produced by accreditation are temporary and cosmetic. Colour schemes and curtains are changed. Doors and walls are patched up. The accreditation people get a guided tour by the administrator or the director of nursing. It is all very chummy. They are treated to lunch. According to nursing-home employees, the accreditation officials do not speak to staff, relatives or residents.

Ambrose Hearn, of the accreditation council, says some surveyors speak to staff, relatives and residents, and others do not. "It's not a requirement." He says homes are accredited in spite of violations of provincial regulations because the accreditation process is different from the government inspection process. "If a home tries to hoodwink us, in many ways it's quite possible," Hearn says. "(Accreditation officials) are not searching for problems. Our report would not look at detail, but at the overall meeting of standards." He says that education is a big part of the accreditation program. Hearn notes that in most cases the cost of accreditation — $1,700 in 1989 — is borne by taxpayers through funding received by nursing homes from provincial governments.

Anne-Marie Johnston, of Concerned Friends, says she has been called at least twenty-seven times by incredulous staff, and told to come and visit a nursing home on accreditation day. The staff call her because they are astonished at the contrast. "When you go in, you say, 'God, is this the same place?'"

Johnston says employees are usually told to come in early on accreditation day. "They make sure all the people have Kleenex, all the bathrooms are cleaned, and flowers are brought in. All the residents who don't look well, no matter how you dress them, are kept in bed. All the residents who can sort of look all right put their best clothes and jewellery on. Hair appointments are made the week before, and they get perms. They all have makeup and nail polish. All the men are shaven and smell of aftershave. When lunchtime comes, instead of the poor souls having the usual dark brown plastic mug they have used for the past five years, there's a real tablecloth on the table, real napkins and cutlery and proper sort of crockery. A big effort is done for the meal. I'm really happy that at least once every two or three years, these poor people are treated to at least one good meal."

Nursing-home operators can ignore regulations and guidelines because they know the government is reluctant to get tough. The demand for nursing-home beds exceeds supply. There is no competition. Alternatives to nursing homes are limited. The operator's success is not dependent on his ability to satisfy customers. "The consumer cannot just pack up and find a better nursing home," Concerned Friends said in a brief to the Ontario government.

"At present, old people in Ontario who truly require placement are at the mercy of private owners who enjoy a virtual monopoly," the advocacy group said. "Demanding accountability creates problems if there is nowhere else to put the residents who suffer when a badly-run home closes and they must be transferred en masse."

In 1985, the Ontario government auditor criticized the health ministry for its casual attitude to nursing-home misdemeanours. The auditor found that one nursing home was charging residents $150 for leaving the home: officials at the nursing homes branch responded by saying that the fee was not uncommon.

The auditor said that random audits at twenty nursing homes showed that residents were being charged for extra services, even though they had not given written authorization, as required under nursing home regulations. Some homes were charging residents a 20-per-cent fee for any item that the home's staff had purchased for a resident. Earlier, the auditor had recommended that the nursing homes branch provide refunds to these residents, but in his report he concluded there was little evidence of compliance.

In 1985, when government inspectors found six people with bedsores in a home that had already been warned to improve its level of care, officials at the nursing homes branch simply telephoned the home and told the administrator to stop reducing his staff. But the health ministry continued to pay the home $6,300 a day.

In Ontario, relationships between nursing-home operators and the government have been close. During the 1987 election campaign, Ontario nursing homes donated at least $89,915 to the Liberal party, according to Ontario NDP research. In May 1989, the *Toronto Star* ran a series of reports on MPP holdings as reported under the Conflict of Interest Statements provided by MPPs. These statements showed that two MPPs and their spouses owned assets in Crownx Inc., the owner of Extendicare, which is the largest nursing-home operator in Canada. Among them was Health Minister Elinor Caplan. Over the years, numerous nursing home and health ministry employees have taken jobs with the nursing-home industry.

Some experts say that conditions in nursing homes are affected by the profit motive of the operators. The nursing-home industry has a higher percentage of private ownership than any other health service in Canada. Almost 40 per cent of nursing-home beds in Canada are operated for profit.

"Quality of care is compromised, accessibility to services is jeopardized, and accountability of providers to consumers is problematic under a service run for profit," Vera Tarman, gerontology instructor at McMaster University, wrote in a 1987 study. "Unless government is willing to alter the proprietary system of nursing home care, any amount of government intervention will only maintain or exacerbate the problematic issues surrounding commercialization." Tarman warns that even the recent reforms in Ontario — a resident bill of rights and public inspection reports — will not greatly improve conditions at profit-making homes.

Several studies have found that profit-making homes have a worse record than non-profit homes. While homes run by governments or non-profit organizations are far from perfect, at least their operating surplus is put back into the home —not into the pocket of an entrepreneur. Accountability also tends to be better in non-profit homes, because they are run by community boards.

A report in 1984 by a Canadian Medical Association task force recommended the elimination of profit-making institutions, and the expansion of non-profit homes. "When an institution becomes the only answer for the care of an elderly person, it must be one that is run on a principle of loving care, not one of tender, loving greed," the report said. "In a comparison between old age homes run for profit and those run by non-profit ethnic or religious organizations, it is the latter that often exhibit a higher standard of care, food, rehabilitation, innovative recreation programs, and at the end of life, compassion, palliative care and respect for the individual."

The Nursing Homes Residents' Complaints Committee, established by the Ontario Government in 1985 to study complaints by residents, also criticized the profit motive in the nursing-home industry. "In a profit-oriented system, operators are motivated to decrease costs — in this case, food, staff, time, luxuries etc. — in order to increase or maintain their profit margin," the committee said, after inspecting 183 nursing homes.

A Winnipeg nurse, who worked in a profit-making Winnipeg nursing home, says she believes non-profit homes offer better care. "They can afford small extras, like replacing staff when they're short, or real orange juice at snack time."

The nursing-home industry argues that the profit motive acts as an incentive to efficiency, cost reduction and flexibility. In some ways, however, profit-making homes are actually more expensive than non-profit homes. A 1984 report by the Social

Planning Council of Metropolitan Toronto noted that the management and administration of profit-making homes can sometimes be more costly, because of the tendency to build expensive head offices and hire a flock of vice-presidents.

The social planning council said that some profit-making homes limit access to what is a universal health service by "cream-skimming" — selecting people who require less care. They discriminate against difficult people, who require a lot of nursing care, by avoiding them or encouraging them to hire private attendants to supplement the care in the nursing home. These people often end up in municipally run homes for the aged, or in the chronic-care wings of hospitals. Hospitals complain that nursing homes refuse to accept difficult cases, causing long delays in hospital for the patient. "A profit-motivated system appears to have a built-in preference for patients who need the least attention," former Ontario health minister Larry Grossman observed in 1982.

The Manitoba Organization of Nurses Associations opposes the establishment of new commercial nursing homes. "Labour relations are much more difficult when the profit motive is there," president Vera Chernecki says. Wages and benefits for the staff of profit-making homes tend to be lower than those at non-profit homes.

In Ontario, the profit-making nursing-home industry has defended itself by promising to be more efficient and cheaper than the government-run non-profit homes for the aged. "We're good at making do," Ontario Nursing Home Association president Harvey Nightingale says. "We know how to stretch a dollar. We have been saving the Ontario government and the citizens of Ontario billions by doing such a good job."

But now, the industry is suing the Ontario government for parity with the higher-funded non-profit homes. If they win, they will gain another $300 million in annual subsidies, and they will cost the government as much as the non-profits.

The Ontario Nursing Home Association, which represents about 90 per cent of Ontario's 339 private nursing homes, has been lobbying the provincial government for the past three decades.

The association, which has a $600,000 annual budget, claims to be launching the suit on behalf of Ontario's 30,566 nursing-home residents. Yet this is the same organization that called the government "irresponsible" for granting more rights to nursing-home residents. The organization said it supported the residents' bill of rights in principle, but said it would be impossible to implement without more government funds. Moreover, the association has fought a proposed new rule which would require nursing-home operators to post their annual profits and losses inside their homes.

Nightingale is a man who does not mince words when it comes to the elderly. He emphasizes how difficult it can be to look after them. "Some of them are not nice people," he says.

Conditions in nursing homes are not perfect, he acknowledges. Nursing-home staff may have given the elderly residents "a slap here and there." But Nightingale argues that many people's complaints about nursing homes stem from a sense of guilt that they cannot look after their relatives at home.

The nursing-home association says it is unfair that municipal homes for the aged receive 33 per cent more subsidies than nursing homes, because both kinds of facilities are looking after residents with the same needs and health conditions. "Right now, the needs of seniors in nursing homes are not being properly met," a 1987 ONHA position paper said. "Funding levels have not kept pace with the changing medical conditions of seniors."

In May 1988, commercial nursing homes received $30.01 a day from the Ontario government for each resident, and an additional $21.58 to $36.73 a day from the residents: a total of $51.59 to $66.74 per day, per resident.

Municipal homes for the aged, on the other hand, received an average total rate in 1987-88 of $87.09 a day per resident. Charitable homes for the aged received a total average of about $62.85 a day. In those years, there were about 29,000 residents in 180 municipal and charitable homes for the aged. Of those,

14,000 were categorized as needing "extended care" — the same level offered in nursing homes.

Municipal homes for the aged also receive government funding for capital costs. In 1988, the Ministry of Community and Social Services announced that $100 million would be spent over the following five years for capital redevelopment to improve the physical structure of homes for the aged.

The increase in nursing-home expenditures over the past fifteen years has been staggering. The Ontario government spent $25 million in 1972 on subsidies to profit-making nursing homes. By 1987, it was spending $346.8 million, and the total revenue of profit-making nursing homes in Ontario was believed to be more than $500 million.

The money keeps pouring in. In 1986, the commercial industry received a special package of $14.3 million for improving recreational activities, incontinence care and staff training. In 1987, the industry received another $88 million to increase nursing and personal care, increase food purchases, hire more kitchen staff and keep up with inflation.

Researchers Rosalie and Robert Kane are skeptical about the nursing-home industry's protestations of poverty. "Although the nursing home industry complains that the reimbursement rate is unconscionably low, each Request for Proposals (to build more homes) seems to prompt a flurry of competitive bids," they wrote. "Somehow the same industry that complains of underpayment is willing to promise to do even more for the same money."

In Ontario, the social planning council report said that nursing homes have profit margins ranging from 10 per cent to 30 per cent. Similarly, a 1984 *Globe and Mail* investigation concluded that nursing homes are big business. "The government subsidy system has turned the nursing home business into a highly profitable one that offers investors unique attractions — limited supply, huge demand, and guaranteed payment — all elements reinforced by government policy," reporter Linda McQuaig wrote. "In the taxi business, it would be comparable to an ever-present and growing line-up of customers ready to jump in as soon as the cab is empty."

McQuaig quoted a real-estate agent who said there is a waiting list of buyers for nursing homes. The buyers often purchase a nursing home on the day it comes onto the market. McQuaig concluded that government control drives up the market value of beds. In 1984, nursing homes were selling for about $30,000 a bed, including the value of the real estate and the value of the government licence.

Anne-Marie Johnston of Concerned Friends says the problem with giving the industry more money is its lack of accountability. She says Concerned Friends cannot figure out what happened to the jackpot given to the industry in 1986 and 1987. While there are more staff in some homes, others have tried to conceal the fact that their staffing levels have not increased, she says. Nursing-home employees have told Concerned Friends that if a worker fails to turn up for a shift, he or she is counted as having worked, but is not replaced.

"Nobody knows where that money went," Johnston says. "We have to take it at face value.We look at the annual report and see a profit. The complaints keep flying in. What guarantees do they give that there will be more staff, that residents will be cared for?"

"It's not free enterprise," Johnston concludes. "It's private enterprise, highly subsidized by the taxpayer. All businesses would love to get into that kind of industry where your income is guaranteed. They know the money will come in, regardless of whether they give good care or don't give good care."

Nightingale says it is a myth that "nursing homes are not caring places, that they're only interested in making profits and cheating people." He says most people who own nursing homes in Canada are well-known citizens in their community and take great pride in their work. However, the numbers suggest that a large percentage of nursing homes are not "Ma-and-Pa" operations. According to the report of an Ontario legislative committee, twenty-five corporate chains operated 18,349 nursing-home beds in Ontario in 1987. That represented 61 per cent of the total in the province.

The chains operated 160 nursing homes — 48.2 per cent of all the homes in the province. The top five chains operated 9,336 beds, or 31.2 per cent of the total. They ran 67 homes, or 20.2 per cent of all the homes. And the top corporate chain — Extendicare — operated 4,687 beds or 15.7 per cent of the total.

As early as 1970, there was mounting concern about the growing corporate ownership of nursing homes. There were already six nursing-home chains in Canada by that year. "It seems to be an unfortunate sign of the times that more people are becoming more interested in the financial return than in the service they are providing…a natural development, I suppose, when people can purchase stocks in larger homes and chains of homes," one cabinet minister said. "At this point, their personal input ceases and becomes strictly a business venture."

Nightingale says he does not know how much money the average nursing home makes or loses. But Dave Cook, former health critic for the Ontario New Democratic Party, says that entrepreneurs have termed this market "grey gold."

In 1980, Extendicare became large enough to swallow the Crown Life Insurance Co., creating a new corporation called Crownx, which now operates internationally. But nursing homes are still a major source of profit for the corporation. Extendicare's profits have increased rapidly in recent years, jumping from $13 million in 1982 to $56.5 million in 1987. And its total revenue reached $620.9 million in 1987, up 12.4 per cent from the previous year.

At the end of 1987, the company operated 63 nursing homes (it calls them "nursing centres") in Canada, and a further 142 homes in the United States and the United Kingdom. It had enough capacity for 8,845 nursing-home residents in Canada and 24,487 residents world-wide. "Canadian nursing centres remained at close to full occupancy," the 1987 Crownx annual report noted. Indeed, the company reported that its nursing homes were operating at 95 or 96 per cent of capacity for the entire period from 1982 to 1987.

"The fees charged by the Company for its nursing centres in Canada are regulated by provincial authorities," the annual report said. "A substantial portion of these fees is funded by provincial programs."

The report boasted that Extendicare's future looked bright. "As a leading provider of long-term care for the elderly, the Extendicare Group expects continued growth in the steadily expanding North American market," it said. "The population over 65 years of age will triple in the next 45 years and a growing proportion of the elderly will require long-term care in either nursing centres or their homes."

Crownx is selling its information-technology businesses and real-estate assets to concentrate on financial services and health care. "Financial services and health care are growth industries in which the company can achieve very satisfactory results," the 1987 annual report said.

Crownx and other members of the nursing-home industry are branching out into home-care services for the elderly. Para-Med Health Services, a division of Crownx, provided 2.2 million hours of home-care service in 1987 — a growth of 30 per cent over the previous year. By January 1989, Para-Med had 40 offices in British Columbia, Alberta and Ontario. "In Canada, the increasing demand for home care services … provide excellent growth opportunities," Crownx said in its 1987 annual report. "Governments are recognizing home care as an integral health care option and are providing more funds for home care programs."

The Ontario Nursing Home Association is anxious for a piece of the home-care action. "Nursing homes should be given the mandate and funding to provide community services," the association said in a position paper. "Nursing homes have … facilities, services, professionally qualified staff, and expertise — to provide many services cost-effectively, such as seniors daycare, meals on wheels, respite care etc."

Another major chain of nursing homes is operated by Central Park Lodges, a wholly owned subsidiary of Trizec Corporation. Trizec is a developer, owner and manager of commercial income properties. According to its 1987 annual report, Trizec Corporation has one of the world's largest property portfolios with assets of $8 billion.

In 1987, Trizec owned and operated forty-two nursing homes and retirement lodges in Canada and the United States, nine home health-care and staff-relief agencies, and three professional pharmacies. Thirteen of its nursing homes were in Canada. Centracare, its home-care division, has evolved into one of the largest Canadian-owned operations of its kind, providing over 800,000 hours of nursing-staff time, the annual report said.

Another major chain, Diversicare Inc., operated 1,408 nursing-home beds in Ontario in 1987. The company is a subsidiary of Counsel Corp., which also holds extensive interests in apartment buildings, office buildings, life insurance and trust companies.

Vera Tarman says diversification makes it difficult to monitor the financial accountability of a company. "It is difficult to ascertain whether the profit made from one type of service is going back into that service, or into another, or not at all," she says.

The chains grow by buying up beds already in existence in smaller companies or "Mom-and-Pop" operations. According to Tarman, "the growing monopolization of nursing homes, as chains grow larger and subsume smaller chains, threatens the choices of consumers."

There is some fear that Canada's free-trade agreement with the United States will usher in even greater private-enterprise ownership of nursing homes. Health economist Pran Manga says U.S. investment in the nursing-home industry is likely to increase as long as the Canadian industry stays profitable. With an aging population, demand for beds will likely continue to grow.

In a 1988 discussion paper published by the Economic Council of Canada, Manga expressed concern about U.S. involvement in Canadian nursing homes. American firms "have not been well disposed towards government regulations," he wrote. "They are likely to resist and indeed alter existing Canadian controls and regulations."

Jody Orr, executive director of the Social Planning Council of Metropolitan Toronto, points out that under the free-trade agreement, American companies must receive the same treatment as Canadian companies in Canada. The management of health-care facilities is included in free trade. A policy paper on free trade by the social planning council said the management of health-care facilities by American companies is undesirable because they tend to have a completely different attitude toward health care. "Canadian social policy may, over time, be increasingly shaped by American management in directions which bear no relation to Canadian needs and wants," the paper said.

David Cook of the Ontario New Democrats says the growth of corporate nursing-home care is undesirable. "Corporations are more likely to view nursing homes as just a business," Cook says. "Managers of chains may be less interested in the local reputation of their homes than in making profit-maximizing decisions." Jody Orr makes the same warning. "The problem in the long run is that as you expand commercialization, you're increasing the potential for social-policy objectives to be influenced by the private sector," she says.

When two Extendicare nursing-home consultants talk about their work, the words that keep coming up are the language of business — operational, division, amalgamate, consolidate. Indeed, in its annual report, Crownx refers to its residents as "operational capacity."

In the new era of corporate care, government efforts to regulate the nursing-home industry "are more likely to confront powerful political and economic opposition," Rosalie and Robert Kane predict. "There is something disconcerting about reading in the business section of newspapers that long-term care is a good place for investing venture capital."

9

Improving the Institutions

Whenever Douglas Rapelje saw something in a nursing home that he did not like, he jotted a note to himself and slipped it into a file folder. After twenty-five years the file was bulging.

"I saw a lot of things that bothered me," says Rapelje, fifty-five. "I wanted to build a facility so people didn't feel as if they were walking into an institution."

Rapelje is director of the Senior Citizens Department in the Regional Municipality of Niagara, Ontario. The department is responsible for services to the elderly of the region, including the six municipally owned homes for the aged. Rapelje has been the administrator of one of these homes for the aged. In total, he has spent thirty-six years working with elderly people.

He is a tall, courtly man who has a reputation for getting things done — within the system. He has improved the long-term care homes and home-support services to the elderly in Niagara region. In doing so, he has earned the admiration of gerontologists and consumers across Canada for his innovative ideas and commitment.

Rapelje particularly disliked large sitting-rooms in nursing homes, where residents "sit and stare at each other." He detested the sight of elderly people herded in big groups to a dining room or an activity room. He considered the lack of privacy in nursing homes dehumanizing.

Rapelje eventually used the contents of his file to build his dream nursing home. (He refers to nursing homes as long-term care facilities.) He visited exemplary facilities in Canada and the

United States, and set up an advisory committee of people who live, work, visit and volunteer in the Niagara homes. Their suggestions contributed to the design of Rapelje's lifelong vision — a nursing home called Gilmore Lodge, in the town of Fort Erie.

Gilmore Lodge opened in August 1988. It probably represents the state of the art in Canadian long-term care homes.

The lodge is an eighty-bed facility that sits on a knoll overlooking a park, children's swimming pool and playground. The average age of the residents is eighty-four, and most of them are women. About eighty volunteers come to the home to spend time with the residents. The lodge is composed of four colonial-style houses with twenty residents each. The houses have front and back porches, and each house has its own dining room, sunroom, living room, kitchen, front garden and back garden. The houses are bright and cheerful, with attractive, homey furnishings and lots of plants and flowers.

Rapelje says twenty-bed houses allow for a reasonable degree of economy, but at the same time provide a more home-like and personal atmosphere. "Twenty-bed houses allow residents to live in small individual communities. This design allows staff and residents to better know each other, to understand and respond to personal preferences and lifestyles," he writes in a description of the home. The smaller size also reduces noise, and eases personality conflicts among residents.

"Staff appear less stressed," Rapelje tells a visitor. "And so do the residents. They're not lining up to get into the dining room. They're not competing with seventy other people."

Except in one wing, residents and visitors enter and leave each house directly from the street rather than through the main lobby. This innovation came about after visitors told Rapelje that it depressed them to have to go through several wings or a main lobby, where they would have to see many other residents before getting to their friend or relative.

Each of the four houses caters to people requiring a different level of care. One house is for people who are fairly independent, requiring only supervision, and perhaps some medication. One house is for residents who require minimal nursing care, one is for people who need a great deal of care, and one is for cognitively impaired residents. Each home is staffed according to the residents' needs; furthermore, the residents are with their peers — a common complaint in nursing homes is that confused residents are mixed in with the mentally aware residents.

Most residents prefer private rooms. Rapelje says the need for privacy increases with age. "Privacy is paramount in preserving dignity. Adjustment to a shared room, communal washrooms and a new roommate is not easy," he has written. "Too often those constructing new facilities skimp in the name of costs. Residents are expected to move into a small room, with limited storage, and give up most of their personal belongings. Often, a shared room is their only personal space.... Space has so much effect on the quality of life, quality of care and quality of programs."

Each house in Gilmore Lodge has twelve private rooms and four semi-private rooms. These bedrooms have large windows and ledges that run the length of the room, so residents can place personal belongings and plants on them. Storage space is generous, by nursing-home standards. Clothes closets are 36 inches wide — up to three times bigger than what other long-term care facilities provide for their residents. The bedrooms also have overhead storage, a built-in wall unit with three drawers that actually lock — a rarity in nursing homes — and a counter which accommodates a 21-inch television.

Each room has a toilet, sink and vanity designed for wheelchair residents. The bathrooms are equipped with fan and heat lights. Each room has its own thermostat — an important feature, as many residents complain that the temperature is too hot or too cold.

One resident transferred to a private room at Gilmore Lodge from a nursing home where she had to share a room with three other residents. Two of her roommates had been so disabled that they couldn't speak. "I like a private room," she said, after she arrived at Gilmore Lodge.

In each house, four of the single rooms have adjoining doors, which allows married couples to live together. The two rooms can be used as two bedrooms or as a bedroom and sitting room.

Residents are encouraged to bring their own furnishings and to personalize their rooms. As an example, one resident had her own easy chair, and desk and chair from home. She had a cozy-looking afghan on her bed, and a reading lamp by the bed. The room looked cheery, clean and neat.

Instead of institutional-looking name plates, residents' rooms are numbered with traditional house numbering and have mailboxes with a slot for the residents' names.

The test of any nursing home is its heavy-care floor, which is for residents who require a great deal of assistance with feeding, washing, dressing and going to the toilet. Often, they are incontinent, and the smell of urine and feces can be strong. Too often, on heavy-care floors, residents sit restrained in wheelchairs for hours on end, staring off into space.

The scene in the heavy-care house at Gilmore Lodge is quite different. Small clusters of residents sit or lie in modern reclining chairs in various lounge areas. They chat or visit with relatives, or watch people come and go through a large window. There is no offensive smell.

In the house for confused residents, one woman with a purse and a determined expression on her face is walking around a circular corridor, with her hand on the handrail. "It bothered me that the only way people could get exercise (in standard nursing homes) was by walking up and down corridors," Rapelje says. The interior of the house has a circular design, with residents' rooms on either side of the corridor and service areas in the centre. The design makes it easier for energetic but disoriented residents to get some exercise without getting lost in dead-end hallways.

Each dining room at Gilmore Lodge has a pantry with hot containers for food, and an area for staff and residents to prepare snacks. Food is brought from the main kitchen. Each pantry has its own dishwasher so dishes are not being transported. This reduces the risk of cross-infection — a common and dangerous occurrence in nursing homes. Each pantry is equipped with a microwave oven to reheat food for residents who are slow eaters. Coffee is made here. On the counter is a basket of apples and oranges, a toaster and a kettle.

The dining rooms have cathedral ceilings, skylights and washable carpeting. As in a restaurant, dining tables vary in size: some are for two people, others for four. There are proper place settings instead of the institutional tray service typical of nursing homes. "The food is very good," says one eighty-eight-year-old woman. "I have no complaints."

The four houses are joined by hallways to a central building which contains the "town square." This is an area of shops and services behind storefronts. Located here are the administration office, bank, library, hairdressing salon, music room, bar, and a small shop with gifts, coffee, cigarettes, candy and toiletries. There is also a cafeteria-style restaurant for residents, staff and visitors.

The square is furnished with attractive and comfortable bamboo furniture and round tables with umbrellas. Large windows overlook a courtyard. The square is used as a lounge, a meeting place and an entertainment site. It features a two-storey wood-beam ceiling with a skylight. There is also a large outdoor patio located at the front of the main building. The central building is air-conditioned.

A small chapel and counselling room for clergy is adjacent to the main square.

One eighty-four-year-old woman who transferred to Gilmore Lodge from a 340-bed nursing home expressed her resounding satisfaction with the new facility. "This is a very nice home," she said. "I've gained weight. It's very comfortable. The girls are very nice and most people are friendly." She says she plays bingo and cards, and enjoys crafts. She also goes out to dinner, shops in a mall and takes bus trips. She likes it better than her former home, because there are fewer people. "I never knew anybody in the other place," she says. "When I had to go to the bathroom, I had to go and wait in line. I ate with thirty-five people. Most of them were in wheelchairs, except myself." She rolls her eyes. "It was quite a place. This is a whole lot better."

Each house also has its own activity room. From the larger homes in Niagara region, Rapelje learned that residents who are frail will not travel a long distance to participate in recreation programs. And if a long distance is involved, staff often don't have the time to take them. Rapelje believes having an activity room in each house saves staff time, and gives activity workers more time to work with individuals or small groups. Each activity room has a video-cassette recorder, so movies and videos can be shown. "If we're to avoid warehousing old people, and provide places where people live, and not just stay until they die, we need to provide sources of stimulation," Rapelje says.

To encourage people to leave the individual houses, activities involving all residents take place in the main square.

Another frequent complaint of residents and their families that Rapelje set out to address was a general shortage or lack of lounges, private visiting areas and rest stations in many nursing homes. The houses of Gilmore Lodge have numerous small alcoves with built-in cushioned seats. At the end of each dining room is a lounge area with built-in furniture and a small library. Each house is also equipped with a small room where residents meet families, clergy and professionals for visits and counselling. This room has a loveseat, two chairs, a table, carpet and venetian blinds. Coffee is available for residents and visitors.

Each house also has its own bathing room with whirlpool baths and showers. The tub room has a skylight.

Poor design of corridors is a major reason for the bleak, institutional atmosphere in many nursing homes. The halls are usually long and sterile. The architects of Gilmore Lodge used special design features to make the corridors appear shorter. The entrances to the rooms are inset, and painted a different colour than the corridor walls. Outside each resident's door is a small shelf where flowers or knick-knacks can be displayed. There are also small cross-corridors and rest stations along the way. The halls are illuminated with skylights.

Instead of a highly visible nursing station which contributes to an environment more like hospital than home, the nursing stations are situated between houses. Each nursing station serves forty residents. Every bedroom and washroom has a call bell. And there is a bedroom in one of the houses for families visiting critically ill residents can stay overnight. Staff are encouraged to wear civilian clothes — again, to help create a non-medical atmosphere.

Instead of a public-address system interrupting sleep and conversations, the intercom is restricted to the town square. The houses are free of signs saying "Dining Room" or "Janitor's Room." These are small touches, but they help dispel the institutional atmosphere. While laundry service is available, there is also a laundromat for residents. "Some ladies like to do their own laundry," says Pauline O'Dell, assistant administrator at Gilmore Lodge.

During a recent visit, the cafeteria in the main square of Gilmore Lodge was serving three kinds of salad (an unusual sight in long-term care homes). These were cole slaw, vegetable salad and green salad. The menu was typical of a good public cafeteria; a cut above the variety and quality of food served in many nursing homes. Included were devilled eggs, pancakes and bacon, mashed potatoes, beans, quiche, soup, fresh fruit, yogurt, jello, blueberry pie and fruit salad. Although there is a staff lunchroom, many employees of the home choose to eat in the main square.

Besides the home's residents, about thirty-five people who live in the community come to the home's day program for seniors. This program allows them to continue living alone in their home, or gives a break to the families who are looking after them.

A common problem in nursing homes with day programs is that sharing facilities with the permanent residents can lead to conflict. For example, day-program people in some homes sometimes annoy the permanent residents by wandering into their rooms. In Gilmore Lodge, the day-program clients have their own lounge, with attractive modern furnishings, fireplace and stereo. The day-program area is equipped with its own washrooms, supervisor's office and kitchen-dining room. Participants in the day program are picked up at their homes by van; spend a few hours doing activities, such as crafts, baking or playing cards; and have a hot meal. The day-program dining room is also available to families who wish to prepare and enjoy a family meal with relatives who live in the nursing home.

There are over 150 people on the waiting list for Gilmore Lodge. A similar home has also been built in Niagara-on-the-Lake.

"Nearly everyone in this home is from this community," O'Dell says. When Gilmore Lodge opened, about thirty-six residents transferred from Sunset Haven in Welland, a 340-bed facility. Some of those residents had been forced to leave Fort Erie to go into a nursing home.

The residents pay a daily charge that ranges from $22.49 to $44.00 a day, depending on the level of care required, and whether they have a private room. Only those who are able to pay are charged full rates. The rest of the cost of care is subsidized by the province.

O'Dell has worked as a nurse and administrator in nursing homes for seventeen years. She says the biggest difference at Gilmore Lodge, compared to other long-term care facilities, is the atmosphere. "It's homey, cheerful, relaxed and friendly. This is the closest I've come to an ideal situation," she says.

Remarkably, despite the amenities, the capital costs of Gilmore Lodge were no higher than those of a typical institutional nursing home. The lodge cost a total of $5.4-million to build and furnish. According to the Ministry of Community and Social Services, which funds and oversees publicly owned homes for the aged, the cost was comparable to that for other homes.

Rapelje points out that there were actual savings in construction costs at Gilmore Lodge, because the houses were not built like institutions, with heavy walls and foundations. "We've been hoodwinked into thinking large institutions are economical," he says.

The hardest aspect of the project was convincing bureaucrats at the provincial level that change was needed to create a more humane and normal environment for residents of long-term care homes. "We get locked into old ideas," Rapelje says. "They said the nursing stations should be in the centre and we hid them in the corridors (between the houses)."

Rapelje believes non-profit and publicly owned homes can provide better care than profit-making nursing homes, and says that he has refused higher-paying jobs in the private sector for that reason. Public accountability and lack of a profit motive contribute to a higher quality of care and a better atmosphere, he says.

It is not just the design of Rapelje's nursing homes that is distinctive. His entire philosophy is innovative. His nursing homes are not necessarily the last stop before death: Rapelje and his staff try to help the elderly residents return to their own homes.

Rapelje says that long-term care facilities are full of people who do not need total care. Some go into a nursing home after an accident or because of depression, after the loss of a spouse, or a reaction to over-medication. Often, they must spend two years on a waiting list before they can enter a nursing home, and after such a long wait, they are afraid to leave.

Rapelje's homes try to rehabilitate residents with therapy. The staff assess the medications the elderly people are taking: too often, inappropriate and excessive prescription drugs are making people physically and mentally ill.

When an elderly person is ready to leave the nursing home, there is a written guarantee from Rapelje that a bed will be waiting if he or she needs to come back. This is the psychological boost many need to step back out into the community. In addition, a former resident is assisted by a wide range of programs provided by the Senior Citizens Department, which helps them stay at home or in a foster home.

Another of Rapelje's goals is to create attractive, safe areas outside his nursing homes, where confused residents can enjoy the outdoors. He recalls one grandchild, on a visit to another nursing home, who wanted "to go back to see (the section) where people try to escape." The child was referring to a bleak area, enclosed by a chain-link fence, designed for residents who are confused and likely to wander.

In the municipally owned homes for the aged in the Niagara region, Rapelje has helped to create outdoor park-like areas, each decorated according to a theme. A Japanese garden at the region's home in Niagara Falls has a bridge, statues, garden, fountain, gazebo, rose garden and bird house. A nautical theme at the region's home in Port Colborne is depicted by an anchor, ship's wheel and 35-foot lifeboat, where the elderly residents can sit and rest. The park also has a weather vane and 5-foot cascading waterfall. Instead of chain-link fences to prevent people from wandering, lattice-type fences and cedar log fences are used.

Mr. Smith, a resident at a nursing home in Winnipeg, yelled and screamed up to 300 times an hour — the staff actually calculated it one day. He threw all his meals on the floor. The man was in his late seventies, and demented from a lifetime of alcohol abuse. The nursing-home employees were at their wits' end.

They tried every trick in the standard nursing-home book. They tied Mr. Smith to a chair for sixteen hours a day. Anti-psychotic drugs and vitamins were pumped into him, until he was receiving up to thirteen different medications a day. They tried giving him crackers and juice to get him to shut up. Sometimes the staff would send Mr. Smith to his room; they would tell him he had to stay there until he was quiet. But, besides being demented, he was taking so many mind-altering drugs that he couldn't remember why he was in his room. He yelled and screamed even louder to get out.

When the Bethania Mennonite Personal Care Home in Winnipeg opened its special-care unit in the fall of 1988, Mr. Smith was the first admission.

The approach of this unit (along with a similar one in Winkler, Manitoba) is considered unique in Canada. It offers a treatment program for people in nursing homes who have behavioural problems because of dementia, brain damage or mental illness. There are other special-care units in Canada, but this program is unusual: using behavioural psychology, it attempts to treat problems, rather than just act as a warehouse for difficult residents. The unit is also distinctive because of its small size. With only ten beds, the staff-to-patient ratio is high. During the day, two nurses and one health-care aide work at the unit.

The director of the unit is Dr. Craig Turner, a psychologist. He trains the nurses and health-care aides in the use of behavioural approaches to deal with elderly people in the special-care unit. Dr. Turner also enlists the help of an occupational therapist, a physician who is an expert in geriatric medicine, and a psychiatrist whose specialty is dealing with the elderly.

The unit hopes to cure behavioural problems such as screaming, physical aggression and dangerous wandering. It accepts residents of Bethania as well as other nursing homes in Winnipeg, and could ultimately open its doors to people outside the nursing homes who need help.

Nursing-home administrators are unanimous in saying that the single biggest problem they face today is caring for residents who have mental problems, many of them associated with Alzheimer's Disease. Their numbers are growing, because people are living longer. Nursing-home operators say they do not have enough staff to properly look after this group. Some mentally confused residents require one-on-one attention — a fantasy, in a nursing home.

The Canadian government recognizes the problem. "Institutions are currently not well equipped or designed to care for the growing numbers of elderly persons with chronic, episodic or acute mental illness," a 1986 federal government paper noted. "The knowledge and attitudes of staff concerning dementia and depression are frequently poor. Access to psychogeriatric consultants is limited."

Mr. Smith — the screamer — had been getting worse and worse at his original nursing home. The head nurse of his ward approached Bethania's special-care unit. She explained that she was responsible for 100 residents. "I don't have the time to look after this one person," she told Dr. Turner. "He's on so many medications I've lost track now as to what's doing what. His quality of life is non-existent."

The relationship between Mr. Smith and the staff of the special-care unit was mutually instructive. After four months, Mr. Smith was practically cured of his destructive behaviour. In return, he provided the special-care unit staff with a remarkable case study of what is wrong with care in nursing homes.

"When he arrived at our facility, he was so constipated that when my physician assessed him, he thought he had cancer," Dr. Turner says. "He had lumps as high as up here." Dr. Turner indicates his own rib cage. "It took us close to three weeks to get him cleared out."

It turned out that the constipation was one of the main reasons for Mr. Smith's obnoxious behaviour. "When something physiologically isn't going right for him, he starts to react aggressively and verbally," Dr. Turner says. "He started to react a few weeks ago, and we found out he was starting to get a cold."

Today, the special-care unit makes a point of doing a complete medical assessment on an elderly person to rule out medical reasons for behaviour problems.

The staff of the special-care unit took Mr. Smith off every medication he was taking. "It made absolutely no difference in his behaviour," Dr. Turner says. "It didn't get worse. What did change for him was that he became more cognitively aware."

Mr. Smith could finally understand what was going on around him. While he was still occasionally confused, because of his dementia, his comprehension and alertness improved. Then came the next step of the treatment — the behaviour program. It worked like this: staff ignored Mr. Smith when he yelled. They paid attention to him when he was quiet. "We got the behaviour to go down to zero rather dramatically," Dr. Turner says.

Dr. Turner says nursing-home residents are so hungry for attention and human contact that attention from members of the staff is a powerful tool in trying to influence behaviour.

Mr. Smith's improved behaviour meant he could eat with the mentally alert residents. In turn, this improved his behaviour even further. He hated being with mentally impaired people. In fact, he had pushed a confused patient in the special-care unit, and broken her wrist, because she had been poking at him with her finger. "He comes out here for mealtimes with the very cognitively aware, and converses very nicely with them, behaves very appropriately. When he's around people that don't communicate he can't stand it," Dr. Turner explains.

After five months, Mr. Smith returned to his own nursing home. When he arrived, members of the staff swarmed around him. "He looks different," they told Dr. Turner. "He acts different. If you can make him look the way he does now, we've got about twenty or thirty other people we'd like you to see."

So far, the special-care unit at Bethania Mennonite Personal Care Home is just a three-year pilot project of the Manitoba Health Services Commission, which funds and monitors nursing homes. What Dr. Turner must prove to the commission is that the special-care unit can admit residents for a maximum of six months, change their behaviour, and maintain those changes.

The special-care unit also provides consultation and staff training to ten other nursing homes in the city, to help them cope with their behaviourally disturbed residents. They are very anxious to receive any assistance the unit can give them, Dr. Turner says. "The majority of the facilities we're dealing with are just clamouring for this stuff. They're saying, 'We don't have the expertise,' and 'We don't have the time to do this.'" By midwinter of 1989, six months after the unit opened, three people had already completed the program, with good results.

Working with Mr. Smith and other patients gave staff an idea of the shocking lack of medical attention received by some residents of nursing homes. The elderly people who arrived at the unit with behavioural problems were not receiving proper medical care at their previous nursing homes, Dr. Turner says. "We're having to do a lot of medical assessment, because it hasn't been done at the nursing home."

One of these patients was Mrs. Zimmerman. The sixty-four-year-old woman suffered paranoia: she believed the Russians, the Gestapo and the Americans were out to get her. To complicate matters, she flatly refused to walk on her own, or to use a walker. At her nursing home, before she was transferred to the special-care unit, the staff insisted that their assessments showed Mrs. Zimmerman was perfectly capable of walking. The staff kept telling her she could walk, and that they expected her to walk. They kept trying to force her to walk, but she would refuse. She would slide out of her wheelchair and fall down. She purposely became incontinent.

"Within a few days of her coming here, we realized she couldn't bear weight, like we were led to believe," Dr. Turner says. An X-ray showed that the entire ball of her hip joint had deteriorated. Pins placed there during a hip operation were protruding into tissue. "Any kind of weight-bearing caused pain," Dr. Turner recalls. "She was unable to rotate or flex her hip, due to pain."

The special-care unit sent Mrs. Zimmerman for a hip-replacement operation. She now gets around so well that she will not be returning to the nursing home. Instead, she is moving into a seniors' apartment.

The nursing-home staff had considered Mrs. Zimmerman a troublesome nuisance, and, assuming she was insane, they had given her anti-psychotic drugs. But when she arrived at the special-care unit, she was taken off the medication. As with Mr. Smith, the medication was doing more harm than good. The special-care unit staff have determined that Mrs. Zimmerman is not a paranoid schizophrenic. She is, however, a survivor of a Nazi concentration camp and an abusive marriage. Her eccentric behaviour "appears to be one of the ways this lady has learned to cope over the years," Dr. Turner says. "She's not going to go out and kill someone."

Another elderly resident of a nursing home had been experiencing dramatic fluctuations in her blood pressure. The staff of the special-care unit were brought in as consultants. The unit staff suspected the woman's fluctuating blood pressure was a reaction to a drug, but when they urged the nursing-home staff to do blood tests, they were questioned about the need for such tests. "We just did them seven months ago, when she was admitted," a member of the nursing-home staff said to the Bethania nurse. The special-care nurse kept trying to explain that it was a matter of life or death. Finally, the nursing home agreed to do the blood tests — when told about a similar problem with another client at the special-care unit.

It is endemic to most nursing homes that the staff members and administrators assume the problems of older residents cannot be solved, Dr. Turner says. The staff believe the residents are crabby, and suffering pain simply because they are old. "The attitude is, 'We'll just keep them warm, and change them and feed them, and they just complain a lot.'"

He says the medical care provided by doctors who visit nursing homes is not always of the highest calibre. Often, the physicians are too busy to spend time with residents. Other doctors don't take the time to investigate the root cause of an elderly person's problem. Most physicians have no special training in geriatrics. "Invariably, medication is the rule of thumb to deal with problem behaviour," Dr. Turner says. "Unfortunately, it often just gets added to another pile of medications. Some physicians fail to take the time to recognize that when you get past three or four medications you're talking about interaction effects, and you're likely making the situation worse."

Doctors tend to rely on nurses to tell them about a resident, and the nurses don't have the time to conduct in-depth assessments. "The staff in nursing homes have so many people to look after — they're on the go constantly," Dr. Turner says. "They don't have the time to sit down and spend a lot of time with each individual person."

The other type of resident referred to the special-care unit is the wanderer. One elderly woman lived in a nursing home that had fifteen exit doors, each of them connected to the alarm-bell system — which the woman was endlessly activating in her efforts to leave the building. "The alarms were going constantly, and someone would have to run after her and get her," Dr. Turner recalls. "That makes staff anxious and uptight. What happens is they start piling on medications to try and deal with that. But chemical and physical restraints don't do the job."

Some nursing homes, confronted with wandering residents, respond by locking all the exit doors. But it can be highly dangerous to lock residents into a nursing home: in the event of fire, the consequences could be disastrous.

One answer to the problem is as simple as placing flaps of paper over the crash bars of the doors. If the confused residents cannot see the crash bars, they do not try to open the doors.

Some progressive homes are putting a tracking device in the clothing of wandering residents. The device trips the alarm when they leave, and helps avoid the problem of locking in all the residents for the sake of a few.

The special-care unit at Bethania is a self-contained ten-bed wing with a fenced-in outdoor area. It is built with hardly any hallways, and a central activity area minimizes wandering by the disoriented elderly.

The unit is expensive, and this may ultimately determine whether such units will become common. Salaries alone amounted to $465,000 in 1988-1989. But there are also cost benefits: there was a significant reduction in drug use among the elderly who entered Bethania. Moreover, the unit has been able to take people out of costly nursing-home beds and rehabilitate them to the point where they can live in less expensive accommodation in the community.

Other special-care units in Canada do not provide treatment. Their goal is simply to segregate mentally disturbed residents and provide a better place for them to live. A good example is the special-care unit in the German Canadian Intermediate Care Homes in Vancouver.

This unit is for people with significant mental health problems such as Alzheimer's Disease. The Alzheimer's sufferers are often physically aggressive, noisy, have bad eating habits and wander.

"These clients present an especially difficult problem ... because existing facilities within the system often refuse them admission or discharge them because of the effects of their disruptive behaviour on other clients," says a report on the Vancouver special-care unit.

In their 144-bed nursing home, the administrators of German Canadian Intermediate Care Homes set aside a wing of the home for sixty-one difficult residents. There, wanderers are given regular physical exercise and walks. Incontinent people are taken to the toilet every two or three hours. Poor eaters are served one course at a time, at a slower pace than usual, and receive more assistance with meals than they had in the nursing-home dining room, where they had been lumped in with other residents. Insomniacs are given a bath late in the day, and a backrub at bedtime to relax them. As in the case of the special-care unit at Bethania Mennonite Personal Care Home, drug use has decreased or entirely disappeared among many of the residents in the Vancouver home.

What is different about this unit is that the staff are specially trained to deal with mentally disturbed residents. They are selected for their sensitivity and patience. They use music as therapy, to stimulate residents and help them enjoy themselves. Even the most severely impaired residents respond to music. Some experts believe that emotional memory is the last part of the memory to disappear in dementia victims. And music touches the emotions.

Perhaps most impressive of all, the Vancouver unit has succeeded in providing special care to confused residents within the budget allocated by the provincial government for its regular nursing-home operation.

In many cases, the typical nursing home is actually increasing the behavioural problems of mentally impaired residents. Strict control is the worst possible approach for confused elderly people. Yet nursing homes usually force residents to follow a rigid bath schedule; force the residents to rise at a fixed time each morning; and restrain the residents at night if they wander. These kinds of strict controls "will usually increase difficult behaviors and turmoil," U.S. gerontologist Dorothy Coons wrote in a 1985 article.

Although it requires a great deal of sustained effort, the administration of the German Canadian Intermediate Care Homes has found significant reductions in behavioural problems. "The residents are definitely easier to manage," a spokesperson for the Vancouver home says. The goal of the special-care unit is to provide a better quality of life for the residents. It seems to be working. Staff say the residents seem happier, more alert and sociable.

Mrs. O'Brien is a frail eighty-six-year-old nursing-home resident who is confined to a wheelchair. She rarely attends the activity programs of the nursing home, because of her severe arthritis, and assorted aches and pains. But there is one function she never misses — pub night. "We better hurry, or we'll have no place to sit," she urged a visitor one evening. "It gets crowded."

It is 7:00 p.m. on a beautiful autumn evening. The dining room of the nursing home is festive with white tablecloths and balloons (albeit emblazoned with the nursing home's corporate logo). There are pink silk flowers on every table. It is clear that the residents have dressed up for the occasion: one woman has a ceramic rose brooch carefully pinned to her blouse; women's faces are touched up with lipstick and rouge; hair is coiffed.

Pub night is a simple idea — an inexpensive way of entertaining elderly residents by providing a pleasant social evening. Yet the vast majority of nursing homes are too institutional and unimaginative to offer such activities. Many are reluctant to spend the small amount of money required for pub nights and similar events.

This nursing home, in suburban Winnipeg, is an exception. On this autumn evening, activity workers are busily wheeling residents into the dining room for pub night. They sit quietly in groups of four, waiting patiently. The musicians, who appear to be in their sixties, arrive in the dining room. They start tuning their instruments — an accordion, an electric guitar and a violin. "They get wonderful talent here," Mrs. O'Brien whispers happily.

Volunteers who work at the nursing home place a paper plate of chips and pretzels on each table. A few wrinkled hands gingerly reach out to take a few of the salty snacks and raise them to their mouths. By 7:20 p.m., about seventy-five elderly residents have assembled. There's not an empty seat in the house.

The musicians stand erect and serious in their short-sleeved burgundy shirts, grey pants and western-style ties. They pause, then launch into a slow waltz. A few hands tentatively start to clap to the beat. The volunteers lead a more robust clap.

One elderly resident leaves behind her walker and steps out onto the dance floor. "She's not supposed to walk!" gasps Mrs. O'Brien. "Where's she going?"

A lively polka is next. Feet in Tender Tootsie shoes start to tap. A woman who appears to be suffering from Alzheimer's Disease begins to bounce in her chair to the rhythm. An elderly resident moves her thin shoulders to the music. Other residents simply clasp their hands over their chests and listen.

A volunteer comes by to take orders for drinks. Gin and 7-Up for a woman with a gracious smile. "Just 7-Up please" for another. "Would you like a little wine?" the volunteer waitress says loudly into the ear of a hearing-impaired resident. The drinks begin to appear: a beer here; a glass of white wine there; some sherry, served in proper glasses. Those residents who are too heavily medicated to drink are given pink, non-alcoholic Shirley Temples. Mrs. O'Brien calls out greetings to people she knows.

"Hello, how are you?"

"Still alive," responds a large woman with a cane.

"That's the main thing," chirps Mrs. O'Brien.

A few voices raise falteringly to join the musicians in a rendition of A Bicycle Built for Two. An activity worker dances over to one of the tables and shouts: "What'll it be, Mabel?" She grabs Mabel and twirls her wheelchair on the dance floor; Mabel's friends wave. Several ladies dance with each other. An elderly male resident stands rooted to the spot, while an activity worker moves his arms to the music. The heat and decibel levels rise and the atmosphere grows giddy. There's more chatter and laughter, and small yelps to the music. Plates of cheese, cold cuts, crackers and olives appear. "I'm not supposed to have salt," Mrs. O'Brien confesses as she swallows a rolled-up slice of ham.

Mrs. O'Brien feels rejuvenated by the pub night. It is a normal, social, adult activity — exactly the kind of activity that should be provided more often in nursing homes.

After a couple of hours, Mrs. O'Brien is ready for bed. She wants to beat the rush out of the dining room. Up in her room, she explains her philosophy. "Never stop dreaming," she says.

"If you ever stop dreaming, you might as well be dead. That's what keeps me going. I dream that I'll walk again. At night, I dream I have a man in my bed making love to me. Sure I do."

Enjoyable activities can keep nursing-home residents healthy and interested in life. Yet the activity programs offered in many nursing homes are unimaginative, childish and boring. Nursing homes typically offer bingo, carpet bowling, sing-songs and crafts. Older people are forced to do silly, meaningless things — making crafts from discarded egg cartons or popsicle sticks. American gerontologist Dorothy Coons says the lack of social and recreational opportunities actually produces stress. "A dearth of activities can only lead to a stark and sterile environment, and sick behaviours."

One interesting example of a nursing home that has explored new and innovative activities is the Jewish Home for the Aged in Detroit. It had six practising artists set up programs in literature, theatre, music, visual arts, poetry and dance.

"Through an art form, the aged person can once again become an active participant in life, learning to be productive, to contribute, and to feel success," an assistant director of the Detroit home has written.

In Peterborough, Ontario, some nursing-home residents have been learning media studies, literature and ethics from their beds and wheelchairs, thanks to a teacher at Sir Sandford Fleming

College. David Fraser has taken education out of the classroom and moved it into institutions for the aged. Fraser says education provides the elderly with the mental stimulation that is often lacking in nursing homes. "Often, seniors are just waiting to die. But this gives them something to live for."

Some nursing homes in Canada have occasional movie nights for the residents, but often the homes do not obtain the popular commercial films that are available for rent on video. Instead, the nursing homes tend to show dull documentaries on wildlife or nature. "It's always some boring thing about owls," says one nurse who works in a Winnipeg nursing home.

Nursing-home residents should be encouraged to maintain their previous hobbies — their woodworking, gardening, baking or bridge. The leisure of advanced years can even be a time to start a new project. Nursing homes must realize that their residents are often capable of taking on new challenges and renewing their lifelong interests.

Grace Dunn, a Winnipeg woman, wrote her first book at the age of seventy-eight, while she lived in a nursing home. It was an autobiography. It helped keep her alive. "I am 78 years old but I feel about 50," she wrote. "Being in a care home is not the dead-end of our lives but the beginning of a new chapter."

10

The Alternatives

Lena sat in the bathtub and wondered if the fire department should be called. The ninety-year-old woman could not get out of the tub. "I felt paralyzed. I got a cramp and I couldn't move."

Lena's husband Mykola, eighty-one, tried to help. "He was shoving pillows and blankets into the water to try to float me to the top," she chuckled, recalling the scene. Somehow, it worked. But Mykola was upset, and swore that Lena's solitary baths were over. They both realized she needed more help than he could provide if she was to remain at home. That was two years ago.

It was the start of home-care services for Lena, who has severe arthritis in her legs. "My legs are no good. If I don't have support — away I go."

Lena and Mykola live in a neatly tended four-room house in Kenora, Ontario. It has a generous backyard with a garden, and across the road are woods.

Once a week, the Red Cross Society, which has a contract with the Ontario government to provide home-care services, sends a bathing assistant to bathe Lena. On Mondays and Fridays, a woman comes in for three hours to houseclean, launder, prepare a light lunch and even bake cookies. There is no charge. "They're wonderful," Lena says.

"That's how we live," adds Mykola. "We rely on the kindness of others."

Canadian statistics show that about one-fifth of people aged sixty-five and over require some help with activities such as bathing, eating, going to the bathroom, preparing a meal, doing housework and managing finances. But, compared to the situation in European countries, home care in Canada is still in its infancy. While all the provinces have home-care programs, most of these are grossly inadequate, underfunded and undeveloped. A 1988 report by the Metropolitan Toronto District Health Council estimated that 5.9 per cent of Canadians over the age of sixty-five live with some type of home-support services. In comparison, 15.6 per cent of elderly Swedes enjoy a semi-independent life with home-support services, while in the Netherlands, the figure is 23.5 per cent. Experts say the lack of sufficient home care is one reason Canada has one of the highest rates in the world of elderly people in institutions.

"Home support services are vitally important to seniors and disabled persons who require some assistance to remain independent in their own homes," says Catharine de Leeuw, senior co-ordinator of the Association of Jewish Seniors in North York, Ontario. "In many situations, there is only one real option — placement in a long-term care institution. Yet that option is not the answer." A survey of 1,000 Ontario seniors found that most want to stay in their homes as long as possible, and that they regard institutionalization only as a last, unwanted resort.

"Most old people are horribly depressed and distressed at the idea of going into an institution," says Patricia Spindel."In that respect, they're no different from you or I. And they shouldn't have to if they don't want to." Researchers have found that elderly people who live in their own homes rather than in a nursing home are happier, because they have some control over their lives. "Living in an institution involves a certain amount of regimentation, and losing control over one's daily schedule is related to low levels of satisfaction among all age groups," says Maureen Baker, author of a book on aging in Canada.

Dr. Lilian Thorpe, a professor of psychiatry at the University of Saskatchewan, says nursing homes contribute to a high rate of depression and suicide among the elderly. She believes that doctors should avoid sending elderly patients to nursing homes, because the loss of independence can result in isolation and loneliness. Dr. James Kirkland, head of geriatric services at Queen Elizabeth Hospital in Toronto, agrees. He says that most people are much better off in their own homes — even without adequate support services — than they are in the average nursing home.

"I feel so fortunate to be at home," Lena says. "A lot of people told me: 'Go to the old folks' home. You'll be better off.' But I told my doctor I wouldn't like to go to the old folks' home. I have my own house."

This sentiment is expressed time and time again. There is an emotional attachment; a sense of comfort, in one's own home. Lena's doctor was sympathetic. "We'll try it," he told her. "We'll try to keep you at home, and give you what's necessary to do that. And if it doesn't work, well..."

For two years,the arrangement has worked. Certainly, it helps that Mykola is able to cook, and drive the car to do shopping. Good neighbours shovel snow, offer half a freshly-baked pie, and make themselves available in case of emergency.

Lena's activities are simple, but she is satisfied with her life. She sleeps until 9:00 a.m., and usually has a breakfast of grapefruit, toast and jam, and coffee. Her husband rises a couple of hours earlier: Lena can hear the familiar sounds of Mykola making coffee in the kitchen. After breakfast, she reads Ukrainian newspapers and novels, then naps until about 11:00 a.m. Mykola fixes lunch — sandwiches and coffee; perhaps some fresh tomatoes and spanish onions with sour cream. After lunch, Lena naps again, then watches a soap opera on TV and telephones a friend. At 4:00 p.m., Lena and Mykola eat a supper of soup or perogies.

After supper and another nap, Lena watches the six o'clock news. If there is a hockey or football game on TV, the elderly couple watch it together: Lena is in bed by 10:00 p.m. Small pleasures are savoured: friends drop in, or the neighbour's cat visits; Lena even went to church for a few minutes, the Easter before last. After the other worshippers left church, she slowly crept up the stairs which have daunted her now for several years. The priest unlocked the door for her, and she whispered a prayer.

Some critics of home care say that it could become very expensive because seniors will drain the program. But Lena is grateful for the service, and careful not to abuse the system. An occupational therapist was coming to visit Lena with a device designed to relieve arthritic pain. When the treatment failed, Lena suggested that the therapist end her visits. "I know someone has to pay for it," she says. "Why should she come and waste time here when she could be with someone who needs her more?"

A cane hangs on the doorknob in the kitchen where Mykola and Lena, dressed in a blue bathrobe, sit with the priest who married them twenty-three years ago. Mykola pulls a bottle of brandy from a kitchen cupboard, and unwraps some cold cooked ham. As they sit and talk about how the years have flown by, Mykola breaks into a Ukrainian song about a miller who also ponders the passage of time. "The wheel is turning," Mykola sings in a strong, gruff voice. The priest joins in. Everyone's eyes mist.

It's Grey Cup weekend in November 1988, and the game is on television. When the crowd roars, Mykola dashes somewhat awkwardly to the living room to see who scored. Mykola is tall and slim, with erect carriage; Lena is slightly shorter and plump, her face a map of soft wrinkles. Both are blue-eyed and white-haired.

They were married two years after Lena's husband of fifty years died. She was sixty-nine; Mykola, sixty. It was his first marriage. "And they lived happily ever after," the priest jokes as they grin broadly. Indeed, they seem compatible mutual helpmates, maintaining each other physically and spiritually, alternately laughing at and cursing old age. Lena gives Mykola much credit for making her final years happy. "I would have been dead long ago, or suffering in the old folks home, if it wasn't for him."

There is a public perception that more nursing-home beds are needed. Canadians tend to think that when people grow old, they should be put into an institution — a perception fed by the belief of many physicians that it is necessary to put the elderly in nursing homes. "Medical schools talk about institutions and how to make them good rather than eliminate them," Spindel says.

Lena's success shows that a nursing home is not inevitable for frail, elderly people. All they need is some help to manage at home. "One of the things we tell people is the nursing-home beds you get now are the ones you're going to live in," Spindel says. "So you think about it."

The Canadian Medical Association sponsored a task force on the allocation of health-care resources. Its 1984 report strongly recommended moving from institutionalization to community alternatives such as home care. "The problem is that at present, in many places, these support systems are grossly inadequate," the task force noted. It predicted that if Canada continues to put old people into institutions at the rate it does now, another thousand 300-bed nursing homes would have to be built by the year 2021. Not only would the costs be staggering, but creating more nursing homes would perpetuate "the callous practice of warehousing the elderly," the task force said. "Old people do not want to live in institutions, even in the best of them."

Vera Chernecki, president of the Manitoba Organization of Nurses Associations, says many elderly people who go into a nursing home are able to stay home, if they get a bit of assistance. Chernecki used to work in a Winnipeg nursing home. "So many people were coming in that could have managed well at home if they had someone coming in to do laundry, prepare a meal, shovel snow or check their medication," she says. "I firmly believe more and more nursing homes are not the answer. Most people would prefer not to be in a nursing home." In 1986, a survey by the Ontario Nurses Association showed that 85 per cent of nurses preferred that government put money into community-based services instead of institutions. Over half of the nurses surveyed described the quality of nursing-home care as fair to bad.

Governments pay a lot of lip service to offering alternatives and keeping people out of institutions. But actions speak louder than words: the more money goes into nursing homes, the less is available for community options.

In 1982-1983, about 94 per cent of the Ontario social services budget for the elderly went to homes for the aged. That left a paltry 6 per cent — $10 million — for home support services. Similarly, in 1986, a Conservative Party task force on human and social services in Ontario found that long-term care services accounted for $800 million in annual expenditures, while community-based services represented $85 million a year.

"There is lack of support, noted at all government levels, for care outside of institutions and still too little interest in alternatives," the 1988 report of the Metropolitan Toronto District Health Council said. Out of about $3.9 billion spent on the elderly by the Ontario government in 1984-1985, only 12 per cent went to shelter and home support to keep seniors at home. Long-term institutional care ate up 21 per cent, hospital and medical health care accounted for 48 per cent and 19 per cent was spent on income support.

Community programs are cheaper than institutions. In 1985, the Ontario government proposed 4,500 new nursing-home beds, which would cost $75,555,000 a year to operate. Concerned Friends said that numerous alternatives to nursing homes could be purchased for almost the same amount. At a cost of about $75,972,000 a year, the consumer group said, Ontario could provide 10 new in-home relief programs, 3,000 attendant-care apartment spaces, 660 new group-home spaces for severely handicapped adults, and 150 advocates and case coordinators.

Manitoba's Continuing Care Program kept about 25,000 people in their homes in 1988, at a cost of about $50 million, or $2,000 a person; in comparison, the Long Term Care program kept about 8,200 people in nursing homes at an average cost of $20,500 per person. In Alberta, a report noted that home care costs the provincial government between $3 and $7 a day per person, compared to $36 to $39 for each person in a nursing home.

Manitoba's home-care program is generally considered to be the best in Canada. It offers a wide variety of health, rehabilitation and home-support services. It develops a personalized care plan for each individual. It is a universal program, free to consumers who are eligible. Usually, it is provided until the point that home-care costs exceed the costs of institutional care. The program is supplemented by a broad range of community-based, non-profit support services, subsidized by the health department, available on demand, and including congregate meals, tenant resource co-ordinators in seniors' apartments, transportation, home maintenance, telephone reassurance and friendly visitors. In June 1987, fifty-nine support services were available to seniors' projects throughout Manitoba; some free, others involving a charge.

A report from one regional program with thirty-eight workers — some volunteer, some paid — described the wide range of services: "They have performed such jobs as lawn and yard clean-up, cleaning and changing windows, house-cleaning, laundry, laying of carpet, hanging pictures and mirrors, cleaning cupboards, moving furniture, snow removal, transportation both locally and to a major centre, visiting, daily phone calls, delivery of groceries, medical prescriptions and mail, typing of letters and reading for the blind, sewing, drivers for the handi-van, etc. The response has been excellent and very rewarding."

In 1986-1987, under the long-term care program, there were 906 people in adult daycare, accounting for 44,194 days of care; and 421 people who periodically entered a nursing home to give their families a break from looking after them. This respite program represented 9,262 days. Both it and the home-care program keep people from permanent institutionalization.

In Ontario, medicare covers eighty hours of home care in the first month, and forty hours of home care for every month thereafter. "Forty hours of home care is not very much," says Patricia Spindel. "Unless you're very wealthy, and you can supplement it with private home care, which is very expensive, you're in a position where you have to put Mum or Dad into a nursing home. And so we're literally driving people into nursing homes when they don't want to go, and when their relatives don't want to put them there."

Statistics show that 80 per cent of the people in Manitoba using home-care services are over the age of sixty-five. Almost 70 per cent are women. More than half live alone, and of those living with others, 35 per cent live with people who have health problems, and 30 per cent live with people who work outside the home. "These findings indicate that the great majority of program clients have limited access to support within their own households," said a 1988 report on Manitoba's Continuing Care Program by management consultants Price Waterhouse. Thirty-seven per cent of home-care users said that without the services, they would have to move from their homes to a seniors' apartment or nursing home.

In 1986-87, 11,827 people in Manitoba were admitted to the home-care program. Of those, 41 per cent would have entered acute-care hospitals; 5 per cent would have gone into extended-care hospitals and 29 per cent would have ended up in nursing homes. That same year, 56 per cent dropped home-care services because their health improved to the point where they could manage their care themselves, or with help from family and friends.

Twenty-eight per cent of elderly people getting home care used only homemaking services. About a third of these people said that homemaking services kept them from moving out of their homes; many said they would otherwise have gone into a nursing home. The consultants noted that homemaking services "probably contributed to the prevention of premature institutionalization."

Amazingly, despite the acknowledged success of the program, the report recommended the provincial government introduce measures that would "serve to encourage clients to meet their needs through their own resources" — measures such as user fees and limited hours of service. The government was also advised to develop independent non-profit cleaning services in all communities. "This effectively should take the program out of the business of providing house cleaning services," the report said. Its justification was that 54 per cent of the 278 people receiving only homemaking services said they would not move from their homes if they lacked these services. In the absence of home care, the elderly using the homemaking service said they would hire help, or enlist family and friends for help.

The government acted on the report's recommendations with alacrity, quickly axing housekeeping services to disabled, elderly people.

Ellen Shannon, ninety, of Winnipeg, started dusting against doctor's orders when her housekeeping services were cut from six to three hours a week. Shannon suffers numerous allergies, diabetes and a blocked ventricle, and is restricted from extended walking due to a series of minor strokes. "If they cut me off (completely) I will have to go into a nursing home," she said.

Another recipient of housekeeping services wept when she found out she was cut off altogether from her bi-monthly government housecleaning service. Sarah Weisman, ninety-two, had tried hard not to be a burden on the system, turning down an offer at one point to increase the service to once a week. "I only hope that God spares me to stay in my own home," she said. "I wouldn't want to be a burden to anybody."

Cutting back on community services is false economy. Not only are home-support services cheaper than nursing homes; there are spin-off savings as well. A 1988 study by the University of Manitoba Centre on Aging found that social services can decrease doctor and hospital costs. During the study, a support-service coordinator worked with about 200 residents at a seniors' apartment building in downtown Winnipeg. The coordinator made people aware of services that exist in the community, and helped them obtain the services they needed. Once residents learned of resources such as home-care nurses, homemakers, Meals on Wheels, handyman services and sitter-attendants, there was a significant increase in their use. "The interesting thing is that their physician and hospital utilization did not increase, despite their declining health," said Neena Chappell, director of the Centre on Aging. "So we had to conclude that the support role of the co-ordinator did in fact work."

Chappell said the elderly apartment residents ended up receiving more appropriate and less expensive services; as a result, there was less dependence on doctors and hospitals.

Rosalie and Robert Kane are American health-care researchers. In a study of Manitoba's home care program they concluded that "universal long-term care benefits were not only a humane and equitable public policy ...but also that universal long-term care benefits with governments as major purchasers of service can lead to high quality care at lower total costs."

The number of commercial homemaking and nursing agencies seems to be growing with increased government funding of home-support services. However, governments should avoid contracts with profit-making operations. The North American experience with profit-making nursing homes indicates that non-profit organizations tend to provide better quality care. The Social Planning Council of Metropolitan Toronto says that for-profit homes cut costs at the expense of staff salaries, and nursing and dietary services to residents. In its 1984 report, the council argued that non-profit services are also less costly. "The increased cost of monitoring private delivery of human services is a further reason to doubt that substantial cost-savings can be achieved by privatization."

Dr. James Kirkland, chief of geriatric services at the Queen Elizabeth Hospital in Toronto, advocates house calls by doctors. He also favours taking mobile hospital equipment to people's homes, if necessary. In New Brunswick, a mobile hospital unit that goes to patient's homes to provide health care is credited with keeping elderly people out of nursing homes.

Another excellent idea is financial support for families who keep their elderly relatives at home. Under a demonstration project, the Nova Scotia government is offering financial assistance to needy families looking after an elderly relative or disabled person. Most municipalities which administer the program offer a maximum of $400 a month or $4,800 a year. As of March 1989, about 600 people were receiving assistance under the program.

"It has been effective in maintaining persons in their own homes who would otherwise require placement in a (nursing home)," says James MacIsaac, administrator of rehabilitation and community services in the Nova Scotia Department of Community Services.

Senior Link is a community-founded home-support agency which has operated in Toronto since 1975. With remarkable flexibility, imagination and volunteer commitment, it helps people stay in their own homes.

Senior Link offers almost any assistance that is requested, from helping to remove a tree from senior citizens' backyards to publishing their memoirs. Statistics in 1984 show that Senior Link staff and volunteers provided 350 seniors with 4,776 drives to such destinations as medical appointments, and shopping and recreation centres. They spent 9,200 hours with 310 elderly people, performing services such as shopping, banking, errands and minor repairs. Over 12,000 hours were spent offering 636 clients counselling, and help filling out government forms or applying for social assistance. About 80 per cent of Senior Link's clients do not have relatives in Metropolitan Toronto.

Hundreds of elderly people received thousands of hours of services such as palliative care, friendly visits, day care for Alzheimer's victims and security checks. Senior Link runs rehabilitative programs, offering exercises and lectures for stroke and arthritis victims.

When the public health department threatened to condemn a house owned by an eccentric man who kept thirty cats, Senior Link cleaned up the house for free — a job for which a private service would have charged up to $5,000. Senior Link respects the independence and right of each individual to make his or her own decisions. "We don't always agree with their lifestyle but we don't write them off," says Gerri Pennie, Senior Link's director of housing.

In the case of a reclusive seventy-four-year-old woman with twenty-one cats, Senior Link had all the animals innoculated.

For those who cannot live at home, Senior Link runs the Hope Centre — a forty-eight-unit seniors' apartment. The main floor is occupied by a community centre which offers imaginative activities, such as amateur theatre. People of many skills —including carpenters, actors, painters and writers — participate in putting on plays.

Senior Link's annual budget in 1988 was about $600,000, of which the provincial ministry of community and social services paid 70 per cent. The rest was raised through donations. Pennie says many of those who are receiving services would otherwise end up in a nursing home. "We're saving the taxpayer a great amount of money," Pennie says. She adds that it doesn't take much to keep some elderly people in their own homes. "People will put up with a lot less to stay where they are. They don't want the niceties."

Another good model for home-support services for the elderly can be found in the Regional Municipality of Niagara, where the Senior Citizens Department is responsible for services to seniors in the area. The region's total population is about 370,000, almost 12 per cent of whom are sixty-five or older.

What makes Niagara unique is that the services are run by the municipality, and provide one-stop shopping for a broad range of services. All services to the elderly are co-ordinated under one roof, which makes it easier for elderly people and their families to get information about programs and be referred appropriately. It also facilitates ongoing assessment to make sure people are getting what they need. In most other areas, support services are fragmented and piecemeal.

The aim of the Seniors Department is to reduce institutionalization and its costs. "We offer choices," says Douglas Rapelje, director of the department. To encourage people who are unsure of their ability to stay home, Rapelje offers a written guarantee that if their health deteriorates to the extent that institutionalization becomes the only alternative, they will get a bed in one of the homes operated by the region.

Services that keep elderly people in the community include the senior day program, which serves elderly people living alone or with their families. They come to any of the regional homes for the aged for the day. There, they get a meal, recreation, referral to other appropriate services, some health care, health education and counselling, on-going assessment of needs — and a ride to and from the home. The program also provides a break for family or friends who are the main caregivers.

A survey of participants in the day program found that 87 per cent of them use the service to avoid institutionalization. One woman has been in the program for eleven years. "It begs the question, 'Do we really have a shortage of beds or are they just used inappropriately?'" Rapelje says. In 1984, 27 per cent of the people enrolled in the region's day program had already been approved for admission to an institution. They chose to remain in the community.

The Senior Citizens Department also offers services such as home and yard maintenance, minor repairs and housekeeping. The department screens and supervises the workers and the elderly person negotiates payment.

Many older people need to know that if something happened to them, it would be noticed. The department provides a couple of security programs. Letter-carriers are asked to watch for unusual signs at a house, such as lights burning, and to inquire at the house or report the situation so that a check can be made. The telephone program involves a daily call: if there is no answer at the prescribed time, a check will be made.

Older people living alone can receive nutritious meals at a nominal cost through Meals on Wheels. The department also helps senior citizens find suitable roommates if they wish to share their homes. A survey of residents in a home for the aged found that 96% of the residents felt home-sharing would give them greater control over their lives, and "relieve loneliness and boredom, provide greater financial independence, greater satisfaction and enjoyment through sharing meals and household chores."

To alleviate loneliness and boredom, the department also links elderly people with visitors, pen pals and volunteer projects such as working with handicapped children. Moreover, the department helps families with elderly people at home. The Alzheimer respite service provides trained people for twenty-four-hour care in the home. Support groups for families caring for elderly relatives are available.

Rapelje says support services are cheaper than nursing homes. He estimates that the department saves about $350,000 a year by having 90 people boarded in private "foster" homes instead of living in nursing homes. The department also saves about $340,000 a year by having 160 people in the day program rather than in nursing homes.

Marguerite Chown, a retired nurse in her seventies, puffs contentedly on a cigarette as she sits surrounded by books, records, native art prints, and a wine collection. Her mobile telephone rings: a newspaper reporter wants to interview her for a series on abuse of the elderly. She graciously complies. The phone rings again — an invitation to come to the opening of a film on the elderly. She promises to check her schedule.

Chown is past president of the Manitoba Society of Seniors, an advocacy group for Manitobans over fifty-five. The society is lobbying for expansion and improvement of home-care services as well as more funding for home renovations for the elderly.

The latter is a subject Chown knows intimately. She is disabled by a spinal ailment and gets around with the aid of a cane, walker and wheelchair. She lived in the same Winnipeg house for forty years, but in 1988, when the stairs became too much for her to handle, she moved into a concrete slab house with one floor and no basement.

The home was renovated to make it easier for her to live there. Doorways were widened to accommodate a wheelchair. New sidewalks were created from wide patio stones, to provide safe footing and wheelchair access. Handrails were installed in hallways, and grab bars were located by the bathtub, and the front and back doors to the house.

Ten months after she moved, the house is attractive, comfortable, wheelchair accessible and crammed with the comforting possessions and memories of a lifetime. "I want to have as much stuff around me that belongs to me as l can crowd in," the widow says. She feels sorry for friends who have moved to tiny apartments and given up dining-room sets or pianos. And others have moved to nursing homes, losing virtually everything.

Chown's home includes a bedroom, guest bedroom, a workroom containing a desk and filing cabinets, bathroom, kitchen, and spacious living and dining rooms. Because there is no basement, the washer and dryer are in the kitchen, and a closet off the kitchen contains the furnace.

There are other conveniences that can help a disabled person, she says. Her home has a microwave oven and bathroom sink located low enough to be accessible from wheelchair level. The sink drain opens and closes with the push of a button. Shelves slide out smoothly on runners. Kitchen-cupboard contents are placed on rotating circular shelves for easier handling. Raised flower-boxes in the yard allow Chown to garden from her wheelchair. "It is expensive," she says. But she points out that some help is available. The Canada Mortgage and Housing Corporation and provincial housing programs offer interest-free or forgiveable loans for renovations for elderly and disabled people.

There are other developments in this area. The Japanese have built a fully automated house designed for the elderly or disabled. A master panel switches lights, appliances and climate control off and on, either automatically or manually. The walls in the house are moveable panels. When an elderly person becomes bedridden, the wall between the bedroom and bathroom is removed, easing access to toilet, bath and sink.

Some provinces in Canada are experimenting with granny flats or garden suites — portable self-contained housing units enabling parents to move into their children's backyards. Some people like the concept of granny flats, but it doesn't win much support from Chown. "It would be like living on a plantation in the southern U.S., where the poor white trash lived."

Dr. Cope Schwenger, professor in the department of health administration at the University of Toronto, says one of the most promising alternatives to institutionalization is supportive housing. This is also called congregate or sheltered housing. It usually consists of individual rental apartments in a specially designed building which provides services such as meals, housekeeping, recreation and possibly an emergency call-bell system. The program is for people who are too frail or lonely to remain at home, but not so disabled that they need to go into a nursing home. It enables elderly people to retain independence, privacy and dignity.

About 5 per cent of the elderly in the United Kingdom live in supportive housing, and in 1986 in England there were 392,000 sheltered units.

The United Kingdom example involves grouped dwellings — apartments or bungalows — and shared dining and recreation facilities. A warden is on call twenty-four hours a day in case of emergency, and there is a call-bell system. There is also extra-care housing for more dependent elderly people, who are provided with meals, care assistants and additional wardens.

"There seems no doubt that the very large quantity of sheltered housing in the U.K. is in large part responsible for the relatively low rate of institutional care and institionalization in the United Kingdom," said the 1988 report of the Metropolitan Toronto District Health Council. The report, by Dr. Schwenger, said: "Although we have the variety in Canada, we have a pathetically small quantity of such assisted accommodation in this country, province and city." Of $3.9 billion spent on the elderly in Ontario in 1984-85, a mere 2 per cent went to promote semi-independent living, providing the elderly with home care, foster homes, renovations and conversions and granny flats.

The United Kingdom is not alone as a pioneer of supportive housing. Municipalities in the Netherlands operate non-profit supportive apartments; rent is deducted from the residents' old-age pensions, leaving a reasonable allowance. Anne-Marie Johnston of Concerned Friends is familiar with these apartments because her mother lives in one. She describes it as simple, yet "so conducive to what a human being needs for thriving."

In the complex where her mother lives, each person or couple has a small apartment consisting of a bedroom, sitting room, bathroom and kitchenette. Unlike a nursing home, the program allows residents to bring their own furniture. To ensure privacy, the door locks. Staff clean the apartments. There is a communal dining room for lunch and dinner. Johnston says excellent food is served in a restaurant-like environment with linen tablecloths and napkins. Staff bring breakfast — meat, cheese and bread — to the apartments, where residents can make their own coffee or tea. At 11:00 a.m., the staff bring consomme, hot chocolate, tea or coffee. "You say what your requirements are and they will be done," Johnston says. "There is a peaceful, relaxed, home atmosphere."

The apartment complex has an attractive lounge, chapel, post office, flower shop, small general store and infirmary. About 200 elderly people live in the building. A registered nurse is on duty on each of the three residential floors, assisted by about seven health-care aides per shift.

Residents who need a great deal of care can also be accommodated. Johnston says she has seen people with Alzheimer's Disease and those dying of cancer remain in the apartment house. Her own mother was near death, but the doctor felt she would be better off staying in the apartment than going to the hospital. Care was provided at the apartment, and she pulled through.

Schwenger says it is important to learn from the European example, because Canada's population is aging. It is estimated that the number of Canadians aged seventy-five or over, living alone, will double in the fifteen-year period between 1981 and 1996. The Toronto health council's report said that the number of institutionalized elderly people could also double in that period. "There are at present relatively few alternatives to institutionalization especially if offspring are not readily available."

Living alone is one of the leading risk factors in premature institutionalization. Aloneness can lead to loneliness, and to inability to handle an emergency, or get care and help when needed. "Involuntary institutionalization or solitary confinement in non-supportive housing often begins a downward emotional spiral of frustration, depression and rapid physical deterioration for the elderly," the report said.

Murray Halkett, director of hospital planning for the Capital Region District of Victoria, B.C., calls supportive housing "one of our finest preventative health care measures." Halkett said his department found that 61 per cent of people in Victoria over age seventy-five want assistance either with meals, shopping or housekeeping. He also notes that supportive housing keeps people out of institutions, and is less expensive. Researchers have found that the cost per square foot of constructing and maintaining a sheltered-housing unit is comparable to the cost of conventional housing — far below that of a nursing home. According to the International Centre for Social Gerontology, care in sheltered housing is about 40 per cent cheaper than nursing-home care.

"Sometimes they'll say, 'Oh Jayne, can you get me a cup of tea?'" Stephenson House coordinator Jayne Walkom, twenty-nine, imitates a plaintive tone. "And I'll say, 'Well, there's nothing wrong with your legs.' And after a few weeks, they're getting tea for each other." Walkom is a fast-talking young woman with long hair and jeans who affectionately addresses her ten elderly charges as "youse." For the most part, they're blue-collar people from Toronto's east end, and Jayne is so cozily unpretentious she could be their granddaughter.

Stephenson House is one of the few non-profit, high-standard group homes for the elderly in Ontario. The innovative project, operated by Senior Link, opened in 1984 as an alternative to nursing homes.

When Senior Link first opened, almost twenty years ago, its founders saw many elderly people go into institutions because they could not look after themselves in their own homes. But many did not need the level of care provided by a nursing home. Distressed by the "almost universal, rapid deterioration of these clients once placed in institutions," according to the agency literature, Senior Link studied European solutions to this need. As a result, the organization developed Stephenson House for those who, with assistance, could maintain themselves with considerable independence.

For example, one eighty-four-year-old man with severe arthritis and Parkinson's Disease, lived in a rooming house. He stored his food in a metal cabinet in the bathroom. He suffered frequent falls. The man was slated for a nursing-home bed but his granddaughter heard about Stephenson House. He lived there for four years before going to a municipally-run home for the aged.

"The main reason they come here is because they can no longer cope at home," says Gerri Pennie of Senior Link. "They would normally be headed to a nursing home, or home for the aged. Lots came off the list."

Staying in the old neighbourhood is important for physical and mental health, Walkom says. "If they move to another part of the city, they refuse to go outside. Their families and churches aren't close by. In their own neighbourhood, they'll go out. They recognize landmarks. They know the girl at the corner store."

Cityhome, a non-profit housing corporation of the City of Toronto, built Stephenson House. Senior Link rents and manages the home. It's indistinguishable from any in a row of red-brick townhouses. The inside is decked out in the worn but serviceable furnishings residents brought with them. "It's hodge-podge, but they like it," Walkom notes cheerily.

During a December 1988 visit, there are seven women and three men. The average age is eighty-seven. Five have memory loss. Seven of ten never married. "As long as they can dress

themselves and keep themselves clean, we can deal with the rest,"
Pennie says.

Stephenson House has three handicapped units for wheelchair
users, who must be able to get themselves in and out of the
wheelchair. A live-in housekeeper and a daytime manager provide
twenty-four hour, non-medical supervision. They help with personal care, supervise baths, monitor medications, cook three
meals a day and co-ordinate volunteers who help cook and clean,
and take the residents on outings. Groups ranging from the Lion's
Club to the Girl Guides volunteer their services. A doctor is
always on call, and comes once a month for check-ups. A bathing
assistant comes in once a week to help with baths.

Staff watch for health problems and refer residents to community health workers when necessary. In one case, after a
psychiatric assessment, a ninety-four-year-old woman, who had
never come to terms with the death of her son twenty years earlier,
received therapy.

Residents have their own bedrooms, for which they are encouraged to bring their own furniture. "Then they're still house-
proud," says Walkom. Each resident shares a bathroom with two
others. The bathrooms and bedrooms are equipped with call bells.

Residents do their own laundry if they're able. "We'll not
overcoddle them," Walkom says. "We won't bring meals to bed
unless they're sick." Residents come and go as they please. The
only house rules pertain to smoking (not in their bedrooms) and
booze — private supplies of liquor are kept locked in the kitchen
and doled out on request. Pets are welcome.

Ann Godward occupied one of the three downstairs bedrooms
for eighteen months. She is one of the project's most dramatic
success stories. Stricken with polio at age three, and confined to
a wheelchair, she last lived at the Queen Elizabeth Hospital for
chronic care, where she shared a room with three senile roommates and became terribly depressed. "She absolutely hated an
institution. Everybody was dying around her," Walkom said. "We
took her off a soft diet and put her on a regular diet." She helped
do menu planning, and taught Walkom to cook. During her stay,

she absolutely refused to leave Stephenson House, even for therapy.

Another eighty-six-year-old woman came from a home for the aged, where she was always crying and getting lost. There were 300 people in the institution — fifty on her floor alone. "In this home they're much more oriented," Walkom says. "They can cope in a smaller environment."

A group home can also accommodate freedom of choice. One woman has breakfast at 10:30 a.m., skips lunch, has a snack in her room, then comes out for supper. Puzzles, cards and dominoes are available. Some residents like to bake. For those in the mood, a woman comes from the board of education once a week to do crafts with the residents.

Each resident pays about $1,278 a month. The entire house can be run for the cost of Ann Godward's former hospital bed.

Senior Link is planning a variation of Stephenson House for people with Alzheimer's. Pennie says they are confident that the same lifestyle can benefit incontinent and wandering residents.

In the heart of Toronto's Jewish community is another good example of a group home for the elderly. The Elm Ridge Group Living Residence opened in 1985 with fourteen beds.

As with Stephenson House, Cityhome built and owns Elm Ridge. The Toronto Jewish Congress operates it. The Jewish Family and Child Service, an agent of the congress, is responsible for day-to-day administration of the home.

The project was based on successful American models in Chicago, Columbus and Philadelphia, and seeks to combine self-reliance with some assistance in day-to-day activities. The home is staffed around the clock and provides a variety of support services.

Eric Kirsh, co-ordinator of the home, says Elm Ridge is a more humane alternative to larger, more impersonal institutions. "We allow people to remain in the community and live independently a while longer," says Kirsh, a social worker. "They use the strengths that are remaining to them, and we enhance those strengths."

Residents prepare their own breakfasts, snacks and tea in kitchenettes, keep their own rooms tidy and dusted, and do their personal laundry. A live-in cook prepares two hot kosher meals daily. A housekeeper comes in twice a week to change and launder the linen, and do heavy cleaning and laundry. Twice a week, a bathing assistant comes in.

The house is comfortable and attractive, with a cathedral-ceilinged living room equipped with television, videocassette recorder and stereo. The room overlooks a spacious backyard. The main floor contains a dining room, with three contemporary tables and velvet-upholstered chairs. A piano is tucked into a hall alcove. Judaic pictures and artifacts decorate the home. "We're strongly culturally identified," Kirsh says. "The kosher part is important." Residents bring their own bedroom furniture. Two share a bathroom, and a kitchenette is usually shared by four residents.

Residents are carefully screened, and come in for a one-month trial. They must be relatively healthy and able to walk. But Kirsh says the incoming residents are less healthy than they expected. "We learned that people who are able and fairly well will not come into a semi-institutional setting."

Most are coming from their own homes, where they were already receiving some homemaker services and Meals on Wheels. They may be experiencing changes in memory, and problems with shopping, cleaning, cooking or getting out socially. Some feel scared at night. Of thirteen residents in December 1988, twelve were women — eleven widowed and one never married. The average age is eighty-three. Others have come from nursing homes. "They were placed too early," Kirsh says.

Mrs. James, seventy-eight, moved to Elm Ridge ten months earlier from an apartment where she lived alone. "I get dizzy spells," she says. "It's quite a trauma to realize you can't look after yourself." Mrs. James says she is happy at Elm Ridge. "What

I like is there are people around for lunch or dinner. And it's small. It's not a large institution."

The cost for a resident with assets is $1,300 a month, excluding telephone and personal expenses. There are five spaces subsidized by the Toronto Jewish Congress so that a person who has only a pension and supplements can pay $700 a month and keep just under $100 a month for themselves.

The residents have a say in the operation of the home. Concerns are raised during weekly meetings with Kirsh. These typically last an hour and a half, with 100 per cent attendance. "People here have a good deal of control over what happens in this house," Kirsh says. "There is argument, conflict, anger, lots of tension and humour too."

Both Stephenson House and the Elm Ridge Group Living Residence have special design features to aid older people. At Elm Ridge, plugs are higher and there are call bells in bathrooms. The windows open, and locks on doors reinforce privacy in rooms and bathrooms. A telephonic-ear system is available during residents' meetings for the hard of hearing.

The home provides some activity programs, such as exercise, crafts and films. Children have come in to make Hanukkah decorations, and families have brought slide shows of travels. There are outings for tea, or to concerts.

Health problems are closely monitored and, when necessary, residents are referred to geriatric specialists. For example, one woman underwent a marked personality change and became anti-social. A psychiatrist discovered that her behaviour was due to a urinary-tract infection which was cleared up by some mild medication.

One elderly woman, who was living alone in an apartment, was eating poorly, becoming depressed, and rarely going outside. Since moving to Elm Ridge, Kirsh says, she has put on weight, visits friends, goes out for lunch and has taken on a leadership role in the home, directing people during fire drills and participating actively in the residents' meetings.

"There's something about a small environment that allows people to feel they have a recognized place in the community and gives them a sense of control," Kirsh says. "Those factors sustain people."

On December 23, 1988, Mykola passed away in a Winnipeg hospital. After his death, Lena was taken to the Kenora hospital to await a nursing-home bed. Whenever relatives or friends are able to stay with her for a few days, Lena leaves the hospital and goes to her beloved home. In April 1989, she was home for a week with a niece who drove in from Edmonton to be with her. As the white-haired woman looked around the small house with its modest furnishings, photographs and mementos, her eyes welled with tears. "If only there was a way for me to stay here," she sobbed. "This is my home."

SOURCES

CHAPTER 1

Christian Labour Association of Canada, *Caring for Our Elderly: An Inquiry into Working and Living Conditions in Alberta Nursing Homes*. (Submission to the Alberta Minister of Hospitals and Medical Care, 1988).

William Forbes, Jennifer Jackson and Arthur Kraus, *Institutionalization of the Elderly in Canada* (Butterworths, 1987).

Health and Welfare Canada, Health Services and Promotion Branch, *Aging: Shifting the Emphasis* (Working Paper, October 1986).

Birthe Jorgensen, *Crimes Against the Elderly in Institutional Care* (unpublished paper, 1986).

Journal of Long Term Care, April 1983.

Manitoba Health Services Commission, *Annual Report, 1987-1988*.

Price Waterhouse, *Direct Nursing Requirements of Extended Care Residents in Homes for the Aged and Nursing Homes in Ontario, Vol. 1* (March 1988).

Proceedings of the Fourth Manitoba Conference on Aging, *Fiction, Fact and the Future* (May 1985).

Judith Wahl, "Access to Nursing Home Residents," *Concerned Friends Quarterly Newsletter*, Autumn 1986.

Winnipeg Free Press, "People in Care Homes Value Old Possessions," March 28, 1989, p. 32.

CHAPTER 2

Canadian Association for Community Living, *Replacing Institutions: The Challenge to End Segregation* (June 1988).

Christian Labour Association of Canada, *Caring for Our Elderly: An Inquiry into Working and Living Conditions in Alberta Nursing Homes*. (Submission to the Alberta Minister of Hospitals and Medical Care, 1988).

Manitoba Task Force on the Young Disabled, *Report to the Minister of Health* (January 1984).

CHAPTER 3

Forbes et al., *Institutionalization of the Elderly in Canada* (Butterworths, 1987).

Regina Leader-Post, "Use of patient restraints should end: professor," Oct. 13, 1988.

Cheryl Ellen Walker, *Residents' Self-Reported Perceptions of Care Outcomes in a Personal Care Home* (University of Manitoba, Thesis for Master's of Nursing, 1988).

CHAPTER 4

Christian Labour Association of Canada, *Caring for Our Elderly: An Inquiry into Working and Living Conditions in Alberta Nursing Homes* (Submission to the Alberta Minister of Hospitals and Medical Care, 1988).

W. Gifford-Jones, "The Doctor Game," *Regina Leader-Post*, May 11, 1989.

Cheryl Ellen Walker, *Residents' Self-Reported Perceptions of Care Outcomes in a Personal Care Home* (University of Manitoba, Thesis for Master's of Nursing, 1988).

CHAPTER 5

Canadian Union of Public Employees, *Health and Safety* (May 1986).

Canadian Union of Public Employees, *Health and Safety Guidelines* (October 1987).

Christian Labour Association of Canada, *Caring for Our Elderly: An Inquiry into Working and Living Conditions in Alberta Nursing Homes* (Submission to the Alberta Minister of Hospitals and Medical Care, 1988).

Forbes et al., *Institutionalization of the Elderly in Canada* (Buttersworths, 1987).

Health and Welfare Canada, Health Services and Promotion Branch, *Aging: Shifting the Emphasis* (Working Paper, October 1986).

Ontario Association of Registered Nursing Assistants, *Who Cares for Our Elderly* (Brief to the Canadian Medical Association Task Force on Allocation of Health Care Resources, January 1984).

Proceedings of the Fourth Manitoba Conference on Aging, *Fiction, Fact and the Future* (May 1985).

Regina Leader-Post, "Staff shortage is bad for seniors' health: workers," January 18, 1989, p. A3.

Cheryl Ellen Walker, *Resident's Self-Reported Perceptions of Care Outcomes in a Personal Care Home* (University of Manitoba, Thesis for Master's of Nursing, 1988).

Beverley M. Wilden, *Nurse and Resident Congruency on Nursing Activities and the Relationship of Congruency to Resident Morale* (University of Manitoba, Thesis for Master's of Nursing, 1988).

CHAPTER 6

Proceedings of the Fourth Manitoba Conference on Aging, *Fiction, Fact and the Future* (May 1985).

Social Planning Council of Winnipeg, *Institutional Pastoral Care in Manitoba* (September 1984).

CHAPTER 7

Concerned Friends of Ontario Citizens in Care Facilities, *A Brief Proposing Items for Inclusion in an Omnibus Extended Care Act* (December 1987).

Concerned Friends of Ontario Citizens in Care Facilities, *Consumer Concerns and Recommendations Related to Nursing Home Care in Ontario* (Brief to Ontario Minister of Health, September 1982).

"Nursing Home Deaths Reviewed," *Toronto Star*, letter to the editor, April 4, 1988, p. A10.

"Self-serving arrogance a slur to residents, workers at nursing home," *Today's Seniors*, letter to the editor, June 1988.

"Seniors group questions deaths at nursing home," *Today's Seniors*, May 1988.

CHAPTER 8

Canadian Medical Association, *Health: A Need for Redirection* (Report of Task Force on the Allocation of Health Care Resources, 1984).

Christian Labour Association, *Caring for Our Elderly: An Inquiry into Working and Living Conditions in Alberta Nursing Homes* (Submission to the Alberta Minister of Hospitals and Medical Care, 1988).

Globe and Mail, "Nursing Home Owners Assail Plan to Alter Law," March 4, 1987.

Globe and Mail, "Nursing Homes Charging Extra, Ontario Auditor Says," November 29, 1985.

Globe and Mail, "Nursing Homes Flourish Under Taxpayers' Umbrella," May 17, 1984.

Robert L. Kane and Rosalie A. Kane, *A Will and a Way: What the United States Can Learn from Canada about Caring for the Elderly* (Columbia University Press, 1985).

Pran Manga, *The Canada-U.S. Free Trade Agreement: Possible Implications on Canada's Health Care Systems* (Economic Council of Canada, Discussion Paper No. 348, May 1988).

Nursing Homes Residents' Complaints Committee, *Report to the Ontario Minister of Health* (March 1986).

Ontario Select Committee on Health, *Interim Report, 1987*.

Crownx Inc., *Annual Report, 1987*.

Jody Orr, *The Free Trade Agreement and Social Policy: A Policy Paper* (Social Planning Council of Metropolitan Toronto, 1988).

Social Planning Council of Metropolitan Toronto, *Caring For Profit: The Commercialization of Human Services in Ontario* (1984).

Vera Tarman, *Looking Behind the Rhetoric: A Political Economic History of Ontario's Commercial Nursing Homes, 1958-87* (University of Toronto, Thesis for Master's of Science, 1987).

Trizec Corporation Ltd., *Annual Report, 1987.*

Woods Gordon, *Review of Inspection and Compliance in Ontario's Nursing Homes* (Report to Ontario Ministry of Health, July 1985).

CHAPTER 9

Dorothy Coons, "Alive and Well at Wesley Hall," *Quarterly: A Journal of Long Term Care*, Vol. 21 (July 1985).

Health and Welfare Canada, Health Services and Promotion Branch, *Aging: Shifting the Emphasis* (Working Paper, October 1986).

Regina Leader-Post, "Nursing homes can be places of learning," May 30, 1989, p. A11.

Cheryl Riskin, "The Role of the Cultural Arts in an Activities Program for Alert and Mentally Impaired Elderly," in *Well Being and the Elderly — An Holistic View* (American Association of Homes for the Aging, 1986), pp. 63-71. Vancouver Health Department, Continuing Care Division, *Final Report of the German-Canadian Care Facility Behaviour Management Project* (October 1986).

CHAPTER 10

Alberta Committee on Long Term Care for Senior Citizens, *A New Vision for Long Term Care* (Alberta Legislative Assembly, 1988).

Maureen Baker, *Aging in Canadian Society* (McGraw-Hill Ryerson, 1988).

Canadian Medical Association, *Health: A Need for Redirection* (Report of Task Force on the Allocation of Health Care Resources, 1984).

Robert L. Kane and Rosalie A. Kane, *Continuing Care Program: Lessons from Experiences in Other Jurisdictions* (unpublished report, 1987).

Metropolitan Toronto District Health Council, *Housing and the Health of the Elderly* (1988).

Price Waterhouse, *Review of the Manitoba Continuing Care Program* (1988).

Winnipeg Free Press, "Study Generates Aid for Seniors," March 14, 1988, p. 15.

Winnipeg Sun, "Depression can be deadly for elderly," May 1, 1989.

Winnipeg Sun, "Senior in Tears," February 24, 1989.